The Mindful Librarian

Chandos
Information Professional Series
Series Editor: Ruth Rikowski
(email: Rikowskigr@aol.com)

Chandos' new series of books is aimed at the busy information professional. They have been specially commissioned to provide the reader with an authoritative view of current thinking. They are designed to provide easy-to-read and (most importantly) practical coverage of topics that are of interest to librarians and other information professionals. If you would like a full listing of current and forthcoming titles, please visit www.chandospublishing.com.

New authors: we are always pleased to receive ideas for new titles; if you would like to write a book for Chandos, please contact Dr Glyn Jones on g.jones.2@elsevier.com or telephone +44 (0) 1865 843000.

The Mindful Librarian
Connecting the Practice of Mindfulness to Librarianship

RICHARD MONIZ

JOE ESHLEMAN

JO HENRY

HOWARD SLUTZKY

LISA MONIZ

Amsterdam • Boston • Heidelberg • London • New York • Oxford
Paris • San Diego • San Francisco • Singapore • Sydney • Tokyo
Chandos Publishing is an imprint of Elsevier

Chandos Publishing is an imprint of Elsevier
225 Wyman Street, Waltham, MA 02451, USA
Langford Lane, Kidlington, OX5 1GB, UK

ISBN: 978-0-08-100555-2

British Library Cataloguing-in-Publication Data
A catalogue record for this book is available from the British Library

Library of Congress Cataloging-in-Publication Data
Library of Congress Control Number: **2015946209**

For information on all Chandos Publishing
visit our website at http://store.elsevier.com/

DEDICATION

This book is dedicated to our fellow librarians and educators. We hope that any insights gained from this book lead them to a greater enjoyment of their lives and work.

CONTENTS

ABOUT THE AUTHOR

Jo Henry is the Information Services Librarian at South Piedmont Community College. Formerly, she has worked at the Charlotte Mecklenburg Library and has over twenty years of experience in sports club management and instruction. She obtained a Master of Library and Information Studies from the University of North Carolina Greensboro and a Master of Public Administration from Georgia Southern University. Ms. Henry is a board member of the Metrolina Library Association (serving as treasurer 2013-2016). She has published in *Public Services Quarterly* and *Library Review* and has presented at the Metrolina Information Literacy Conference and the North Carolina Library Association Conference. Additionally, she is co-author of **Fundamentals for the Academic Liaison** and **The Personal Librarian: Enhancing the Student Experience**.

Lisa Moniz, MLS has 21 years of experience working as a school library media specialist in both public and independent schools. She has served students of all ages and from all walks of life, from prekindergarten through grade 12. Her special interests in the field of education include technology integration in the classroom, bibliotherapy, and global studies. In addition to her teaching licensure, Moniz is also certified to work in public libraries in North Carolina. While living in Winston-Salem she served on the Friends of the Greensboro Public Library board, was an active member of AISL (Association of Independent School Librarians) and served for two years as Secretary of the Forsyth School Media Association. She is currently a member of NCSMLA , ALA, AASL, and the Metrolina Library Association. She lives in Charlotte N.C. with her husband, Richard, and their three children.

Joe Eshleman received his Master of Library and Information Science degree from the University of North Carolina at Greensboro in 2007. He was the Instruction Librarian at Johnson & Wales University Library–Charlotte from 2008 through 2015 and has been Head of Reference at Johnson & Wales University's Providence campus from 2015 to present. In addition to leading hundreds of instruction sessions, Mr. Eshleman completed the Association of College and Research Libraries' Immersion

Program in 2009. He is a coauthor of **Fundamentals for the Academic Liaison** and a contributor to **The Personal Librarian: Enhancing the Student Experience** and contributed a chapter to the book **Not Just Where to Click: Teaching Students How to Think About Information**.

Howard Slutzky attended University of Maryland at College Park having graduated Magna Cum Laude with a Bachelor of Arts degree in Psychology. He earned a doctorate degree from Georgia School of Professional Psychology (now called Argosy University) with a focus on general adult psychology. He has worked in a variety of clinical settings including community mental health, college counseling, and private practice. He is currently a full-time associate professor at Johnson & Wales University, but offers numerous health and wellness workshops to students on topics such as relationships, stress reduction, time-management, grief and loss, fitness and weight loss, and coping with medical issues. In addition to teaching, Dr. Slutzky has a part-time private practice and he also conducts disability evaluations for Social Security.

Richard Moniz, MA (History), MLIS, EdD served as Director of Library Services for Johnson & Wales University's North Miami campus from 1997 – 2004 and has been the Director of Library Services at Johnson & Wales University's Charlotte campus since 2004. He has taught undergraduate history classes ay JWU. Additionally, since 2006, he has served as an adjunct instructor for the MLIS program at the University of North Carolina at Greensboro. Dr. Moniz has published in numerous periodicals such as College & Undergraduate Libraries, Reference and User Services Quarterly, North Carolina Libraries, Library Journal, and Library Leadership & Management. He is sole author of the textbook **Practical and Effective Management of Libraries**, co-author of **Fundamentals for the Academic Liaison** and co-author and co-editor of **The Personal Librarian: Enhancing the Student Experience**. He also has a contributed chapter in **Mid-Career Library & Information Professionals: A Leadership Primer** and in **Advances in Library Administration and Organization** (2015 edition). He is actively engaged in the profession and has held a number of committee and board responsibilities within ALA LLAMA, ACRL CLS, and Metrolina Library Association (including serving as President of this organization in 2007 and 2015) in addition to other non-profit organizations such as Carolina Raptor Center, Charlotte Museum of History, and Charlotte's Arts & Science Council. He has done several regional and national presentations related to his involvement in these organizations.

ACKNOWLEDGMENTS

We would first like to thank George Knott for having faith in our idea for this book and encouraging us to pursue it. We would also like to thank Harriet Clayton, Omer Mukthar, Project Manager from Elsevier and Lakshmipraba Manimaran, Project Manager from MPS Limited, who also helped in the editing process and made the book reach completion.

Beyond our gratitude for the support we received from friends and family, we would also especially like to thank Lisa Kendall, Kenny Harmon, Charles Butler, and Lindsay Bridges. These individuals have at various points encouraged and inspired us to pursue this topic.

INTRODUCTION

Acclaimed author and US Representative Tim Ryan (D-OH) states at the beginning of his popular book, *A Mindful Nation*, "I am not a Mindfulness Instructor."[1] We too are not mindfulness instructors, but rather experienced librarians (and a psychology professor!) who have come to develop a deep appreciation for what mindfulness can do for us and our profession. I can relate deeply and personally to Ryan's desire to get the word out on what is a revolution in modern thinking, at least in the Western world. I have struggled with anxiety and issues related to a lack of mindfulness all my life. In terms of school, it seems as though I was racing to finish getting my bachelor's degree in history while thinking more about getting my master's, then finishing my master's in history while thinking about getting a doctorate or a master's in library science. Then, after getting the MA and MLIS, I worked on my doctorate, most of the time just wishing it was done! Don't get me wrong. I benefited immensely from each of these undertakings, but I don't believe my mind was very often in the present. At other times in my personal life I also believe I have not been especially mindful. I would oftentimes not be fully present with my family, worrying or ruminating about something that needs to be done or even something I had done in the past that could have been done differently. Unfortunately, it turns out that my challenges are not unusual. As we will learn in this book, there is a big difference between thoughtful planning and incessant, unnecessary, and unproductive worrying. This exploration of mindfulness, again, has been something of a personal mission, not just for me, but for my fellow writers as well. We know that becoming more mindful has helped us in our personal and professional lives and believe that it has great potential for helping others. In fairness, it is not a panacea, nor is it just something to add to a to-do list. It ultimately boils down to a different way of viewing the world. It's a lens of sorts, but one that can encompass everything we do. For me, it is also an ideal, a way of being that I would like to spend more time "in."

I first encountered mindfulness as a formal practice in early 2012. Two well-respected colleagues and instructors at Johnson & Wales University

---

[1] Ryan, T., 2012. A Mindful Nation: How a Simple Practice Can Help Us Reduce Stress, Improve Performance, and Recapture the American Spirit. Hay House, Carlsbad, CA, p. xxi.

in Charlotte, where I have served as the director of library services for more than a decade, informed me about their efforts to integrate mindfulness into the classroom. I was extremely interested in attending some of their sessions and beginning to explore readings and brief workshops on mindfulness. I began doing short meditations every day, took yoga classes and workshops, and completed both t'ai chi and mindfulness-based stress reduction (MBSR) courses. It was the science, however, that finally sold me on the power and possibility of integrating mindfulness into my personal and professional life, and this led me to pursue it in earnest. Quoting Tim Ryan once again, "My own experience took me most of the way to believing the power of mindfulness to effect change, but what the researchers showed me sealed the deal."[2] The recent research efforts connected to mindfulness are mindboggling (no pun intended)! This text will be peppered with many of the interesting findings in this regard, but even so, it still fail to be exhaustive. Our goal here is rather to get you, as a librarian or future librarian, started down this path, and for those who may be a bit more skeptical, as we were, to show you how something like a functional magnetic resonance imaging (fMRI) can illustrate demonstrably positive changes to the brain in real time as a result of practicing mindfulness. We want to help others in our profession, and we felt that writing this book was a way to do just that.

So, in a sense, we need to tell you what mindfulness is as we see it. There are numerous definitions, but one we gravitate toward is that by Susan Smalley and Diana Winston in their book *Fully Present: The Art, Science, and Practice of Mindfulness*. They state, "Mindfulness is the art of observing your physical, emotional, and mental experiences with deliberate, open, and curious attention."[3] To extend this a bit further, we might add, in the words of Jon Kabbat-Zinn (one of the seminal figures in the mindfulness movement), "mindfulness is a *way of being*, one that requires consistent cultivation…mindfulness is not merely a good idea."[4] Indeed, what we are discussing in this text is explored in the hope that it will be transformative. As we delve deeper, we will come to see the many ways that librarians can specifically benefit. Writing for *Library Journal*, Michael

---

[2] Ibid., 41.

[3] Smalley, S., Winston, D., 2010. Fully Present: The Science, Art and Practice of Mindfulness. DaCapo Press, Cambridge, MA, p. 11.

[4] Kabbat-Zinn, J., 2012. Mindfulness for Beginners: Reclaiming the Present Moment and Your Life. Sounds True, Coulder, CO, p. 64.

Stephens states, "Reflective practice is mindfulness to the *n*th degree. Be thoughtful about the decisions you make, about the projects you take on, and about how you put yourself out there...Those things become part of your practice as well."[5]

The implications here are manifold. For us, that means that this book will be a creation in which we have tried to put our words into practice by further integrating mindfulness into our writing and our lives. As you will see, there are many natural places in which mindfulness can also be appropriately and meaningfully tied to our profession. Our goal is lofty. We are hoping that by focusing on librarians, we are helping students as well. According to one study, "The fast-paced library environment has called for more than what the professionals did in the past both in their personal and professional lives, coupled with the fast development of information technology now being introduced in the profession.... These have turned the library and information professional [into] a high-risk profession."[6] Furthermore, regarding students, "Researchers have found that anxiety can impede cognitive processes that are essential to their research abilities."[7]

One of the best books addressing students specifically, many points of which will be discussed in this book, is *The Mindful Way to Study: Dancing with Your Books*, by Jake and Roddy Gibbs. This father-and-son team does a masterful job at sharing some of their thoughts and ideas directly with both students and educators. In a discussion of Zen and its focus on the present moment, for example, they highlight how ironic it is that we tell college students to "pay attention" without really instructing them how to do so.[8] Another excellent book worth exploring is *The New Science of Learning: How to Learn in Harmony with Your Brain*, by Terry Doyle and Todd Zakrajsek. Not specifically targeting mindfulness per se, they have chapters on "mindsets toward learning" and "paying attention." They state "You can only learn when paying attention. Unfortunately, paying attention is not as easy as it might

[5] Stephens, M., 2014. Reflective practice. Libr. J. Available from: <http://lj.libraryjournal.com/2014/01/opinion/michael-stephens/reflective-practice-office-hours/#_.1>.

[6] Ajala, E., 2011. Work-related stress among librarians and information professionals in a Nigerian University. Libr. Philos. Pract. (e-journal).

[7] Kwon, N., Onwuegbuzie, A.J., Alexander, L., 2007. Critical thinking disposition and library anxiety: affective domains on the space of information seeking and use in academic libraries. Coll. Res. Libr. 68 (3), 269.

[8] Gibbs, J., Gibbs, R., 2013. The Mindful Way to Study: Dancing with Your Books. O'Connor Press, pp. 30–31.

seem. The human brain is wired to attend to whatever is most interesting at a given time.... If you are under the age of 30, you have lived your entire life in a media-based culture that is full of short bits of information…and constant exposure to these snippets has wired your brain to deal with information that comes at you for shorter periods and a continual basis."[9] While these books have focused primarily on students, we believe that a focus on ourselves as librarians is necessary. Each chapter will offer some additional recommended readings and resources to help you explore further. Throughout your reading, however, you may wish to consider these additional questions: How are we to teach our students to pay attention if we have not considered this more deeply ourselves? How do we better model mindful behavior and a thoughtful, caring, and contemplative approach to life?

Again, while we do address the needs of students in this book, our focus is more on librarians themselves and the impact we can have. Indeed, all of the literature on mindfulness has a "begin with yourself" bent to it. Previous books written by myself and other contributors to this text have focused on faculty or students (i.e., *Fundamentals for the Academic Librarian* and *Personal Librarian: Enhancing the Student Experience*). It seems fitting, then, that we come full circle and explore ourselves as librarians. We believe that there are a variety of ways that, as librarians, we can connect to a deep practice of mindfulness. We believe that if you listen to what we have to share and the insight within yourself, the result could have deep repercussions in your own personal life. We have tried to make this a practical reflection on how mindfulness is connected and relevant to the profession. At the same time, we have provided evidence supporting the current outlook of science on the topic of mindfulness.

The first chapter of this text briefly explores the recent history of mindfulness, its integration into health care, and some of its central tenets or concepts. Critical to this story is the creation of the MBSR clinic at the University of Massachusetts Medical Center in 1979 by Kabbat-Zinn, as well as his numerous publications such as his book *Full Catastrophe Living*, published in 1990 and considered a "watershed" text within the mindfulness movement.[10] Other important developments include the implementation of mindfulness techniques and approaches in the halls of medicine and areas far beyond. This is, however, not just the story of implementation

---

[9] Doyle, T., Zakrajsek, T., 2013. The New Science of Learning: How to Learn in Harmony with Your Brain. Stylus, Sterling, VA, p. 100.

[10] McCown, D., Reibel, D., Micozzi, M.S., 2011. Teaching Mindfulness: A Practical Guide for Clinicians and Educators. Springer, New York, NY, p. 4.

in these areas, but noted and significant benefits and successes. While its primary purpose is to lay the foundation for the rest of the text, Chapter 1 also contains a minor connecting thread on the roots and history of librarianship. Librarianship as a profession has a natural fit with mindfulness. In the broadest sense, we believe that the need to be present in the service of others is of central importance in librarianship. Being more aware of our natural connection as librarians to mindfulness is something that can help us move forward toward being more effective and happy in our roles as librarians and in our own personal lives.

Chapter 2 of this book continues the discussion of mindfulness in education. Since librarianship is fundamentally connected to teaching and learning, it is necessary to explore this area in more detail, paying specific attention to studies and programs that have improved student learning in ways that could readily connect to what we do, especially in the school and academic library environment. One of the interesting points that we hear about from authors such as Ellen Langer is that much of what mindfulness means in education requires "unlearning" bad habits.[11] We explore in some detail how contemplative practices in the K–12 and college classroom have the potential to change the educational climate. A variety of creative practices will be shared, as well as student feedback regarding the implementation of mindfulness practices in various classroom settings.

Chapter 3 describes the process of writing a research paper and explores common student anxieties as they face this challenge for the first time at the college or university level. It is here that we deviate some to address students more directly. Our hope is to quickly and directly connect some of the concepts explored in education and mindfulness to a common task that librarians are often involved in. One of the authors of this book has been involved in the process of "creating a more mindful research paper." His experiences in this regard will be shared in great detail, with the hope that you might have an immediate and practical takeaway. For example, a student's ability to quietly and calmly reflect on a topic for research at the beginning of the research process can be affected by adopting mindfulness techniques such as meditation and simple breathing exercises. Evidence is provided demonstrating how ratcheting down student anxieties in the process of writing a research paper leads to better work and deeper learning.

Chapter 4 of this text explores the connection between mindfulness and the new Association of College and Research Libraries Framework

---

[11] Langer, E., 1997. The Power of Mindful Learning. Addison-Wesley, Reading, MA.

for Information Literacy for Higher Education. Mindfulness teaches that we need to pay attention to our lives now, not just to what might come next. The new framework emphasizes research as a process and one that should be valued and appreciated in its own right. Taking from the framework still further, a librarian can see the tenets of mindfulness whereby one is expected to accept the world as it truly is as relating to a student's ability to be open to new information and perspectives on a given topic. The connections are many. The creators of this new framework have intended it be an ongoing discussion among library professionals, and we can think of no better way to enhance this than by connecting it to the practice and meaning of mindfulness.

As Chapter 4 draws out the deep connections between mindfulness practice and information literacy or library instruction efforts, Chapter 5 applies mindfulness to our work at the reference desk. Every librarian has had to study and practice the Reference and User Services Association (RUSA) *Guidelines for Behavioral Performance of Reference and Information Service Providers* at one time or another. These standards focus on fine-tuning approachability, interest, listening, searching, and follow up.[12] When looked at more carefully, they all connect to one key element—paying attention to the present moment. It would be hard not to see the direct and relevant connection to mindfulness! Nonetheless, this chapter will explore what is meant by a mindful approach to reference connecting to each of the steps within RUSA's guidelines. It also includes multiple anecdotes and examples.

Chapter 6 focuses on mindfulness in relationships. In our previous books, we have discussed in great detail ways by which librarians can be connected to faculty and students. The mindful approach that we have taken here focuses on aspects of communication that affect faculty–librarian relationships, with a special emphasis on the states of mind of each communicator and how this in turn affects the exchange of information between them. One tenet of mindfulness is the idea that we should apply deep listening to our interactions with our faculty colleagues. Therefore, mindful listening and interpersonal synchrony are both discussed.

Chapter 7 continues where Chapter 6 left off in terms of developing the library and its staff in a new light. It explores what mindful leadership and management means. While the implication is for the library staff and director taking a mindful role in the campus or educational enterprise as

---

[12] Reference and User Services Association. Available from: <http://www.ala.org/rusa/resources/guidelines/guidelinesbehavioral>.

a whole, the special focus here is on applying leadership *within* the library. For example, Lyn Hopper states, "Mindfulness may expand a leader's perceptions and lead to authenticity." She goes on to quote Charles Scwenk: "Deep knowledge about yourself enables you to be consistent, to present yourself authentically, as you are."[13] It is very important for library directors, deans, and administrators to be caring and thoughtful about what they do on a daily basis. They too must learn the tenets of accepting who they are and being open to greater awareness.

Finally, Chapter 8 provides a unique exploration of what specific challenges are aligned with being a "solo librarian." This applies less to the academic library environment and more to those in which school and special librarians find themselves. According to one school librarian, "I was a bundle of mixed emotions: enthusiastic and filled with the hope that comes with a new beginning, yet completely overwhelmed about the task that I had been entrusted with…*alone*."[14] It seems to us that these solo acts often have the greatest need for what mindfulness has to offer. School librarians and special librarians must display tremendous resilience and resolve without the collegial network of support that is familiar to most academic librarians.

Finally, we conclude with some further thoughts on what the process has meant to us. We also suggest some possibilities where mindful practice may applied in the future.

FURTHER NOTES ON THIS TEXTBOOK

We have attempted to insert into many chapters concrete narratives that, we hope, ground some of the ideas that we are trying to communicate. For example, Chapter 5, focusing on reference services, describes several such encounters, highlighting both how being more present and mindful helps and ways in which it might be missing.

Each chapter also contains a list of recommended readings or resources. The literature on mindfulness is exhaustive, and our attempt, as good reference librarians, has been not to overwhelm you, but rather share just a few other places to look for books, videos, or articles that you may find helpful. Most of the chapters include some element of formal mindfulness practice, such as a suggested meditation.

---

[13] Hopper, L., 2010. Mindful leadership. Ga Libr. Q. 47 (2), 15; Schwenk, C. as quoted by Hopper, Mindful leadership, pp. 15–16.

[14] Bishop, L., 2013. The solo act. Know. Quest 41 (5), 31.

Again, we are not formal mindfulness instructors, but we have paid great care and attention to utilize the information and experience available to us and adapt it to our world as librarians. Some of our ideas may work for you, and some may not. Feel free to pick and choose. In order to make this a more contemplative experience, we have also inserted in appropriate locations questions for you to consider. This journey is, after all is said and done, deeply personal and subjective. It is our sincere hope that you consider using this text as a workbook of sorts in this regard. Finally, Dr Howard Slutzky, a practicing psychologist, psychology professor, and coauthor of this book, has included some basic clinical or classroom advice in each chapter based on his experiences. Our hope is that this book will improve your life, your work in the library, and your deep enjoyment of both.

Richard Moniz

REFERENCES

Ajala, E., 2011. Work-related stress among librarians and information professionals in a Nigerian University. Libr. Philos. Pract. (e-journal)

Bishop, L., 2013. The solo act. Knowl. Quest 41 (5), 30–35.

Doyle, T., Zakrajsek, T., 2013. The New Science of Learning: How to Learn in Harmony with Your Brain. Stylus, Sterling, VA.

Gibbs, J., Gibbs, R., 2013. The Mindful Way to Study: Dancing with Your Books. O'Connor Press, USA.

Hopper, L., 2010. Mindful leadership. Ga Libr. Q. 47 (2), 15.

Kabbat-Zinn, J., 2012. Mindfulness for Beginners: Reclaiming the Present Moment and Your Life. Sounds True, Boulder, CO.

Kwon, N., Onwuegbuzie, A.J., Alexander, L., 2007. Critical thinking disposition and library anxiety: affective domains on the space of information seeking and use in academic libraries. Coll. Res. Libr. 68 (3), 268–278.

Langer, E., 1997. The Power of Mindful Learning. Addison-Wesley, Reading, MA.

McCown, D., Reibel, D., Micozzi, M.S., 2011. Teaching Mindfulness: A Practical Guide for Clinicians and Educators. Springer, New York, NY.

Reference and User Services Association. Guidelines for behavioral performance of reference and information service provider guidelines. Available from: <http://www.ala.org/rusa/resources/guidelines/guidelinesbehavioral>.

Ryan, T., 2012. A Mindful Nation: How a Simple Practice Can Help Us Reduce Stress, Improve Performance, and Recapture the American Spirit. Hay House, Carlsbad, CA.

Smalley, S., Winston, D., 2010. Fully Present: The Science, Art and Practice of Mindfulness. DaCapo Press, Cambridge, MA.

Stephens, M., January 13, 2014. Reflective practice. Libr. J. Available from: <http://lj.libraryjournal.com/2014/01/opinion/michael-stephens/reflective-practice-office-hours/#_1>

CHAPTER 1

A Brief Introduction to Mindfulness: Origins, Science, the Brain, and Practice

Richard Moniz and Howard Slutzky

ROOTS OF MINDFULNESS IN MODERN WESTERN SOCIETY

Mindfulness is a central element within a multitude of religions and spiritual traditions, but it is most closely associated with the 2500-year-old Buddhist tradition. While our focus as authors of this text for simplicity is primarily on Buddhist practices, we do recognize that many traditions have made similar contributions in the much broader context of world history.

While at least a handful of Buddhist-related texts related to mindfulness had been translated into English from other languages by the late nineteenth century, it wasn't until the latter half of the twentieth century that the idea of mindfulness began to spread to the masses in the United States and other Western countries such as the United Kingdom. The intent in this transition and in our writing is to share some of the tenets of mindfulness and to help librarians in their lives and work. We intend no disrespect and, in fact, share the deepest awe and reverence for the varied traditions from which mindfulness concepts and practices have arisen. In perhaps the most famous example of the introduction of such practices into Western society, Maharishi Mahesh Yogi briefly popularized mindfulness practice in the United Kingdom in the 1960s when he traveled there and taught meditation techniques to the members of the Beatles and other celebrities.[1] What follows is a very brief introduction to mindfulness and how it spread in the West. Also described is the transition of mindfulness as part of a religious tradition into something of a more secular approach or lens for viewing the world and oneself, at least by many modern Western adherents.

---

[1] Barker, I., Close your eyes and think of....nothing at all. The Times Educational Supplement 5017, 20.

The Mindful Librarian.
1

The purpose of our content below is to share the concept of mindfulness and to help librarians in their lives and work. An early figure of some importance in developing awareness of mindfulness-based practice was Nyanaponika Thera. Thera was a German-born Buddhist monk who actively spread the teachings and practices of Buddhism until his death in 1994.[2] His most famous book, published in 1973, was *The Heart of Buddhist Meditation: A Handbook of Mental Training Based on the Buddha's Way of Mindfulness;* it made the claim that many practical benefits could arise from adoption of these ancient practices. "These benefits, he states at various points in the book, include mental clarity, freedom, energy, well-being, happiness, quietude, balance, self-control, [and] the avoidance of rash words and actions."[3]

The pivotal work of Vietnamese Zen Buddhist monk Thich Nhat Hahn cannot be understated either, in the early days of the contemporary mindfulness movement in the West. In what would be the first of dozens of books written by Hahn, he described the importance of mindfulness in his very first text, *The Miracle of Mindfulness!* In it, he states:

> I like to walk along country paths, rice plants, and wild grasses on both sides, putting each foot down on the earth in mindfulness, knowing that I walk on the wondrous earth. In such moments existence is a miraculous and mysterious reality. People usually consider walking on water and in thin air a miracle. But I think the real miracle is not to walk either on water or in thin air, but to walk on earth. Every day we are engaged in a miracle we don't even recognize: a blue sky, white clouds, green leaves, the black curious eyes of a child...[4]

Clearly, one may draw a connection from Hahn's writing to the American literary tradition and authors such as Henry David Thoreau and Ralph Waldo Emerson. Like these American-born counterparts, Thich Nhat Hahn's writings on mindfulness connected appreciation for the everyday world that we inhabit to a belief in religion. While we are explicitly not advocating any particular religion and wish to give all due respect to both

[2] "Nyanaponika." 2014. Contemporary Authors Online. Gale, Detroit. Available from <http://ic.galegroup.com/ic/bic1/ReferenceDetailsPage/ReferenceDetailsWindow?failOverType=&query=&prodId=BIC1&windowstate=normal&contentModules=&display-query=&mode=view&displayGroupName=Reference&limiter=&currPage=&disable Highlighting=false&displayGroups=&sortBy=&search_within_results=&p=BIC1&action=e&catId=&activityType=&scanId=&documentId=GALE%7CH1000073834&source=Bookmark&u=gree35277&jsid=6c55c163f6c056fcb1a468cf35335824>.
[3] Wilson, J., 2014. Mindful America: The Mutual Transformation of Buddhist Meditation and American Culture. Oxford University Press, Oxford, p. 26.
[4] Hahn, T.N., 1987. The Miracle of Mindfulness. Beacon Press, Boston, p. 12.

the Christian and Buddhist traditions in which these various individuals believed, the intent here is on the secular application of mindfulness, one that may be derived from each of these aforementioned writers. During a talk given to Loyola University students in 2003, Thich Nhat Hahn stated, "With mindfulness, we are able to be fully present, fully alive.... Mindfulness is knowing what is going on."[5] To this day, and with that in mind, even with all the other books and materials in existence related to mindfulness, *The Miracle of Mindfulness!* remains a straightforward and practical guide. It discusses, for example, the application of mindfulness in a variety of contexts such as washing dishes, washing clothes, making tea, cleaning one's house, and taking a bath.[6] In terms of Hahn's impact in the United States and beyond, it should be noted that his particular approach of connecting mindfulness to nonviolent protest and resistance to oppression led Dr Martin Luther King Jr. to nominate him for the Nobel Peace Prize in 1967.[7] In fact, the two became good friends and allies until King's untimely death in 1968.

Another key individual in the mindfulness movement in the West has been the Dalai Lama. As the spiritual leader of Tibetan Buddhists, the Dalai Lama was forced to flee Tibet when it was occupied by the Chinese in 1959. On the world stage, it would be hard to find many other individuals who have had as deep and powerful an impact on the lives of others. Earning the Nobel Peace Prize in 1989, the Dalai Lama has traveled far and wide.[8] One notable contribution in this context is that he helped create the Mind and Life Institute, based in Hadley, Massachusetts, in 1987. According to its web site:

Since the first Dialogue with the Dalai Lama, Mind and Life has held 26 others that bring together scientists and contemplatives on a wide range of critical subjects: addiction, ecology, ethics, attention, neuroplasticity, destructive emotions, altruism, economics, and more. Additionally, over the past 30 years, Mind and Life's work has extended beyond the Dialogues. The Institute has become a direct funder of individual research via its grant and scholarship programs. It convenes an annual Summer Research Institute, as well as the field's marquee biannual conference: the International Symposium for Contemplative Studies. In the process, Mind and Life has become more than just a leader in the field of contemplative science; it has become an incubator for discovery in all of the fields this new science touches.[9]

[5] Hahn, T.N. as cited by Schlumpf, H., 2003. Practicing Peace: Famed Buddhist Monk Urges Overflow Crowd to Live Mindfully, National Catholic Reporter, 12 September, p. 12.
[6] Hahn, T.N., 1987. The Miracle of Mindfulness, pp. 85–86.
[7] Hahn, T.N., 2000. Contemporary Heroes and Heroines, vol. 4. Gale, Detroit.
[8] Quezzaire, P., 2006. Dalai Lama. History Reference Center, pp. 1–3.
[9] Mind & Life Institute. Available from: <http://www.mindandlife.org/mission/>.

The Mind and Life Institute is one of many such organizations that has played a key role in spreading mindfulness and contemplative practice throughout the world. It also serves as an important bridge between the religious practices of mindfulness that have been passed down for centuries and the recent attempts by science to quantify and study the effects of these practices. As such, more resources and connections to this organization will appear throughout this book.

Despite the work of Nyanaponika Thera, Thich Nhat Hahn, the Dalai Lama, and other critical figures, the watershed moment for mindfulness in the Western world is largely credited to the establishment of the first mindfulness-based stress reduction (MBSR) clinic at the University of Massachusetts Medical School in 1979 by Dr Jon Kabbat-Zinn. He is credited with being the first to separate the practice of mindfulness from any direct or explicit religious context and establish nontheological professional training for MBSR teachers. Interestingly, as it relates to the history of librarianship, Boston, Massachusetts, is where the American Library Association (ALA) had been chartered exactly 100 years earlier.[10] Focused on improving the health of its patients, the goals of the Center for Mindfulness at the University of Massachusetts were similarly altruistic to that of the ALA, with its focus on service to others. In addition, the professionalism sought by ALA in creating its charter parallels the professional or clinical application of mindfulness by Kabbat-Zinn. While completing his doctorate in molecular biology, he became heavily involved in yoga and meditation. He states, "I loved science…I also saw there were multiple ways of knowing things. It prompted me to want to understand the biology of consciousness itself."[11] His original intent was to target a wide variety of chronic medical conditions to scientifically determine if mindfulness could help ordinary people live improved lives. According to Pickert in a recent article in Time magazine "Even if you couldn't alleviate their symptoms, Kabbat-Zinn speculated that mindfulness training might help patients refocus their attention so they could change their response to pain and thereby reduce their overall suffering."[12]

Largely due to the promise that this type of practice held within the medical field, dissertations on the topic exploded in the 1980s.[13] By 2005,

[10] American Library Association. Charter of 1879. Available from: <http://www.ala.org/aboutala/history/charter-1879-revised-1942>.
[11] Kabbat-Zinn, J. as quoted by McCluskey, E., 2005. Jon Kabbat-Zinn, PhD '71. Technol. Rev. 108 (11), 42.
[12] Pickert, K., 2014. The art of being mindful. Time 183 (2), 42.
[13] Wilson, J., Mindful America, 37.

nearly 16,000 people had gone through MBSR training at the University of Massachusetts.[14] In 2003, there were just 52 publications on mindfulness in academic journals, but by 2012, the number of yearly journal publications had reached 477.[15] Furthermore, by 2014, there were more than 1000 certified instructors (many trained by Kabbat-Zinn himself) in every state in the United States, as well as 30 additional countries.

So, what is MBSR, and why has it gained so much credence in the West in recent years? MBSR is an eight-week program led by a certified professional. Individuals may choose to participate on their own or be referred by a doctor for treatment of a wide range of ailments, including general anxiety and stress, struggling with the loss of a loved one, chronic pain conditions, post-traumatic stress disorder (PTSD), and numerous other conditions. Over the course of eight weeks, participants agree to attend one in-person session that can run approximately 2 h. They also agree to do "homework" by practicing the techniques they learn in class.

In MBSR programs, patients are taught how to eat mindfully. This first entails eating a raisin very slowly, attempting to explore its texture and taste to a much greater degree than one usually does. The connection here is the need to slow down in our lives and to appreciate and recognize experiences through our senses in any given moment. More will be shared on mindful eating in the next section.

Another technique taught through MBSR is mindful breathing. Short stints of closing one's eyes and paying close attention to one's breathing are gradually expanded to include longer sessions. In a recent story for the television program *60 Minutes*, Anderson Cooper participated in MBSR training. He noted the difficulty that nearly everyone encounters when beginning this practice. As soon as you sit still, your brain begins producing thoughts of various kinds. These could be anything from "I am bored" to worrying about things that need to be done in the future or events that have occurred in the past. The key to mindfulness, however, is to live in the present as much as possible. Therefore, early instructions include the need to acknowledge thoughts as they arise, but to allow them to come and go. Each time this occurs, one is then encouraged to refocus attention on the breath.[16] Since mindful breathing meditation is a central practice in mindfulness, it will also be addressed again later in this chapter.

[14] Mind-Body Medicine, 2005. Therapy Today 16 (9), 4.

[15] Pickert, K., The art of being mindful, 45.

[16] Cooper, A., 60 Minutes, CBS News. Available from: <http://www.cbsnews.com/news/mindfulness-anderson-cooper-60-minutes/>.

Another critical element of MBSR is body scan meditation. Like breathing meditation, body scan meditation can be especially challenging to beginners. Over varying periods of time (with 45 min being common), one is led by an instructor to focus the attention on each part of the body and finally the whole body as a system. The intent of this practice is to get one to move from avoidance to acceptance, especially in dealing with pain. Practitioners believe that while we all experience pain, it is our secondary response to that pain that can determine how we view it, or even the general quality of our lives. Feelings are to be considered as fleeting elements spurred by the thoughts and interpretations that we provide. Again, as this is a central practice, it will be discussed in more detail later.

Yoga is yet another practice taught within MBSR training. While yogic practice can vary considerably, MBSR places emphasis on working within the limitations of one's own body and comfort. The intent is to synchronize breathing with movement and develop a deeper appreciation and understanding of the mind and body connection.

Finally, the practice of mindful walking is introduced. Unlike the walking that we do every day to get somewhere, the intent of mindful walking is to simply pay attention to our movements as we walk. This is often done within the confines of a specific room or outdoor space. One typically walks very slowly (although speed can vary), paying attention to each movement, even so far as to noting the lifting of the foot, the forward movement of the leg, and the placement of various parts of the foot on the ground. A brief description of this process is provided at the end of this chapter for those interested in giving it a try.

The development of MBSR is important because it extracted and established mindfulness in a context outside explicit religion. Further studies, as will be noted next, have provided evidence that the specific practices mentioned here, as well as others associated with mindfulness, can affect individuals positively in a variety of ways. Furthermore, while experts or those who participate in more involved programs such as MBSR can realize great benefits from these practices, they have been shown to have positive effects even when they are used to a lesser degree in life. Some of the simplest suggestions related to this practice will be offered at the end of this chapter.

IMPORTANT MINDFULNESS CONCEPTS

Beginner's Mind

Before delving into the science behind mindfulness and everyday practice, some concepts related to mindfulness are so central to the practice that they deserve special mention and a brief discussion. The "beginner's mind" is one of these. Shunryu Suzuki is frequently credited with spreading knowledge and awareness of this concept in the United States. In 1967, he founded the first Zen Buddhist monastery in the United States. His book *Zen Mind, Beginner's Mind*, published in 1970 (just 1 year before he died), outlines the practice of Zen in relation to the concept of the beginner's mind.[17] Some of the best descriptions of the concept have been in its application to therapy and medical practice. An article in *Therapy Today* written by Charles Gordon-Graham states, "Beginner's mind is a mind that is open, fresh, curious, present here and now, natural, free and uncluttered… with beginner's mind comes a sense of wonder…Beginner's mind, being open and curious, promotes empathy; the related quality of compassion—awareness of other's suffering and a wish to help them—is surely a driving force for many therapists."[18] Likewise, the medical literature encourages physicians to consider the concept as well. Aaron Hauptman has stated, "One crucial part of 'a [medical] practice' is the challenge of advancing one's understanding while retaining a sense of openness and uncertainty. I would posit that the best kind of growth entails the balance between these seemingly dichotomous modes of thinking and being."[19] He goes on to warn that this could help us overcome "the risks of our own hubris" and that "to grow in medicine is to balance extraordinary knowledge with a real and honest sense of not-knowing. When we begin to think that we know with certainty, we do a great disservice to our own function as practitioners: we cut off options…."[20]

The "beginner's mind" concept plays a critical role throughout this text when we consider our role as librarians. For example, it is important that we convey openness and empathy at the reference desk and consider each student and his or her questions with a free and open mind. We need to understand students' needs when we perform instruction as well. It is also imperative that we consider trends (for instance, within a given cohort or

[17] "Shunryu Suzuki." 2004. Contemporary Authors Online. Gale, Detroit. Available from: <http://ic.galegroup.com/ic/bic1/ReferenceDetailsPage/ReferenceDetailsWindow?fail OverType=&query=&prodId=BIC1&windowstate=normal&contentModules=&display-query=&mode=view&displayGroupName=Reference&limiter=&currPage=&disable Highlighting=false&displayGroups=&sortBy=&search_within_results=&p=BIC1&action= e&catId=&activityType=&scanId=&documentId=GALE%7CH1000153340&source= Bookmark&u=gree35277&jsid=87f3387ab3af71283ac2f99207e37f58> (accessed 12.12.14.).

[18] Gordon-Graham, C., 2014. Beginner's mind. Therapy Today 25 (5), 22, 24.

[19] Hauptman, A., 2013. Medicine as practice: notes on keeping the mind of a beginner despite becoming an expert. J. Religion Health 53 (5), 1297.

[20] Ibid., 1297, 1298.

demographic) that may foster a different view of information skills that we hope to teach them. When library managers address the personal needs of library staff, they must not rush to judgment based on past experience and really listen to the *staff member*'s perspective.

Dr Howard Slutzky and Beginners Mind

Many of us have heard the advice of trying to live everyday as if it were our last. While this morbid approach is intended to give us perspective, it is the opposite of beginner's mind. Instead, I encourage my students and clients to live everyday as if were their first. With this approach, we can begin reclaiming the ability to see the world with curiosity, excitement, and without the distortion of preconception. One of my favorite Christmas songs (by Gloria Estefan) called "Christmas Through Your Eyes" captures this sentiment in the following lyric: "I see the rain, you see the rainbow hiding in the clouds."[21] The innocence and curiosity of a child's perspective is something that most unfortunately lose as we age, but with mindfulness practice, we can begin to reclaim it.

Part of the curriculum for Introductory Psychology is the concept of Schemas. A schema is a cognitive framework that helps us to organize and interpret information. In essence, schemas are preconceptions that we have for categories of people, places, and situations based on our past experiences. While they provide a mental short-cut for simplifying the world around us, schemas come with a cost ... they distort our perception. Furthermore, schemas can reduce our ability to consider new information that does not conform to our established ideas about the world.

An extremely simple example involves proofreading. It has long been recommended that we have someone else proof read our writing. The reason for this is that our preconception of what "should" be there blinds us to any errors we may have made. If our preconceptions can blind us to something as simple and concrete as words and sentences on a page, the potential for this type of error with more complex situations is great.

I share an activity with my students in which they are shown the sentence, "The snake is in the the grass." The first five words (the snake is in the) are on one line and the last two words (the grass) are on the second line just beneath the first. This is flashed on the screen for on second and students are asked to write down what they saw. Most people omit or exclude the redundant word (the) from the sentence.

I share another activity with my students in which I tell them the following brain teaser: "A boy and his father are driving down the highway returning from a winter ski trip. The father doesn't realize that the roads

[21] Estefan, G., 1993. Christmas through your eyes, CD, Epic Records.

have iced up and he takes the exit ramp too quickly. The car slides off the side of the road over an embankment. The father is unfortunately killed upon impact. His son, sustaining serious injuries, is rushed to the local hospital where it is determined that he needs emergency surgery. The surgeon takes one look at the boy and says, 'Oh my God! That's my son!'" I then ask my students to work individually to generate the possible explanations for this situation. The majority of students come up with one or more of the following:

1. There are two fathers, a biological father and a stepfather.
2. There are two fathers, it is a gay couple.
3. It is a case of mistaken identity, the boy resembles the surgeon's own son.
4. It is a priest in the car, you never said "his son," you only said a father and "a son".

But few if any come up with one of the most plausible answers to this scenario… that the surgeon is his mother. The schema for "surgeon" includes the gender of male for most people, even women. In fact, I shared this brainteaser with the head of the E.R. of a prominent hospital in North Carolina…who happened to be female. She gave the same responses as the majority of my students but was unable to consider that the surgeon was the boy's mother. Needless to say she was shocked, and admittedly disappointed in herself for being susceptible to the power of this schema distortion.

During my first graduate program, I was involved in a real-world experience that further demonstrated the distortion of schemas. I was 25 years old and driving home from my graduate program to visit my parents for the weekend. I looked a lot different than I do now. I had long hair pulled back in a ponytail, I had facial stubble, and two earrings. I was wearing a baseball cap, jean shorts, and a t-shirt. I was driving down a main road heading towards the Baltimore beltway entrance ramp. There was a bad intersection there with the traffic light just over a small peak and decline in the road. The light was only visible once over the peak. When traffic was backed up, this made for a dangerous situation. As I was approaching the peak before the light, I realize that traffic was backed up and I had seconds to screech to a complete stop. I looked in my rear view mirror and saw a Volvo station wagon coming towards me at what appeared to be full speed. As I feared, the car hit me, causing a five-car collision. The woman was traveling with two small children. All three got out of the car and her son began getting sick on the side of the road (apparently from the dust released when the airbag deployed). Her car was literally attached to my bumper. As I stepped out of my car, the women from the three cars in front of me started yelling at me, with one asking me "What were you thinking?" I sarcastically replied, "I'm thinking it sucks to be rear ended!" The three women finally "saw" what was in their sight the entire time. They were admittedly shocked that they didn't even see the women, her two kids, or the Volvo station wagon attached to my car. I share this story with my students as another example of the impact schemas have on our perception. A schema was activated for this women triggered by my youth and my appearance. As such, the evidence inconsistent with their schema was literally deleted from their reality.

So, one aspect of mindfulness involves acknowledging the powerful influence of schemas. Recognizing the flaws in our perception is a powerful first step to reclaiming beginner's mind. By doing so, we are able to increasingly challenge our automatic perceptions in exchange for a more open and uncontaminated view of reality.

Presence

Most people know, at least conceptually, what it means to be mentally present. Still, it is something that we are not really taught through traditional Western education to *practice*. In fact, the exact opposite is true. We are taught to pay attention to a wide variety of stimuli and to multitask, both at work and at home. According to Susan Smalley and Diana Winston, authors of *Fully Present: The Science, Practice, and Art of Mindfulness*, "Despite extraordinary advances in science and technology, from mapping our genomes to information access via the Internet, we live in an age of increasing anxiety and increasing doubt in our capacity to make decisions and affect change, whether in our bodies, our lives, or the world around us.... In addition to the stresses of ambiguous decision-making, constant interruptions from cell phones, Blackberries, Facebook, Twitter, and so on, are creating another source of stressful thinking, multitasking."[22] In a similar fashion, Jane Pickert states, "In a time when no one seems to have enough time, our devices allow us to be many places at once—but at the cost of being unable to fully inhabit the place where we actually want to be."[23] In a sense, the lack of presence in our societies could be deemed the single most critical reason for us to explore and consider mindfulness practice.

Jon Kabbat-Zinn dedicates much of his work to addressing the problems mentioned here and how mindfulness can help us handle these modern challenges. In his compact text *Mindfulness for Beginners: Reclaiming the Present Moment—and Your Life*, he states, "Most of our lives we are absorbed in doing: in getting things done, in going rapidly from one thing to the next

[22] Smalley, S.L., Winston, D., 2010. Fully Present: The Science, Art, and Practice of Mindfulness. Da Capo Lifelong, Cambridge, MA, p. 178.
[23] Pickert, K., The art of being mindful, 42.

or multitasking—attempting to juggle a bunch of different things at the very same time."[24] In one of many interpretations of how to be more fully present in the moment we are in and how to focus on it, he states, "Mindfulness reminds us that it is possible to shift from a *doing mode* to a *being mode* through the application of attention and awareness."[25] While many practices are connected to being present, and much of this concept will weave its way through this book, what is important is the need to live in the present moment. We frequently get caught up in the past or future, or, as noted previously, we are distracted by the things around us and the Western tendency to "be productive" at all times. Being present, however, ultimately allows one to live life more productively, not in the sleepwalking fashion to which many of us are accustomed. The implications and importance of presence for librarians is a theme that is woven throughout this book as well. It is especially important when we are connecting with patrons.

Making Conscious Choices

Natalia Karelai and Jochen Reb, contributors to the upcoming book *Mindfulness in Organizations*, write:

> to the extent that individuals and organizations are mindless, their judgments and choices are more habitual and reactive as opposed to proactive, and they are less likely to notice that there is a decision to be made. As a result, actors are likely to continue with the status quo, potentially missing important decision problems or opportunities.... Mindful decision makers are capable of recognizing their habitual reactions to certain "triggers" (e.g., conflict situation, angry customer) and by doing so, are less like to act automatically according to pre-established behavioral scripts.[26]

While they focus on the workplace setting, paying closer attention to how one makes decisions can have a relevance to and impact on all aspects of life. Stephen Covey, in his seminal book *The 7 Habits of Highly Effective People: Powerful Lessons in Personal Change*, emphasizes the need to be proactive versus reactive. His concept is that in each and every moment, we make choices. These may be mindless or reactive, or they may be deliberate, thoughtful, and proactive based on our core values and beliefs.[27]

---

[24] Kabbat-Zinn, J., 2011. Mindfulness for Beginners: Reclaiming the Present Moment–and Your Life. Sounds True, Louisville, CO, p. 18.

[25] Ibid., 18.

[26] Karelaia, N., Reb, J., 2015. Improving Decision Making Through Mindfulness. Cambridge, Cambridge University Press, p. 166.

[27] Covey, S., 1989. Seven Habits of Highly Effective People: Powerful Lessons in Personal Change. Fireside, New York, NY, p. 65.

What many mindfulness practitioners believe is that we can make choices, especially relating to how we interpret events in the world. According to Daniel Siegel, a well-known neuroscientist "With the dissolution of automatic patterns, the mind seems to be freed to acquire new levels of self-regulation. This is the power of mindfulness to alter our affective responses."[28] A central component taught in any MBSR program—in fact, it is brought up in the very first meeting—is that if we look more carefully, there is almost always a space between something that occurs and our reaction to it. According to Rick Hanson and Richard Mendus, authors of *Buddha's Brain: The Practical Neuroscience of Happiness, Love, & Wisdom*, "First darts are unpleasant to be sure. But then we add our reactions to them. These reactions are 'second darts'—the ones we throw ourselves. Most of our suffering comes from second darts."[29] A belief that we can inhabit this space through mindful practices and the development of greater awareness is of great importance to many, if not most, people who choose mindfulness as a way of being that can, among other things, improve the quality of choices they make in their lives on a moment-to-moment basis. There are numerous applications of this principle for librarians in both their personal and professional lives. For example, a library manager who recognizes the space that exists to consider an action in any given circumstance will make better decisions than one who makes them based solely on emotions, or even experience.

Mindfulness and Your Brain: What the Science Tells Us

The following discussion is not intended to be an exhaustive review of the research on mindfulness and its impact on one's brain and health. It is necessary, however, to illustrate the bridge between mindfulness and brain function. While research in the general area has been prolific, it is also just beginning in many respects. After considering how research in this area is being conducted, we will explore some of the more recent studies illustrating the positive impact of mindfulness on specific structures of the brain and consider the possibilities that may be brought about through additional research.

In one critical exploration of the scientific research on mindfulness, John Dunne, Antoine Lutz, and Richard Davidson state at the outset that

---

[28] Siegel, D., 2007. The Mindful Brain. WW Norton & Co, New York, NY, p. 101.

[29] Hanson, R., Mendus, R., 2009. Buddha's Brain: The Practical Neuroscience of Happiness, Love, & Wisdom. New Harbinger Publications, Oakland, CA, p. 50.

"from the vantage point of the researcher who stands outside the tradition [of Buddhism], it is crucial to separate the highly detailed and verifiable aspects of traditional knowledge about meditation from the transcendental claims that form the metaphysical or theological context of that knowledge."[30] They emphasize the need for scientific research on mindfulness to be separated from its original theological context. They go on to distinguish three critical elements that we must consider relative to mindfulness research: "(1) the claimed production of a distinctive and reproducible state that is phenomenally reportable, (2) the claimed relationship between that state and the development of specific traits, and (3) the claimed progression in the practice from the novice to virtuoso."[31] Their work is also helpful in identifying and illustrating the relevant methods by which we have come to explore mindfulness in the lab.

While the electroencephalogram (EEG) provided the ability to monitor brain activity while it is occurring for the first time, it is limited by the way that it externally measures brain activity. In that procedure, electrodes are placed on one's skull to monitor brain activity. Positron emission tomography (PET) is more sophisticated, since it measures "radioactively labeled chemicals that have been injected into the bloodstream and uses the data to produce two- or three-dimensional images of the distribution of those chemicals throughout the brain."[32] Functional magnetic resonance imaging (fMRI) lacks PET's ability to pinpoint neurochemicals, but it is a leap forward in terms of what scientists are able to study. "An fMRI scan can produce images of brain activity as fast as every second or two… Thus, with fMRI, scientists can determine precisely when brain regions become active and how long they remain active."[33] Additional means of studying the impact of mindful practice include the measuring of immune systems and self-reported surveys. Interestingly, these latter surveys have been studied to determine several key shared aspects of mindfulness that researchers are looking at for further exploration: "(1) nonreactivity to inner experience; (2) observing/noticing/attending to sensations/ perceptions/thoughts/feelings; (3) acting with awareness/(non) automatic

---

[30] Dunne, J., Lutz, A., Davidson, R., 2007. Meditation and the neuroscience of consciousness: an introduction. In: Thompson, E., Moscovitch, M., Zelazo, P. (Eds.), Cambridge Handbook of Consciousness. Cambridge University Press, Cambridge, p. 3.

[31] Dunne, J., Lutz, A., Davidson, R., Meditation and the neuroscience of consciousness: an introduction, p. 4.

[32] Ibid., 37.

[33] Ibid., 37.

pilot/concentration/nondistraction; (4) describing/labeling with words; and (5) non-judging of experience."[34] Thanks to these varied techniques, we are actually able to study changes in the brain in relation to mindful practices from a number of angles.

One study by Lazar et al. (2005) that used fMRI to study the brains of experienced meditators discovered two areas of the brain, the middle prefrontal area and the right insula, which were more fully developed than in the brains of nonpractioners. They concluded that "initial results suggest that meditation may be associated with structural changes in areas of the brain that are important for sensory, cognitive, and emotional processing. The data further suggest that meditation may impact age-related declines in cortical structure."[35] So, at least in experienced practitioners, higher-level brain functioning occurs to such a degree as to affect the aging of the brain.

It is important to diverge somewhat at this point to explain what we are looking for when examining the brain. According to Daniel Siegel, "Neurons fire when we have an experience. With neural firing, the potential is created to alter synapses by growing new ones, strengthening existing ones, or even stimulating the growth of new neurons that create new synaptic linkages."[36] This process, referred to as *neurogenesis*, denotes the possibility that we all have to be able to alter the structure of our brains in profound ways.

Another study by Richard Davidson, and reported by Daniel Siegel, discovered that "there was a left anterior shift [within the brain] in function during emotion-provoking stimuli tests, reveal[ing] that mindfulness practice enable individuals to regulate their emotions in a more positive manner with approach rather than withdrawal."[37] Again, this illustrates the ability of the brain to change in profound ways with time and practice.

Other studies, such as those associated with MBSR programs, "show that mindful awareness training over an eight-week period could significantly improve the executive function of attention in adults and adolescents with genetically loaded forms of attention-deficit hyperactivity disorder."[38] The implication, of course, is that it could benefit anyone's executive functioning, not just those with a deficiency in this area.

[34] Siegel, D. The Mindful Brain, p. 91.
[35] Lazar, S.W., Kerr, C.E., Wasserman, R.H., Gray, J.R., Greve, D.N., Treadway, M.T., McGarvey, M., et al., 2005. Meditation experience is associated with increased cortical thickness. Neuroreport 16 (17), 1893.
[36] Siegel, D., The Mindful Brain, p. 30.
[37] Ibid., 32.
[38] Ibid., 111.

As various studies continue to demonstrate, structural changes in the brain occur as a result of mindful practice over time. The thickness in the middle prefrontal area, right insula, and possibly other locations shows that the brains of mindful practitioners are different than nonpracticing people. Furthermore, the substantive changes to the brain indicate "how a state can become a trait."[39]

Still other research has demonstrated the existence of mirror neurons. This means that our brains are capable of experiencing brain activity based on the vicarious experience of watching another person do something. This has important implications regarding our ability to develop empathy and introception through mindfulness.[40] Other research has demonstrated the potential for mindful practice in altering "anterior cingulated activation" and "orbitofrontal and superior temporal activation" within the brain.[41] Again, while the exact meanings and conclusions may remain murky, the potential is incredible. We can change our brains through mindfulness-based activities.

Researchers such as Richard Davidson and Sharon Begley described numerous preliminary research projects, as well as the potential for much more progress in this area, in their book *The Emotional Life of Your Brain: How Unique Patterns Affect the Way You Think, Feel, and Live—and How You Can Change Them*. While they admit the limitations of current studies since they vary based on the level of experience of the proponents of mindfulness, the length of the studies, the number of participants, the use or lack of control groups, the application of different methodologies and tools, and numerous other shortcomings, they clearly believe that mindfulness can help alleviate suffering and help us live more effective and better lives. Davidson states, "My research on meditatators has shown that mental training can alter patterns of activity in the brain to strengthen empathy, compassion, optimism, and a sense of well-being—the culmination of my promise to study meditation as well as positive emotions. And my research in the mainstream of affective neuroscience has shown that it is these sites of higher-order reasoning that hold the key to altering these patterns of brain activity."[42]

---

[39] Ibid., 121.
[40] Ibid., 168.
[41] Ibid., 220.
[42] Davidson, R., Begley, S., 2013. The Emotional Life of Your Brain: How Unique Patterns Affect the Way You Think, Feel, and Live—and How You Can Change Them. Plume, New York, NY, p. xix.

In conclusion, John Dunne, Antoine Lutz, and Richard Davidson sum up the current status of scientific research on the brain as it relates to mindfulness:

> the collective evidence…underscores the fact that many of our core mental processes, such as awareness and attention and emotion regulation, including our very capacity for happiness and compassion, should best be conceptualized as trainable skills. The meditative traditions provide a compelling example of strategies and techniques that have evolved over time to enhance and optimize human potential and well-being. The neuroscientific study of these traditions is still in its infancy, but the early findings promise both to reveal the mechanisms by which such training may exert its effects and underscore the plasticity of the brain circuits that underlie complex mental functions.[43]

Thus, we know that brains can change. This is referred to as *plasticity* or *neuroplasticity*. We also know that mindful practice induces change, as noted in some of the more specific studies or examples provided earlier in this chapter. Knowing, however, is not enough. We must practice mindfulness to gain its benefits. What follows are some examples of practices in this regard.

According to Dr Sagar Sethi, a practicing psychiatrist for the past 30 years, many of the problems and challenges that we face as adults could be solved when we were younger. Through his study and research, he has come to believe that the application of mindfulness practice at an early age would "reduce or eliminate the need for many of the medications which need to be prescribed later on for a variety of conditions." He feels that if guided breath meditation, proper exercise and diet, and yoga were taken up by more people at a younger age, we could dramatically alter our society in a profoundly positive way.[44]

SELECTED MINDFULNESS TECHNIQUES

This section briefly describes techniques that can assist one in becoming more mindful. There are numerous books and other resources that can take you further. The intent of this discussion is to get you started with some basic techniques and approaches that you may do right away. Following this section are some even shorter tips or pointers, including some suggestions that one should easily be able to incorporate into a regular routine.

---

[43] Dunne, J., Lutz, A., Davidson, R., Meditation and the neuroscience of consciousness: an introduction, p. 41.
[44] Dr Vidya Sethi, personal interview with author, January 16, 2015.

Breath Meditation

Breath meditation is probably the most fundamental techniques of mindfulness-based practice. It is easy to get started with this. According to Jon Kabbat-Zinn, "The breath plays a very important role in meditation and healing… The easiest and most effective way to begin practicing mindfulness as a formal meditative practice is to simply focus on your breathing…."[45] Perhaps Daniel Siegel put it even better:

> *Breath is a fundamental part of life. Breathing is initiated by deep brainstem structures and is impacted directly by our emotional states. Yet breath can also be intentional. And for all of these reasons, breath awareness leads us to the heart of our lives. We come to the borderline between body and mind. Perhaps for each of these reasons, pathways toward health include the mindful focus on the breath as a starting point on the journey.*[46]

If you want to try this activity unguided, you could set an alarm for 5–10 min (perhaps increasing the time later, as you grow more experienced). Then, simply sit upright in a chair with your hands at your side or on your lap and pay attention to your breath for this time period. For beginners, this activity is not easy. Your mind *will* wander—and that is OK. What you need to do is simply keep bringing your attention back to your breath. It is important not to be too hard on yourself or judge yourself as you go (e.g., "I am doing this wrong. I just can't quiet my mind like other people can…."). You can pay attention to your nose, your chest or whatever you would like to focus on. The idea is to notice *each* individual breath coming in and going out. One variation is to count your breath in and out based on a specific number of breaths.

Many people find it especially hard to do an unguided meditation in the beginning. There are many guided meditations that you may find on the Internet, some of which are listed at the end of this chapter. The benefit of the guided meditation is that it works as "training wheels," in a way. The voice of the meditation guide will help bring you back to your breath and to let go of the various thoughts that arise.

Since the purpose of a breathing meditation is to remain as focused as possible, you should seek out the quietest place possible to practice. If you can set up a comfortable place at home, that is great. For many people, however, this is not an option. If this is the case for you, most YMCAs

---

[45] Kabbat-Zinn, J., Full Catastrophe Living: Using the Wisdom of Your Body and Mind to Face Stress, Pain, and Illness, pp. 48, 51.

[46] Siegel, D., The Mindful Brain, p. 176.

have a chapel that is open to members for meditation. Other options can even include meditating in your car or a library study room.

There are a variety of opinions as to the best time to meditate, but the best time is really whatever works for you. Meditating in the morning can be a great way to start your day and gain a focus to carry with you throughout the rest of the day and evening. Meditating at night can help you settle into a calmer state and place the day's events behind you. Sometimes meditating in the middle of the day can help you gain a second wind. Again, whatever works best for you is fine. Ideally, however, having some set times will help you be consistent with your practice.

Loving Kindness Meditation

Loving kindness meditations, sometimes referred to as "metta" meditations,[47] vary from breath meditations in that your focus is on the well-being of yourself and others. The intent of this practice is to help you develop compassion and understanding within the context of overall mindfulness. A typical loving kindness meditation can be as short as 10 min. A link to a guided meditation of this type, posted by the Health Services Department of the University of New Hampshire, is noted at the end of this chapter. It is possible, however, to do this on your own. Thinking about yourself, simply repeat the words "May I be happy. May I be well. May I be peaceful. May I be loved." As you say these words, it is important to try to gain a sense that you deserve these things. After repeating these statements about six times, you can then consider a close loved one. After bringing up a picture of this person in your mind, simply say to yourself six times, "May you be happy. May you be well. May you be peaceful. May you be loved."

After finishing this part of the exercise, stop and reflect for a moment on the feelings that arise within you. Then, consider someone you don't know well. It might be helpful to think of a library patron whom you interact with on occasion. After bringing up a picture of him or her in your mind, simply say to yourself six times "May you be happy. May you be well. May you be peaceful. May you be loved." Next, you should consider someone you are having difficulty with. This could be a colleague or anyone in your life that you feel that you could have a better relationship with. This is perhaps the most challenging step, but after considering

---

[47] Ibid., 62.

a visualization of this person in your head, say to yourself six times, "May you be happy. May you be well. May you be peaceful. May you be loved." At last, you may briefly reflect on how you feel and how you might bring a greater sense of compassion into your work in the library, as well as your personal life. This exercise may seem a little uncomfortable at first, but it really works well. You should notice more rewarding interactions as a result. After mentioning how we are all connected, Jon Kabbat-Zinn states, "The path to developing our capacity to express love more fully is to bring awareness to our actual feelings, to observe them mindfully, to work at being non-judgmental and more patient and accepting."[48] Other authors also have pointed to this type of meditation as helping eliminate bias towards others and helping induce a state of being "both more stable and more engaged with aiding others."[49]

As with breath meditation, it is important to find a good quiet place to do a loving kindness meditation, and it can be done any time of day. Some strategically placed times could be just before a meeting, before doing library instruction, or before going out to help patrons at the reference desk. Empathy and compassion are two very central skills in librarianship, and this exercise will help build your "muscles."

Body Scan Meditation

A body scan meditation has similar requirements to the other meditations already mentioned thus far. You need to find a quiet and secure place to perform this activity. Body scans can last 10–45 min or anything in between. They have one key additional element, which may be done lying down. While you could lie on a bed or couch, a yoga mat is ideal. There are many guided versions that you can find on the Internet (one example is provided at the end of this chapter). The idea is to really pay attention to each part of your body in a way that you may never have done before. Most scans start at the top of your head and work their way down. It is important to stop and take a moment at each location. For example, you might notice tension in your forehead and then slowly shift your attention to your jaw and tongue, noticing whether they are relaxed or tense. Finally, you can consider your body as a whole and might end by stretching a bit or moving your legs and arms. The body scan meditation

[48] Kabbat-Zinn, J., Full Catastrophe Living, p. 224.
[49] Dunne, J., Lutz, A., Davidson, R., Meditation and the neuroscience of consciousness: an introduction. pp. 17, 18.

is intended to help build some reserve for dealing with normal aches and pains, in addition to any other chronic conditions you may have. By learning to accept and not avoid sensations, the idea is that pain can be experienced in a different way, and one can focus on other aspects of one's life and work instead.

Walking Meditation

A walking meditation may be done alone or with a group. If you have never done this activity, it will seem strange at first. The biggest difference between a walking meditation and regular walking is that you are not walking to get anywhere. While walking mindfully (e.g., paying attention to the trees, the birds, or the wind) is helpful, a walking meditation is something more specific. According to Kabbat-Zinn, "Walking meditation involves intentionally attending to the experience of walking itself. It involves focusing on the sensations in your feet or your legs or, alternatively, feeling your whole body moving. You can also integrate awareness of your breathing with the experience of walking."[50]

In a walking meditation, you may walk only 15 or 20 steps in one direction, turn around, and walk straight back. While it is typically done very slowly, one can do mindful walking at varied speeds. It helps to set a timer or alarm so that you can focus on what you are doing without worrying how much time you have spent. Again, while walking in nature has its own mindfulness rewards, and one can do a walking meditation outside, the intent of this exercise is to focus on your body and each distinct movement. For instance, you might say to yourself, "Lifting my right leg. Placing the heel of my right foot on the ground. Placing my right toes on the ground…." This exercise requires a tremendous amount of patience for some. At the same time, some people prefer it to other types of meditation since it involves movement. One of the challenges in walking meditation is finding a place to do it where you are comfortable. Since it requires more space, this isn't always easy. Doing walking meditation in a group can sometimes help overcome some of the anxiety in doing this for the first time since others are similarly engaged.

Mindful Eating

Like other mindfulness techniques, mindful eating can be awkward for beginners. We usually rush through our meals, barely tasting what we eat.

---

[50] Kabbat-Zinn, J., Full Catastrophe Living, p. 114.

This can lead to overeating, lethargy, and indigestion. We also distract ourselves by talking, watching TV, or checking email on our phone while we eat. When we engage in mindful eating, we do not allow any distractions. While it is a practice often done with others, no talking is involved. The idea is to take your time to smell and taste *each* bite of food or *each* sip of drink. Formal mindful eating is not something you need to do every day, but, if done on occasion, it can help you become more aware of your senses at other times as well. It also has the practical benefit of aiding digestion.

Yoga/T'ai Chi

It would be a bit beyond the purview of this book to describe specific yoga or t'ai chi techniques as we have with the other techniques mentioned so far in this chapter. Many people have found these techniques incredibly helpful, however, so they merit a mention. Yoga can be practiced in a wide variety of ways. According to yoga instructor and author Goldie Oren, "The word yoga means 'yoke' or 'to unite,' and the discipline aims to the mind and body into sync with each other…. By practicing yoga, you can improve your posture, balance, flexibility, and strength."[51] Some approaches or classes can involve considerable manipulation of the body. Others can be incredibly gentle and can be done by senior citizens, individuals with disabilities, or individuals struggling with chronic pain. T'ai chi likewise has variants that are more or less difficult and involved. It "embodies a deep philosophical tradition with a dynamic form mindful movement."[52] Classes on t'ai chi can easily be found that target a gentle approach.

Both yoga and t'ai chi may be thought of as forms of moving meditation. There are a number of great videos to get started with either of these techniques. Amazon Prime, YouTube and other web sites offer other streaming video examples. Since these are more involved than other mindfulness techniques mentioned so far, however, your best bet is to have the guidance of an instructor. Yoga and t'ai chi classes can be found in special studios, as well as at the YMCA, community colleges, and other community-based organizations. It is important to try different approaches if you wish to practice because there are so many options. It really is not one size fits all—you should tailor the program to your needs.

[51] Oren, G., 2013. Yoga: The Trainer's Guide to Your Workout. Hinkler Books, Melbourne, pp. 8, 9.
[52] Seigel, D., The Mindful Brain, p. 268.

TEN QUICK TIPS FOR BECOMING MORE MINDFUL

1. **Just breathe.** No other single thing that you can do will be mentioned as frequently in the literature on mindfulness as paying attention to your breath. Taking even a few short breaths when we feel stressed, are stuck waiting in a long line, are stuck waiting in traffic, or have a long line of patrons waiting for assistance in front of you at the reference desk can make you more calm and mindful.

2. **Consider doing chores mindfully.** Instead of rushing to get dishes washed, clothes folded, laundry ironed, floors mopped, rooms vacuumed, or leaves raked, consider performing these actions in a calm and thoughtful way. Pay attention to your breathing and do each task as if it were the most important thing you could be doing.[53]

3. **Pay attention to your senses.**[54] Close your eyes and listen to the sounds around you. Feel the sunlight on your face. Open your eyes and appreciate the world around you. Stop and enjoy the food you eat or any pleasant smells that arise.

4. **Don't overcommit your time.**[55] So often, we have trouble saying no and prioritizing. One of Steven Covey's seven habits is to put first things first.[56] We need to make sure that we are focused on the things that really matter to us. One way to do that is by not planning to do more than you can handle.

5. **Spend time in nature.**[57] This point is pretty obvious to some, but it is very important nevertheless. In conjunction with paying attention to one's senses, spending time in nature can be helpful toward building a reserve for mindfulness and appreciating the miracle of the world as it is.

6. **Be thankful.** It is almost impossible not to be mindful or to have a bad attitude when one dwells on people in your life that one is grateful for. Appreciating events and the things you have can also help. Sometimes this can be done in a very deliberate way. For example, challenge

---

[53] Hahn, T.N., The Miracle of Mindfulness! pp. 85–86.

[54] Smith, M., What's the buzz about mindfulness?, Heretohelp.com. Available from: <http://www.heretohelp.bc.ca/visions/wellness-vol7/whats-the-buzz-about-mindfulness>.

[55] Ibid.

[56] Covey, S., 7 Habits, p. 145.

[57] Smith, M., What's the buzz about mindfulness?

yourself to send three meaningful thank-you messages by email every day, or write three positive things each night before going to sleep.

7. **Be mindful of your thoughts.** While the more involved practices mentioned previously, such as breath meditation, can help with this activity, it also helps to simply be cognitively aware as much as possible that thoughts are constantly streaming through your brain. If you can recognize them as just thoughts, especially when they are thoughts that are self-judging (e.g., I should have done this instead; I should have said that instead; if only I had considered….), you will be practicing mindfulness.[58]

8. **Choose to start your day.**[59] We often get up in the morning and the "rat race" begins before we know it. We need to get the kids ready, walk the dog, pack lunch for work, get dressed, and numerous other small tasks. Instead of jumping up at the sound of the alarm clock and starting to race along, in one continuous motion, until you climb back in bed that night, try sitting up, taking a few breaths, stretching, and welcoming a new day.

9. **Transition well.**[60] Take a moment to breathe when switching from one project to the next, arriving at work, or arriving home. Again, we tend to race from one thing to the next without giving respect and appreciation for what we have done or what we are about to do. We need to cultivate awareness in small but effective ways.

10. **Commit to listening to those around you.** Steven Covey framed this point by explaining that we should first seek to understand, and only then seek to be understood.[61] We should simply focus more on understanding others. We can be much more mindful and compassionate in our relationships if we slow down and take the time to listen to what others have to say. You could also take this a step further. Set aside a day each week to take a colleague or friend out for coffee and really focus on listening to what this person has to say or is feeling.

---

[58] Ibid.

[59] Marturano, J., 5 Tips for practicing mindfulness at the office. Mindful Magazine (online). Available from: <http://www.mindful.org/mindful-voices/on-leadership/5-tips-for-practicing-mindfulness-at-the-office>.

[60] Ibid.

[61] Covey, S., 7 Habits, p. 235.

RECOMMENDED RESOURCES

Kim Eng's 10-minute guided breath meditation exercise is a great place to start with this type of meditation. Available from: <https://www.youtube.com/watch?v=67SeR3LxtdI>.

Sponsored by the University of New Hampshire's Health Services Department, this video is a great place to start with a 10-minute loving kindness meditation. Available from: <https://www.youtube.com/watch?v=sz7cpV7ERsM>.

Greg Devries's body scan meditation is excellent for beginners. Available from: <https://www.youtube.com/watch?v=obYJRmgrqOU>.

MINDFUL MAGAZINE

Rinzler, L., 2014. The Buddha Walks into the Office: A Guide to Livelihood for a New Generation. Shambala, Boston, MA.

BIBLIOGRAPHY

American Library Association, Charter of 1879. Available from: <http://www.ala.org/aboutala/history/charter-1879-revised-1942> (accessed 09.12.14.).

Barker, I., Close Your Eyes and Think of.... Nothing at All. The Times Educational Supplement 5017: 20.

Cooper, A., CBS News: 60 Minutes. Available from: <http://www.cbsnews.com/news/mindfulness-anderson-cooper-60-minutes/> (accessed 15.12.14.).

Covey, S., 1989. Seven Habits of Highly Effective People: Powerful Lessons in Personal Change. Fireside, New York, NY.

Davidson, R., Begley, S., 2013. The Emotional Life of Your Brain: How Unique Patterns Affect the Way You Think, Feel, and Live—and How You Can Change Them. Plume, New York, NY.

Dunne, J., Lutz, A., Davidson, R., 2007. Meditation and the neuroscience of consciousness: an introduction. In: Thompson, E., Moscovitch, M., Zelazo, P. (Eds.) Cambridge Handbook of Consciousness, Cambridge University Press, Cambridge, pp. 499–555.

Estefan, G., 1993. Christmas Through Your Eyes. Epic Records, CD.

Gordon-Graham, C., 2014. Beginner's mind. Therapy Today 25 (5), 22–25.

Hahn, T.N., 1987. The Miracle of Mindfulness. Beacon Press, Boston, MA.

Hanh, T.N., 2000. Contemporary Heroes and Heroines, vol. 4. Gale, Detroit.

Hanson, R., Mendus, R., 2009. Buddha's Brain: The Practical Neuroscience of Happiness, Love, & Wisdom. New Harbinger Publications, Oakland, CA.

Hauptman, A., 2013. Medicine as practice: notes on keeping the mind of a beginner despite becoming an expert. J. Relig. Health 53 (5), 1297–1299.

Kabbat-Zinn, J., 2009. Full Catastrophe Living: Using the Wisdom of Your Body and Mind to Face Stress, Pain, and Illness. Delta Trade Paperbacks, New York, NY.

Kabbat-Zinn, J., 2011. Mindfulness for Beginners: Reclaiming the Present Moment–and Your Life. Sounds True, Louisville, CO.

Karelaia, N., Reb, J., 2015. Improving Decision Making Through Mindfulness. Cambridge, Cambridge University Press.

Lazar, S., Kerr, C.E., Wasserman, R.H., Gray, J.R., Greve, D.N., Treadway, M.T., et al., 2005. Meditation experience is associated with increased cortical thickness. Neuroreport 16 (17), 1893.

Marturano, J., 5 Tips for practicing mindfulness at the office. Mindful Magazine (online). Available from: <http://www.mindful.org/mindful-voices/on-leadership/5-tips-for-practicing-mindfulness-at-the-office> (accessed 24.12.14.).

McCluskey, E., 2005. Jon Kabbat-Zinn, PhD '71. Technol. Rev. 108 (11), 42.

Mind-Body Medicine, 2005. Therapy Today 16 (9), 4–7.

Mind & Life Institute, Mission. Available from: <http://www.mindandlife.org/mission/> (accessed 10.12.14.).

Nyanaponika, 2014. Contemporary Authors Online. Gale, Detroit, Available from: <http://ic.galegroup.com/ic/bic1/ReferenceDetailsPage/ReferenceDetailsWindow?f ailOverType=&query=&prodId=BIC1&windowstate=normal&contentModules=&d isplay-query=&mode=view&displayGroupName=Reference&limiter=&currPage=& disableHighlighting=false&displayGroups=&sortBy=&search_within_results=&p=BI-C1&action=e&catId=&activityType=&scanId=&documentId=GALE%7CH1000073 834&source=Bookmark&u=gree35277&jsid=6c55c163f6c056fcb1a468cf35335824> (accessed 15.12.14.).

Oren, G., 2013. Yoga: The Trainer's Guide to Your Workout. Hinkler Books, Melbourne.

Pickert, K., 2014. The art of being mindful. Time 183 (2), 42–46.

Quezzaire, P., 2006. Dalai Lama. History Reference Center. pp. 1–3.

Schlumpf, H., September 12, 2003. Practicing peace: Famed Buddhist Monk urges overflow crowd to live mindfully. National Catholic Reporter.

Seigel, D., 2007. The Mindful Brain. WW Norton & Co, New York, NY.

Shunryu Suzuki, 2004. Contemporary Authors Online. Gale, Detroit, <http://ic.galegroup. com/ic/bic1/ReferenceDetailsPage/ReferenceDetailsWindow?failOverType=&query =&prodId=BIC1&windowstate=normal&contentModules=&display-query=&mode =view&displayGroupName=Reference&limiter=&currPage=&disableHighlighting= false&displayGroups=&sortBy=&search_within_results=&p=BIC1&action=e&catId= &activityType=&scanId=&documentId=GALE%7CH1000153340&source=Bookma rk&u=gree35277&jsid=87f3387ab3af71283ac2f99207e37f58> (accessed 12.12.14.).

Smalley, S., Winston, D., 2010. Fully Present: The Science, Art, and Practice of Mindfulness. Da Capo Lifelong, Cambridge, MA.

Smith, M., What's the Buzz About Mindfulness? Heretohelp.com. Available from: <http:// www.heretohelp.bc.ca/visions/wellness-vol7/whats-the-buzz-about-mindfulness> (accessed 24.12.14.).

Wilson, J., 2014. Mindful America: The Mutual Transformation of Buddhist Meditation and American Culture. Oxford Press, Oxford.

CHAPTER 2

The Mindfulness Movement in Education

Richard Moniz and Howard Slutzky

INTRODUCTION

How often do we see students that struggle at all levels of education because they face problems that are not fundamentally academic? Issues as basic as time management or where to start with a research project are challenges that librarians and teachers see students face every day. On a more basic level, we know, both in what we see in the classroom and from our own personal experiences, the powerful role that self-regulation (or lack of), distraction, self-efficacy, and other concerns can pull us and our students away from being in the moment and learning as effectively as possible. The mindful or contemplative movement in education provides us with an alternative way to view education. It is not by any means a quick fix or something to add on to an already busy day. That is, it should not just be considered busy work. It is, rather, a different way of viewing the world and education that has tremendous promise for enhancing the way we all learn. Take, for example, the following quote by Daniel Rechstaffen, author of *The Way of Mindful Education: Cultivating Well-Being in Teachers and Students*:

> Students are told to pay attention a thousand times in school, but rarely taught how. We tell our kids to be nice to each other again and again, without ever teaching them the incredibly accessible exercises that cultivate empathy and forgiveness. We tell students not to be so reactive, and even put them in juvenile detention centers, all because they can't regulate the disturbances within their own bodies. There are methods for teaching impulse control, attention, and empathy, but young people have rarely been taught them. Mindfulness has been effectively training these qualities for millennia…[1]

Other authors have encapsulated this theme as well. Gavriel Salomon and Tamar Globerson once termed the gap that exists between what

[1] Rechtschaffen, D., 2014. The Way of Mindful Education: Cultivating Well-Being in Teachers and Students. WW Norton & Co., New York, NY, p. 10

students are capable of learning and what they actually learn the "zone of proximal learning." According to these experts, this gap exists primarily due to a lack of mindfulness. They state:

> One entertains the implicit assumption that if individuals have a fair mastery of knowledge and skills, that they are likely to apply them when the opportunity arises. But such an assumption faces difficulties. The painful truth is that more often than not individuals do not make good use of what they know and master...In many situations they are often not very mindful, thus manifesting poorer learning and transfer than they could have, would they have been more mindful during the learning and/or transfer process.[2]

Indeed, if one were to look at Western education in general, it has in many ways actually *removed* mindfulness from the curriculum. By doing so, it has ignored important facets of how people view the world and how they learn. Take, for example, the prevalent perspective of education, which generally assumes that all of us are always rational beings. According to Jake and Roddy Gibbs, authors of *The Mindful Way to Study: Dancing with Your Books*, "Although the ability to think at the rational level is of great benefit, and everyone should develop the ability to use reason, most of the thinking done by people is not at the rational level...Research shows that many of us do not think at the rational level most of the time."[3] Other popular authors, such as Dan Ariely in his book *Predictably Irrational: The Hidden Forces That Shape Our Decisions*, have driven this home as well. We are constantly subject to unforeseen biases and distracted in all manner of ways that affect our ability to think, learn, and make decisions.[4] Steven Rockefeller at Middlebury College notes the words of the liberal Christian philosopher Friedrich Schleiermacher: "...every person is born with a capacity to experience directly the mystery, wonder, and beauty of the world, which is essential to human well-being, and a sense of joy and the meaning of life. However ... this capacity is 'crushed' out of children in the course of their education by the modern."[5] The implication is that

---

[2] Salomon, G., Globerson, T., 1987. Skill may not be enough: the role of mindfulness in learning and transfer. Int. J. Edu. Res. 11 (6), 623, 624.

[3] Gibbs, J., Gibbs, R., 2013. The Mindful Way to Study: Dancing with Your Books. O'Connor Press, New York, NY, p. 20.

[4] Ariely, D., 2010. Predictibly Irrational: The Hidden Forces That Shape Our Decisions. Harper Perennial, New York, NY, pp. 1–384.

[5] Rockefeller, S., 2006. Meditation, social change, and undergraduate education. Teach. College Rec. 108 (9), 1779.

we are not mindful, so we sleepwalk through much of the learning process in the various contexts in which learning occurs, among other aspects of our lives. Furthermore, while teachers (and librarians for that matter) face all of the issues that nonteachers face in this regard, they also directly face problems or challenges that are peculiar to the profession as well. To cite just a few examples:

- Watching students misbehave and feeling ineffective when you try to intervene.
- Getting chewed out by your Principal [or other administrator in higher education] when you feel you didn't deserve it.
- Having to cover (again) for a colleague who shirks responsibilities.[6]

While Daniel Rechstaffen's book focuses on K–12 education, much creativity and experimentation is occurring in the area of integrating contemplative practices in higher education as well. Daniel Holland, in a report of contemplative practices in education in both the United States and Austria, states:

The confluence of these trends provides an opportunity for a quiet revolution across many educational settings. Such a revolution could involve the integration of contemplative practices into the traditional higher education settings for the purpose not only of retaining reflection, creativity, and meaning in the learning process, but also promoting health and psychological well-being among those within these educational settings.[7]

Clearly, there is an opportunity for us to help ourselves and our students by integrating a mindfulness-based approach in the classroom. According to Zenner et al. (2014), the authors of one meta-analysis of research on the topic, "Mindfulness can be understood as the foundation and basic pre-condition for education."[8] Libraries, as part of the education landscape, can have a role to play as well. This chapter is intended to provide an idea of the kinds of activities and developments that are occurring in both K–12 and higher-education classrooms and campuses.

---

[6] Schoeberlein, D., 2009. Mindful Teaching and Teaching Mindfulness: A Guide for Anyone Who Teaches Anything. Wisdom Publications, Boston, MA, p. 101.

[7] Holland, D., 2006. Contemplative education in unexpected places: teaching mindfulness in Arkansas and Austria. Teach. College Rec. 108 (9), 1843.

[8] Zenner, C., Herrnleben-Kurz, S., Walach, H., 2014. Mindfulness-based Interventions in schools—a systematic review and meta-analysis. Front. Psychol. 5, 2.

DEVELOPMENT IN K–12

The Western roots for integrating mindfulness into the K–12 curriculum owes much of its inspiration to American psychologist Daniel Goleman, who is best known for highlighting the importance of emotional intelligence. According to Goleman, "Emotions that simmer beneath the threshold of awareness can have a powerful impact on how we perceive and react, even though we have no idea they are at work…people who cannot marshal some control over their emotional life fight inner battles that sabotage their ability for focused work and clear thought."[9] His fundamentally important concept is that various forms of emotional intelligence are not fixed; rather, they can be taught. One can easily see the natural fit between such thinking and the more recent discovery of neuroplasticity of the brain. The term *neuroplasticity* refers to the now-well-proven biological capability to literally change one's brain in order to live a more thoughtful, compassionate life.

Beginning as far back as the 1960s, schools began experimenting with Goleman's concepts in the social emotional learning (SEL) movement. Over time, these programs have demonstrated the ability "to support emotional regulation, social competency, and resiliency, as well as increase academic achievement."[10] This is accomplished by targeting five critical competencies:

- Self-management
- Self awareness
- Social awareness
- Relationship skills
- Responsible decision making.[11]

Linda Lantieri is a proponent of Goleman's views on the importance of emotional intelligence and mindfulness in schools. As the founder of the Collaborative for Academic, Social, and Emotional Learning (CASEL), she has helped operationalize this approach in a classroom setting. According to Lantieri, the primary focus of the aforementioned bullet points boils down to "relaxing the body" and "focusing the mind."[12] Many

---

[9] Goleman, D., 1995. Emotional Intelligence: Why it Can Matter More Than IQ. Bantam, New York, NY, pp. 55, 36.

[10] Rechtschaffen, D., The Way of Mindful Education: Cultivating Well-Being in Teachers and Students, 17.

[11] Ibid., 17.

[12] Lantieri, L., 2008. Building Emotional Intelligence. Sounds True, Louisville, CO, p. 9.

other initiatives have arisen in primary education since the foundation of CASEL. A few of these are mentioned next as a sample of some of the pioneering efforts related to mindfulness that are occurring in schools.

MindUP Curriculum

According to the program web site for the MindUP curriculum:

MindUP is a research-based training program for educators and children. This program is composed of 15 lessons based in neuroscience. Students learn to self-regulate behavior and mindfully engage in focused concentration required for academic success. MindUP lessons align with all state standards, including Common Core, and support improved academic performance while enhancing perspective taking, empathy and kindness as well as fostering complex problem-solving skills.[13]

Founded by Goldie Hawn and supported by the Hawn Foundation, MindUP has locations throughout the United States and other countries, such as the United Kingdom, Hong Kong, China (as well as Hong Kong), Serbia, Australia, and Venezuela. The MindUP web site points to a recent study that explored mindfulness-based education programs designed along the same lines as MindUP (i.e., teaching mindful breathing and other techniques). The study of 246 fourth to seventh graders, conducted by Kimberly Schonert-Reichl and Molly Lawlor, determined that these interventions had significant benefits for the students involved, and that students and teachers seemed to buy into them significantly over time as well:

Results also revealed that pre- and early adolescents who participated in the ME program, compared to pre- and early adolescents who did not, evidenced significant and positive improvements in their positive emotions, namely optimism…. the ME program teachers told us that they found the "core" mindful attention exercises easy to implement, and that frequently their students reminded them to stop their regular classroom instruction and do their "mindful breathing" lesson each day. Teachers also commented to us that they often saw an immediate change in students' behaviors—and that students were able to focus and pay attention to their academic lessons more easily.[14]

---

[13] The Hawn Foundation. MindUP. Available from: <http://thehawnfoundation.org/mindup/>.

[14] Schonert-Reichl, K.A., Stewart Lawlor, M., 2010. The effects of a mindfulness-based education program on pre-and early adolescents' well-being and social and emotional competence. Mindfulness 1 (3), 149–150.

In addition, Dr Schonert-Reichl utilized self and peer reports of fourth and fifth graders specifically enrolled in MindUP and reported the following:

- 82% of children reported having a more positive outlook
- 81% of children learned to make themselves happy
- 58% of children tried to help others more often.[15]

.b Curriculum

The *.b* in the name *.b Curriculum* stands for "Stop, Breathe, and Be!" It is part of a broader initiative known as the Mindfulness in Schools Project, created by experienced schoolteachers Richard Burnett, Chris Cullen, and Chris O'Neil.[16] Teachers that employ this curriculum participate in mindfulness-based stress reduction (MBSR) or similar programs and have their own personal mindfulness-based practice prior to teaching in this way. Divided into nine specific lessons on topics such as paying attention, recognizing worry and anxiety as it occurs, and being present, its purpose is to help students to calm their minds, concentrate, deal with and manage stress effectively, and generally lead happier lives.[17] According to the web site, .b has gained international recognition and has been translated into Dutch, Danish, Finnish, French, and German.[18] The British Parliament has even discussed wider national initiatives to integrate mindfulness in the classroom based on the success of this specific program.[19]

Learning to BREATHE Curriculum

The Learning to BREATHE Curriculum was created by Dr Patricia Broderick. Dr Broderick currently serves as a research associate at the Penn State Prevention Research Center and has also served as the former

---

[15] The Hawn Foundation. MindUP. Available from: <http://thehawnfoundation.org/mindup/>.

[16] Mindfulness in Schools Project. About. Available from: <http://mindfulnessinschools.org/about/our-story/>.

[17] Mindfulness in Schools Project. What is .b? Available from: <http://mindfulnessin-schools.org/what-is-b/>.

[18] Mindfulness in Schools Project. Our story. Available from: <http://mindfulnessinschools.org/about/our-story/>.

[19] If moral judgement had a mark scheme…. The Times Educational Supplement, July 11, 2014. Available from: <https://www.tes.co.uk/article.aspx?storycode=6437112> (accessed 02.01.15.).

director of the Stress Reduction Center at West Chester University of Pennsylvania.[20] According to the web site promoting this program:

Learning to BREATHE is a mindfulness-based curriculum for adolescents created for a classroom or group setting. The curriculum is intended to strengthen emotion regulation and attention, expand adolescents' repertoire of stress management skills, and help them integrate mindfulness into daily life. Each lesson includes age-appropriate discussion, activities, and opportunities to practice mindfulness skills in a group setting.[21]

The program consists of six themes, including developing students' abilities to manage stress, regulate their emotions, and focus their attention.[22] A comprehensive study of the effectiveness of Learning to BREATHE, which included 216 high school students, reported the following:

The results of this study support the hypotheses that Learning to BREATHE has a positive effect on measures of emotional regulation, self-regulation efficacy, psychosomatic complaints, and self-report stress level. Students in the treatment group reported small yet statistically significant reductions in emotional regulation difficulties, psychosomatic complaints, and self-report stress level, while moderately increasing self-regulation efficacy of emotions compared to their counterparts.[23]

MBSR training for the teachers in advance was considered an important element of the program's success.[24] Furthermore, additional research determined that teacher participation in the MBSR program in preparation for teaching students was highly beneficial for the teachers themselves:[25]

Relative to the control group, teachers who participated in the MBSR program demonstrated significantly greater levels of self-kindness, mindfulness, and overall

---

[20] Learning to Breathe. Available from: <http://learning2breathe.org/background/parent>.

[21] Learning to BREATHE. Available from: <http://learning2breathe.org/about/introduction>.

[22] Learning to BREATHE. Available from: <http://learning2breathe.org/about/program-goals>.

[23] Metz, S.M., Frank, J.L., Reibel, D., Cantrell, T., Sanders, R., Broderick, P.C., 2013. The effectiveness of the Learning to BREATHE program on adolescent emotion regulation. Res. Hum. Dev. 10 (3), p. 267.

[24] Metz, S.M., et al., The effectiveness of the Learning to BREATHE program on adolescent emotion regulation, 268.

[25] Frank, J.L., Reibel, D., Broderick, P., Cantrell, T., Metz, S., 2013. The effectiveness of mindfulness-based stress reduction on educator stress and well-being: results from a pilot study. Mindfulness, 7.

self-compassion. Similarly, levels of self judging and over-identification showed significantly greater declines for treatment group participants compared to controls. Interestingly, the most consistent and strongest benefits related to participation in the MBSR group were found related to improvements in teacher sleep quality.[26]

Skills for Life

One of the best-known proponents in the United States of adopting mindfulness in general has been Democratic Congressman Tim Ryan. According to Ryan:

We need to raise our children in a nation that teaches them to be mindful, that teaches them about the importance of kindness and being connected to their fellow human beings and the environment that sustains them. A nation that teaches them to appreciate their basic human goodness in others.[27]

Ryan was largely responsible for securing $982,000 in funding to implement the mindfulness-based education initiative known as Skills for Life in Youngstown and Warren, Ohio (Ryan's home state). According to kindergarten teacher Denise Roberts, "The first year we did it, we found that we had a much better-behaved classroom than we did the year before."[28] In the second year of the program, she noted, "not only do I have a better-behaved class, I also have a class that's reading higher and writing higher than I ever had before."[29] The program for kindergarteners incorporates elements such as 5-minute group meditations and a "peace corner," where students may go when they experience stress.[30] Ryan has continued to spread the word and sees higher education as playing a key role. In a 2014 talk at the University of Miami, he stated, "I got into politics to change things, to make a difference. When you find something that can make a change, you want to push it out."[31]

---

[26] Frank, J.L., et al., The effectiveness of mindfulness-based stress reduction on educator stress and well-being, 7.

[27] Ryan, T., 2012. A Mindful Nation: How a Simple Practice Can Help Us Reduce Stress, Improve Performance, and Recapture the American Spirit. Hay House, Carlsbad, CA, p. 172.

[28] O'Brien, D., Ryan takes 'mindfulness' to inner-city schools. The Business Journal, April 13, 2012. Available from: <http://businessjournaldaily.com/education/ryan-takes-%E2%80%98mindfulness%E2%80%99-inner-city-schools-2012-4-13>.

[29] Ibid.

[30] Ibid.

[31] Tim Ryan as quoted in "Congressman Tim Ryan visits UM to share his vision for a mindful nation," University of Miami College of Arts & Sciences, November 11, 2014. Available from: <http://www.as.miami.edu/news/news-archive/congressman-tim-ryan-visits-um-to-share-his-vision-for-a-mindful-nation-.html>.

DEVELOPMENTS IN HIGHER EDUCATION

Mindfulness in education is by no means limited to K–12. A wide variety of initiatives have burgeoned within higher education as well. These efforts run the gamut; they can involve any of the following: creating a space or spaces on campus where students, faculty, and staff may engage in mindful activities such as meditation; staff, faculty, and student committees or campus mindfulness groups that meet on a regular basis; bringing in outside mindfulness experts for an occasional workshop; faculty that insert a few "mindful moments" strategically into a traditional class; a course or courses that integrate mindfulness or highlight related concepts as a fundamentally central component of the course or courses; and full concentrations or majors in contemplative studies. Below are some specific examples of the kinds of initiatives taking place.

Contemplative Spaces

One of the simplest ways that colleges and universities have begun implementing mindfulness-based initiatives is by providing a place on campus for students, faculty, and staff to meditate. At Carnegie Mellon University, for instance, there is a mindfulness room, with a waterfall and plants. Those entering the room are asked to leave electronic devices outside. The emphasis is on providing a quiet place for reflection or meditation. Bentleigh College, in Melbourne, Australia, is another similar example. It offers a regular space for students, faculty, and staff to utilize for meditation purposes, which is also occasionally used to host classes or short workshops on meditation.[32]

At Johnson & Wales University in Charlotte, North Carolina, faculty from the School of Science and Liberal Arts have collaborated with the library staff to convert a faculty conference room into a room supporting contemplative practices. While the conference room may be booked for traditional activities, such as meeting with students or working on research and writing, the room is also used for individual and group meditation. A small water fountain, as well as other appropriate décor such as a Japanese shoji screen and a scroll with a quote from the Dalai Lama, decorate this room.

---

[32] A place to be mindful on campus. Mindful Magazine, November 18, 2014. Available from: <http://mindful.org/news/a-place-to-be-mindful-on-campus>.

Campus Mindfulness Groups or Committees

Margaret DuFon and Jennifer Christian first began discussions to create a contemplative practices interest group among the faculty at California State University's Chico campus in 2005. By 2008, the group began meeting more formally every other week, taking on the title "Faculty Initiative for Transformative Learning."[33] Through financial support from their Center for Excellence in Learning and Teaching, they were able to bring workshops and awareness to campus faculty regarding mindfulness practices in a classroom setting. By 2010, they were able to introduce a Campus Day of Meditation during final exams. This initiative included the reservation of meditation space. By 2011, the group was also able to bring in outside meditation teachers and start offering more direct opportunities to students.[34] According to DuFon and Christian:

> The Mindful Campus continues its efforts towards raising awareness in the daily lives of faculty and students. We believe that mindful living and contemplative pedagogy have the potential to effectively enhance student learning and achievement, as well as foster an innovative environment that can create fuller and richer learning for students, greater satisfaction for educators, and a more nurturing environment in our university and community.[35]

Largely due to the efforts of Steven Rockefeller, a professor at Middlebury College, students at Middlebury College were introduced to meditation on a voluntary basis through workshops and other initiatives. He emphasizes the critical need for administrative support from the institution and the establishment of an appropriate committee or structure for mindfulness initiatives. Among other recommendations, he states, "This support could involve a policy of allowing staff time for meditation during the workday and creation of a space or spaces for it in buildings where people are working."[36]

At Johnson & Wales University in Charlotte, efforts began in the 2011–2012 academic year to create a campus committee that would initially involve the faculty and staff in contemplative practices. Later expanded to students, the initiative was led by a core group of Arts & Sciences faculty, most notably Kenny Harmon and Lisa Kendall (see sidebar). Their efforts

---

[33] Dufon, M., Christian, J., 2013. The formation and development of the mindful campus. New Dir. Teach. Learn. 134, 66.

[34] Ibid., 69–70.

[35] Ibid., 72.

[36] Rockefeller, S., 2006. Meditation, social change, and undergraduate education. Teach. College Rec. 108, (9), 1785.

were soon supported by myself, as the director of library services, and three additional librarians. Over time, the committee came to be known as the campus's "BREATHE group."

The BREATHE group began by offering weekday meditations one afternoon every week. As mentioned previously, a faculty conference room in the library was rededicated to the purpose of supporting this initiative. While the afternoon sessions continued over time and included an ever-changing group of faculty, staff, and students, an additional evening session was introduced and held in the Student Union. While the daytime group had more staff involvement, the evening session drew significantly larger numbers of students. Both groups experimented with different varieties of short meditations, although breathing meditations were most common. Meditation sessions were always followed by short periods of reflection led by a faculty member that allowed people to share how they felt about their meditation experience. It should be noted that over time, some of these sessions have been guided by myself, other librarians, or both in the absence of a faculty guide.

The core group of staff and faculty involved in the campus BREATHE initiative later also helped sponsor and create a special Mindfulness Day workshop to kick off Faith and Spirituality Week. The library was utilized during a time in which it would otherwise have been closed. The day session proceeded with the following agenda:

9 am—Mindful Morning Mixer,
9:15 am—Beginning Yoga,
10 am—Breathing Meditation,
10:30 am—Tea Meditation,
11:00 am—Walking Meditation,
12 pm—Wrap-up and Discussion.

In addition to sessions being led by faculty and staff from other areas, the tea meditation was led by Jean Moats, one of the Johnson & Wales Charlotte campus librarians. In addition to her participation in the campus BREATHE group, Jean had also recently attended a retreat for educators involved in contemplative practices. She utilized knowledge from this conference to share her experience with the students who attended this part of the day. In the end, the day was deemed successful, with about 25 students participating. In addition, the library was able to make students aware of mindfulness-related resources as part of the event. A book cart was used beforehand to collect books and DVDs related to mindfulness in general, meditation, yoga, and other relevant topics. The attendees were encouraged at the beginning and end of the event to check out materials (even though the library was closed, one student employee and I remained available to assist with checkout).

Dr Howard Slutzky and Contemplative Spaces

A common misconception of the mindfulness practice of meditation is that it involves quieting the mind through breathing exercise and discipline. In reality, mindfulness really involves focused attention on the present. It involves honest reflection. It involves taking a break from our busy schedules and mindless activities. It involves recognizing and honoring our thoughts and emotions without judgment and without attachment. As this chapter has indicated, many college campuses have spearheaded initiatives to set up "contemplative spaces" for students, faculty, and staff to meditate. One variation to some of the traditional mindfulness meditations involves guided imagery. I offer a stress-reduction workshop that incorporates a guided imagery component. I find that this more active approach to mindfulness can be easier for those new to mindfulness practices.

While there are numerous approaches to guided imagery, I use one that incorporates multiple components that all begin with closed eyes and focused breathing. I typically conduct this exercise in a group fitness room with the use of yoga mats. I simply have students focus on their breathing. I instruct them to observe the sensation of the air coming in and out of their nose, the difference in the temperature of the air between the inhalation and exhalation, and the sensation of their chest and diaphragm as they expand and contract. I then give the suggestion that with every breath, they are becoming more and more relaxed. As they inhale, they are breathing in relaxing, healing, nurturing energy. As they exhale, they are releasing any stress, worries, and frustrations.

I then invite them to see a door. Through this door is a staircase that leads down to an "inner sanctuary," which for this exercise is a beach. As they walk through the door and down the steps, I prompt them to feel more and more relaxed with each step they take down the staircase. Once they reach the beach, I guide them to experience their surroundings through each of their five senses (i.e., the smell of the salt air, the sound of the waves crashing and then receding, the sensation of the sun gently warming their skin). I then guide them through an exercise to get in touch with their "inner child." Participants are prompted to invite their inner child into their inner sanctuary (the beach). They are instructed to simply greet their inner child with an open heart and to pay attention to anything that child may be trying to tell them or ask of them. Oftentimes, students feel a pull to hug their inner child and to tell it that everything will be okay. Other times, they are prompted by their inner child to be more playful or to take things less seriously. Following this portion of the guided imagery, I lead participants though some additional breathing exercises and suggestions of healing, nurturing, and relaxing energy before inviting them to return to the staircase, where they make their ascent back to the "door" to the group fitness room.

An alternative to guided imagery that still allows for inner-child work is an empty chair activity. I have used this technique with many clients for whom there are injuries, disappointments, and unfinished business from childhood. The best way to describe this activity is to illustrate one of my most memorable cases. I was working with a college student whose father cheated on his mother and ultimately abandoned both of them to live with his mistress. Through my work with this client, we traced a lot of his current emotional and social difficulties back to this abandonment. I asked my client if he would be interested in doing some inner-child work (carefully explaining to him what this would entail), and he seemed both curious and motivated. I asked him to recount an experience that most wounded him, and he recalled a time when his father promised to pick him up for a father–son weekend but never showed up.

I asked my client to invite this child counterpart into our therapy session, having set up an additional chair for this purpose. I asked my client to look at the chair and to describe his child counterpart to me (age, clothing, and physical features). I then asked him to describe what his child counterpart was thinking and feeling. My client (who typically expressed little to no emotion during our sessions) began to cry as he described the sadness, disappointment, and pain of his child counterpart. I then asked my client if there was anything he wanted to say to his child counterpart. Initially he began expressing his response to me, but I directed him to say it directly to his child counterpart. He proceeded to say "I love you. I'm here for you. Everything is going to be okay." Like many people, my client had disowned his childhood injuries. Doing so may have the short-term benefit of decreasing pain and suffering, but it ultimately inhibits healing and impedes interpersonal, emotional, and identity development.

So, another crucial aspect of mindfulness involves identifying and reclaiming aspects of ourselves that we have disowned. Doing so is a prerequisite to healing, growth, and authentic connection with others. Guided imagery and empty chair exercises are excellent ways to accomplish this goal. While some inner-child work is often best done in the supportive context of psychotherapy, there are numerous guided imagery CDs and downloads available online. Self-help books such as *Banished Knowledge: Facing Childhood Injuries* by Alice Miller, and *Legacy of the Heart: The Spiritual Advantage of a Painful Childhood* by Wayne Muller, are excellent resources as well.

Interview with Faculty on Contemplative Practices

Kenny Harmon, associate professor of English at Johnson & Wales University's Charlotte campus, noticed "a lack of focus and unity" in his students' writing and decided to take action. "Both writing and textual analysis require long periods of sustained focus if one is to do them well. From conversations with students in my classes, I found that they were listening to music, watching YouTube videos, chatting with friends on Facebook, and other distracting activities, all while attempting to write an essay for class. What many of them would submit as a final draft was a jumbled mess (perhaps not surprisingly). While an individual paragraph might be well written at the sentence level, the essay lacked unity. Perhaps there wasn't a clear thesis or connections between the ideas of each paragraph were not clear."

According to Harmon, "the process [of finding a solution] began with reading, conversations with colleagues, and observation of changes in student performance…Reading led me to topics of technology and culture and its effects upon the individual mind, body, and spirit (particularly the brain and neuroscience)." As a result, he has implemented a number of exercises in his class, including meditation and reflective blogging, and has noticed a difference in the focus of his students. He states, "I think it certainly improved the atmosphere of the classroom. Not only did students seem more relaxed, attentive, and ready to work, but I did as well."[37]

Lisa Kendall, associate professor of English at Johnson & Wales University's Charlotte campus, also shared her experiences with mindfulness. "I began introducing meditation in my Foundations of Leadership classroom a few years ago as a way for students to center themselves and focus on their learning. It was a way for overworked/overwhelmed students to take a moment to catch a breath and be present to what was going on in the classroom and with each other… It was also an effort on my part to create a more collaborative environment and to encourage supportive relationships among the students…This year, after a talk by our campus Student Health and Counseling Center in which the director shared disheartening statistics about the number of students on our campus (and across the country) struggling with anxiety and depression, I decided to offer a Leadership Challenge assignment, in which one of the challenges a student might choose would be meditation. Students were directed to Jack Kornfield's book, *Meditation for Beginners*, and invited to create their own contemplative practice over the course of the term. Anecdotally, students report that the meditation seems to be helpful.

[37] Harmon, K., Email message to author, January 20, 2015.

They're not limited to meditation, though, and may opt to develop other contemplative practices such as yoga or qi gong. One student, a runner, has begun meditating prior to an early morning run and claims that it helps her to clear her head, and makes for an exceptional run as well."[38]

Mindfulness in the Classroom

Integrating mindfulness-related practices directly into the classroom has been the primary way by which contemplative practices have come into higher education in recent years. The efforts that have been undertaken by faculty have run from simple and basic to layered and exceptionally creative. A brief exploration of what has been occurring is in order. First, it should be noted that some of these initiatives may be adapted for use by librarians. In other cases, librarians may play a supporting role. In still others, simple awareness of what is occurring on campus may help inform other library activities in this regard.

Marc Perry recently reported in the *Chronicle of Higher Education* on a number of smaller and creative initiatives related to mindfulness or contemplative practices. For example, one instructor, Megan Hill at the University of Washington, in a class entitled "Information and Contemplation," has students carefully consider their use of technology. She has them set aside specific times for instance for checking email (as opposed to constant monitoring). They even watch videos of themselves multitasking and engage in discussions over how that may affect their emotions and attention. A similar approach is taken by the Koru program, which teaches mindfulness to students at Duke University. According to Holly Rogers, "It is useful for [students] to see that it is as much the way they think about time as it is the way they spend their time that creates stress for them."[39] Awareness of multitasking and its potential detriments in this context seem especially poignant. Perry also reports the implementation of programs similar to Hill's by other faculty in addition to one of the more common practices, inserting short meditations into the classroom experience. In one circumstance, he notes, "Those who had received meditation training were less fragmented in their work, switching tasks less

---

[38] Kendall, L., Email message to author, February 13, 2015.

[39] Rogers, H., 2013. Koru: teaching mindfulness to emerging adults. New Dir. Teach. Learn. 134, 79.

frequently and spending more time on each one. They also showed less stress and better memory."[40]

In an exploration of mindfulness in higher education, Mirabai Bush notes that the roots of mindfulness in the West can be traced to John Dewey and William James. In addition to mentioning the emphasis by both on the first-person experience of learners, Bush provides an oft-cited quote by James from 1890: "The faculty of voluntarily bringing back a wandering attention, over and over again, is the very root of judgment, character, and will…. An education which should improve this faculty would be the education par excellence. But it is easier to define this ideal than to give practical directions for bringing it about."[41] The most recent critical development, according to Bush, was the creation of the Center for Contemplative Mind in Society in 1997. It has offered fellowships that have led to many of the experiments mentioned in this chapter.[42]

Amy Cheng, a professor at the State University of New York (SUNY), has attempted to connect mindfulness to art. Students meditated and reflected on "making something new, original or unexpected; renewing or sustaining what already exists; healing and making things whole."[43] Likewise, at Syracuse University, Anne Beffel teaches meditation connected to the arts. She has students practice "paying attention and opening awareness to their connections with their surroundings and each other."[44]

Creative implementation of mindfulness in the classroom is occurring in places outside the arts as well. At Bryn Mawr, chemistry professor Michelle Franci is teaching budding scientists to be more mindful and contemplative when it comes to sound. She engages them in exercises whereby they explore the sounds closest to them and work their way out from there. Al Kaszniak, a professor of psychology at the University of Arizona, utilizes breathing meditations, mindful listening, and reflective journaling in his classes. These different practices are explored in layers as the course develops. According to Bush in reporting on Kaszniak's class, "The final session met in a contemplative garden, where they practiced mindful attention and discussed how natural and built environments relate to the expression or inhibition of empathy and compassion."[45]

---

[40] Perry, M. 2013. You're distracted. Chron. Higher Edu. 56 (29), A26, A28.

[41] William James, as quoted by Mirabai Bush, Mindfulness in higher education. Contemp. Buddhism 12 (1), 185.

[42] Ibid., 187.

[43] Ibid., 189.

[44] Ibid., 189.

[45] Ibid., 192.

One faculty member at the University of Arkansas, Daniel Holland, studied the integration of mindfulness in the classroom at his own institution and the implementation of the same measures at Facchochschule-Joanneum, a university in Graz, Austria. He specifically introduced "contemplative practices of sitting meditation, guided body scan, walking meditation, and mindful movement exercises."[46] The course in Arkansas further targeted students with disabilities. According to Holland, this is an especially important population to provide support for, as "students with disabilities are at an increased risk for more stressful and less rewarding college experiences because of persistent social marginalization."[47] An element of the courses at both locations that was deemed critical for success was dedicating a significant amount of course time to directing classroom discussion of student experiences that were related to the various practices explored.[48]

The efforts discussed here are diverse. Mindfulness-related efforts in education, in addition to being diverse, transcend national boundaries. For example, mindfulness meditation has become a part of positive psychology taught around the world. According to Nicole Albrecht, Patricia Albrecht, and Marc Cohen, "A typical program focuses on experiencing and reflecting on gratitude, acts of kindness, flow, mindfulness activities, hope, optimism, signature strengths, and savouring experiences. Universities such as Victoria University in Australia teach well-being in schools through the framework of Positive Psychology to pre-service education students studying the subject."[49] In many ways, teacher training in higher education takes us full circle, connecting K–12 and higher education. Another program available in Australia is referred to as "Meditation Capsules." Created by Janet Etty-Leal, this program is designed to build the mindfulness skills of teachers over the course of 10 sessions. The hope is that due to participation in this or similar programs, teachers would then integrate mindfulness-based practices in the classroom.[50] If we are to truly integrate mindfulness into our society, it must be done at the elementary, secondary, and postsecondary levels.

---

[46] Holland, D., 2006. Contemplative practices in unexpected places: teaching mindfulness in Arkansas and Austria. Teach. College Rec. 108 (9), 1844.

[47] Ibid., 1845.

[48] Ibid., 1850.

[49] Albrecht, N., Albrecht, P., Cohen, M., 2012. Mindfully teaching in the classroom: a literature review. Aust. J. Teach. Edu. 37 (12), 6.

[50] Ibid., 8.

Labyrinths have been around for many years. While they serve many purposes, these structures are intended in this context to be used for a walking/mindful meditation based on the shape and design provided. Many universities, and even libraries, have begun providing access to labyrinths. For example, the W. E. B. Dubois Library at the University of Massachusetts at Amherst (UMass Amherst) has one on the ninth floor. According to the UMass Amherst web site, "The Sparq labyrinth is an interactive mindfulness tool designed to counteract stress and promote wellness in computer-centric work and school environments."[51] According to the Perkins School of Theology at Southern Methodist University (SMU), which also provides students access to a labyrinth, "During the past two decades, labyrinths have undergone a dramatic revival" and may be found in "communities of all types: hospitals, health care facilities, spas and retreat centers, schools and universities, public parks, memorials, healing gardens, prisons, and even progressive businesses."[52]

Mindfulness Programs or Concentrations

While programs or concentrations on mindfulness exist, they still appear to be relatively rare, at least in relation to other attempts to ingrate mindfulness into education—specifically higher education (as previously noted). Furthermore, since these programs are so comprehensive, they lie somewhat outside the scope of this book. It is worth noting, however, that they seem to be gaining popularity within health care, and thus within related healthcare education programs. To share just one example of creative work being done in other areas, Ed Sarath at the University of Michigan has managed to spur the creation of a Bachelor of Fine Arts degree in jazz and contemplative studies. In this program, 25 credits of students' coursework come from classes related to meditative practice.[53] Clearly, there is virtually no limit to the possibilities that such a program demonstrates for other disciplines as well.

---

[51] UMass Amherst Libraries, W. E. B. Library installs Sparq Meditation Labyrinth for stress reduction, March 26, 2014. Available from: <http://www.library.umass.edu/news/announcements/sparq-labyrinth/>.

[52] SMU School of Theology. Available from: <https://www.smu.edu/Perkins/About/Labyrinth>.

[53] Sarath, E., 2006. Meditation, creativity, and consciousness: charting future terrain within higher education. Teach. College Rec. 108 (9), 1818.

Student Testimonials: Higher Education

While some basic feedback has been provided by students in the various K–12 iterations of mindfulness in education, feedback in higher-education experiments tends to be a bit more detailed and insightful due to the later developmental stage of the participants. Before concluding, it is worth sharing some of their comments. Daniel Holland's study, mentioned earlier in this chapter, had students explore a wide variety of mindfulness-based techniques. Here are a couple of especially pertinent excerpts from reflections shared by students:

> We are always either worrying over things in the past or anxious about things in the future. We are never (at least without effort) just in the moment. How did I live my whole life without realizing this? Why didn't someone explain this monumental concept to me before now?[54]
>
> I begin to consciously attempt to be in the moment as I drive to and from class. I notice the colors of the trees, the sky, the cars that go by. I note the temperature outside, the breeze of the air conditioner, the softness of my seat. I stop there and try not to go further…non-judging, beginner's mind.[55]

Finally, this quote comes from a student who has regularly participated in the weekly meditations at Johnson & Wales University:

> Being able to get involved into mindfulness awareness I was able to finally find something that relaxes me. Having fibromyalgia created problems that had no solution until I started practicing meditation. Being able to get involved with meditation, yoga, and learning how to control my body really provides me with a positive outlook. I no longer take all the medications I used to and I feel better about myself and my surroundings. Developing these skills was exactly what I need to create a healthier and happier life.

CONCLUSION

Clearly, there are many exciting efforts occurring in education relative to mindfulness. What is most striking is the relatively recent explosion of innovation and research. Despite its historical roots, the science of mindfulness has spurred many of these developments. However, there remain many challenges moving forward. For example, one comprehensive review of the literature has noted that more needs to be done: "It is obvious that more research, especially larger and randomized studies, if possible with active controls, is needed. Also, longer follow-up measures would

[54] Holland, D., Contemplative education in unexpected places, 1856.
[55] Ibid., 1856.

be appropriate, primarily to see if benefits are lasting, but also to investigate potential effects of triggering developmental steps."[56] Indeed, much research in education lacks long-term longitudinal data. The more available data exist, the greater a case can be made for specific (and perhaps overlapping) educational initiatives. Another issue that is apparent is the reliance on self-reporting in much of the data on mindfulness. Of course, the resolution to this problem is not clear due to the nature of development of mindfulness skills and experiences being somewhat subjective. Finally, one author has noted the problem that some participants in various mindfulness-related interventions have a tendency to spend dramatically different amounts of time on their own, practicing outside class.[57] This could obviously affect the results.

Again, while the challenges are daunting, the potential rewards are worth it. Robert Thurman eloquently sums up the goal of the mindfulness movement in education:

"We would like for people to develop contemplative states that increase contentment, detachment, tolerance, patience, nonviolence, and compassion, which simultaneously decrease feelings of anger, irritation, and paranoia. We would like them to develop more wisdom, more freedom, and more capacity for responsibility and creativity by seeing through the constructed realities in which our materialist culture has enmeshed us."[58] He goes on to eloquently state "The question, then, for academic institutions is not a question of adding a desirable frill to their vast smorgasbord of offerings. Rather, it is a matter of their effectively fulfilling their duty to provide a liberal-that is, a liberating and empowering-education. The ideal pedagogical process is first to learn something really well, using memorization and broad study; then to reflect upon it internally, assisted by energetic debate and discussion with teachers and other students; and finally to meditate upon the first tentative understandings in a sustained and focused way in order to develop insight to a transformative depth."[59]

If viewed this way, mindful education is not so far off the beaten path relative to traditional goals pursued in education. The part that mindfulness emphasizes the most is the reflective and transformative piece. It does so in a way that has not received much formal attention in the past. That is, it gives us tools or exercises that can be employed to improve

---

[56] Zenner, C., et al., 2014. Mindfulness-based interventions in schools, 18.

[57] Helber, C., Zook, N., Immergut, M., 2012. Meditation in higher education: does it enhance cognition. Innov. Higher Educ. 37, 355.

[58] Thurman, R., Meditation and education: India, Tibet, and Modern America. Teach. College Rec. 108 (9), 1766.

[59] Thurman, R., Meditation and education: India, Tibet, and Modern America, 1772.

and deepen the educational experience. As libraries serve a critical role in educating our children and our citizens, there is much to be learned and much yet to be explored.

PRACTICAL IDEAS TO GET STARTED

Take up mindfulness yourself. As an educator, a librarian, or both, the benefits of mindfulness are best experienced firsthand. Try meditating using online clips. Take a yoga class. If you are really ambitious, explore what MBSR programs are available in your area. There is much to be said in favor of modeling practice for students.

Try inserting a short breathing meditation in class. At the beginning of an instruction session try a short meditation. If students are unfamiliar with this practice, explain some benefits and have them try it for 5–10 min.

Insert a reading about mindfulness in class. This could be done in a variety of ways. If it's a class focused on information literacy or science, students could read and discuss an article that examines scientific research on mindfulness. If it's a class in American or comparative literature, one could read an excerpt by Henry David Thoreau or Thich Nhat Hahn. An instructor is only limited by his or her own creativity.

Join a mindfulness group on campus. Many campuses already have initiatives that one can join. If you are unaware of any such initiatives, the health services department is a good place to contact first.

RECOMMENDED RESOURCES

For an interesting video on the MindUP program. Available from: <http://www.scholastic.com/livewebcasts/teacher_talks/marc_meyer.htm>.
Ariely, D., 2010. Predictibly Irrational: The Hidden Forces that Shape Our Decisions.. Harper Perennial, New York, NY.
Gibbs, J., Gibbs, R., 2013. The Mindful Way to Study: Dancing with Your Books. O'Connor Press, New York, NY.

BIBLIOGRAPHY

Albrecht, N., Albrecht, P., Cohen, M., 2012. Mindfully teaching in the classroom: a literature review. Aust. J. Teacher Educ. 37 (12), 1–14.
A place to be mindful on campus. Mindful Magazine. November 18, 2014. Available from: <http://mindful.org/news/a-place-to-be-mindful-on-campus> (accessed 03.01.15.).
Ariely, D., 2010. Predictibly Irrational: The Hidden Forces that Shape Our Decisions.. Harper Perennial, New York, NY.
Bush, M., 2011. Mindfulness in higher education. Contemp. Buddhism 12 (1), 183–197.
Congressman Tim Ryan visits UM to share his vision for a mindful nation. University of Miami College of Arts & Sciences, November 11, 2014. Available from: <http://

www.as.miami.edu/news/news-archive/congressman-tim-ryan-visits-um-to-share-his-vision-for-a-mindful-nation-.html> (accessed 03.01.15.).

Dufon, M., Christian, J., 2013. The formation and development of the mindful campus. New Dir. Teach. Learn. 134, 65–72.

Frank, J.L., Reibel, D., Broderick, P., Cantrell, T., Metz, S., 2013. The effectiveness of mindfulness-based stress reduction on educator stress and well-being: results from a pilot study. Mindfulness 12, 1–9.

Gibbs, J., Gibbs, R., 2013. The Mindful Way to Study: Dancing with Your Books. O'Connor Press, New York, NY.

Goleman, D., 1995. Emotional Intelligence: Why it Can Matter More Than IQ. Bantam, New York, NY.

The Hawn Foundation. MindUP. Available from: <http://thehawnfoundation.org/mind-up/> (accessed 24.12.14.).

Helber, C., Zook, N., Immergut, M., 2012. Meditation in higher education: does it enhance cognition. Innov. Higher Educ. 37, 349–358.

Holland, D., 2006. Contemplative education in unexpected places: teaching mindfulness in Arkansas and Austria. Teach. College Rec. 108 (9), 1842–1861.

If moral judgement had a mark scheme.... The Times Educational Supplement. Available from: <https://www.tes.co.uk/article.aspx?storycode=6437112> (accessed 11.07.14.).

Lantieri, L., 2008. Building Emotional Intelligence. Sounds True, Louisville, CO.

Metz, S.M., Frank, J.L., Reibel, D., Cantrell, T., Sanders, R., Broderick, P.C., 2013. The effectiveness of the learning to BREATHE program on adolescent emotion regulation. Res. Hum. Dev. 10 (3), 252–272.

Miller, A., 1991. Banished Knowledge: Facing Childhood Injuries. Anchor Books, New York, NY.

Muller, W., 1992. Legacy of the Heart: Spiritual Advantages of a Painful Childhood.. Fireside, New York, NY.

O'Brien, D. Ryan takes 'mindfulness' to inner-city schools. The Business Journal, April 13, 2012. Available from: <http://businessjournaldaily.com/education/ryan-takes-%E2%80%98mindfulness'%E2%80%99-inner-city-schools-2012-4-13> (accessed 02.01.15.).

Perry, M., 2013. You're distracted. Chron. High. Educ. 56 (29), A26–A28.

Rechtschaffen, D., 2014. The Way of Mindful Education: Cultivating Well-Being in Teachers and Students. WW Norton & Co., New York, NY.

Rockefeller, S., 2006. Meditation, social change, and undergraduate education. Teach. Coll. Rec. 108 (9), 1775–1786.

Rogers, H., 2013. Koru: teaching mindfulness to emerging adults. New Dir. Teach. Learn. 134, 73–81.

Ryan, T., 2012. A Mindful Nation: How a Simple Practice Can Help Us Reduce Stress, Improve Performance, and Recapture the American Spirit. Hay House, Carlsbad, CA.

Salomon, G., Globerson, T., 1987. Skill may not be enough: the role of mindfulness in learning and transfer. Int. J. Educ. Res. 11 (6), 623–637.

Sarath, E., 2006. Meditation, creativity, and consciousness: charting future terrain within higher education. Teach. College Rec. 108 (9), 1816–1841.

Schoeberlein, D., 2009. Mindful Teaching and Teaching Mindfulness: A Guide for Anyone Who Teaches Anything. Wisdom Publications, Boston, MA.

Schonert-Reichl, K.A., Lawlor, M.S., 2010. The effects of a mindfulness-based education program on pre-and early adolescents' well-being and social and emotional competence. Mindfulness 1 (3), 137–151.

Thurman, R., 2006. Meditation and education: India, Tibet, and Modern America. Teach. College Rec. 108 (9), 1765–1774.

Zenner, C., Herrnleben-Kurz, S., Walach, H., 2014. Mindfulness-based interventions in schools—a systematic review and meta-analysis. Front. Psychol. 5, 1–20.

CHAPTER 3

Applying Mindfulness to the Undergraduate Research Process

Joe Eshleman and Howard Slutzky

WHAT IS MINDFUL RESEARCH?

An exercise that exemplifies the focused aspect of mindfulness is the close scrutiny of words: what they mean, how they are used, and their intent. What is being referenced or conceptualized when we talk about "mindful research"? Throughout *The Mindful Librarian*, the value of developing a conscientious and intentional approach has been stressed and the influence on our thoughts, actions, health, relationships, work, and practically all parts of our lives has been pointed out. Although mindfulness can be narrowed down to a basic, simplified definition, there are many different aspects associated with it. When some of these are considered, such as attentiveness, awareness, being observant, reflective, nonjudgmental, and hyperconscious, then tasks take on a deeper meaning. As with other definitions, it can be easier to describe something by qualifying its negation—that is, what it is *not*. A research paper that lacks mindful elements would be written poorly, be unclear, lack proper evidence to support its propositions (if they are present at all), and most disappointedly, would be devoid of any voice, conviction, or deep connection to its creator. Work that shows evidence of a mindful actor exemplifies the ability to take full ownership of its creation.

Consistently developing a mindful position begins with the ability to be in the present moment; that is, understanding, appreciating, and responding in a balanced way to what is occurring "right now." Even with the current change toward the Framework for Information Literacy for Higher Education, the research process traditionally maps to the Association of College and Research Libraries (ACRL) Information Literacy Competency Standards in a general way. Created by ACRL in 2000, the standards state the importance of knowing when one has an information need, how to locate information effectively and efficiently, and the value of evaluating the information and using it responsibly. The use of mindful principles can enhance the appropriate application of

The Mindful Librarian.

standards, and therefore, the research process. This chapter explores the mindful approach and examines how students, faculty, and librarians can use mindfulness to move toward an improved research experience.

Later in this chapter, a cursory look at the development and prominence of the college research paper in English composition classes in the United States will be undertaken. This review will help to illuminate how it enters this conversation. For the time being, it is sufficient to state that research that is done mindfully by an undergraduate would exhibit qualities such as a thoughtful adherence to assignment requirements, a developed voice, and an organized, coherent structure. Serving as a minimal definition (but not necessarily a nuanced one), mindful undergraduate research would include searching for, collecting, evaluating, and using information in a thoughtful and directed manner in tandem with an approach unencumbered by self-conscious judgment. This nonjudgmental aspect is a crucial linchpin for those students who have trouble beginning assignments and find the research process frustrating. Often, this self-critical attitude both impedes full ownership of scholarly work and diminishes the value of the research experience. What are the elements that make up a mindful approach to the writing and researching aspects of composing a research paper? It can be revealing to examine the design of the research paper in a mindful way because the realization that it is not typically built for the mindful approach becomes apparent. At a minimum, it can be very difficult to do even one of the multiple tasks associated with it mindfully, especially for most undergraduate students.

Presenting students with a lead-in paragraph on an assignment that spells out the attributes of a mindful research paper would not necessarily result in all the desired outcomes. Teaching students how to write a paper in a state of heightened dedication to "being in the moment" would not magically eliminate patch-writing or automatically lead to excellent research projects. Interestingly, mindfulness needs to be practiced to be fully realized. There is a layer of actualized mindfulness that needs to be brought to the entire process by both teacher and student in order to produce a greater learning experience. And, ideally, there is an equally mindful part for the librarian to play in the creation of the research project. Each of these three perspectives and their interrelated pieces will be explored in order to lead to a mindful whole. The key point, in this case, is to remember that mindfulness is not just a tool or a competency, but a complete shift of perspective and state of being that works best when it is understood collectively by all parties involved.

One clear-cut nomination for an activity that would be difficult to make mindful, especially for a uninterested student, is writing a research paper. This consideration of how to help "fix" the research paper can come across as trite if it only amounts to an expectation that the work will be so much better once students pace themselves through the research process. This is difficult work, and cajoling students into a mindset that produces a better research paper experience for them when there are so many barriers to begin with is a tall order. But, as this book contends with regard to numerous facets of librarianship and life, mindfulness opens pathways to seeing almost any activity with fresh eyes.

How can a required assignment that carries within itself aspects of time (deadlines, due dates) be approached in an intentional way that focuses on the present moment? How can an assignment that will be graded divorce itself from judgment by its creator? How can you both fully concentrate on one thing at a time (i.e., selecting a topic, finding and synthesizing information, and writing) and center on the whole of the research paper writing experience? These are difficult questions to answer, and yet a most important and central idea to keep in mind is that they do not need to be singularly addressed by the student. Faculty and librarians who also bring a mindful stance can be valuable allies and need to help students view the research process in a different way.

In his book *The Curious Researcher*, Bruce Ballenger begins with an introduction entitled "Rethinking the Research Paper." He points out that the assumptions about how a research paper is "*supposed* to be done"[1] need to be reevaluated and "are often misleading, incomplete, or downright unhelpful."[2] He goes on to point out that these preconceptions "have a huge effect on how you approach the assignment. No doubt many beliefs have some truth to them. Other beliefs, however, may need to be unlearned if you're going to take your research writing to the next level. Keep these beliefs out in the open, where you can see and evaluate them to determine if you have some unlearning to do."[3] Unlearning can be much more difficult than learning. Students can be taught the basic tenets or directed to various theories and definitions of mindfulness and may even be able to grasp the general ideas. But old habits are hard to break, and mindful habits can take time to develop. Even when given the

---

[1] Ballenger, B., 2015. The Curious Researcher. Pearson, Boston, MA, p. 3.
[2] Ibid.
[3] Ibid.

mindful blueprint for clearing the muddled ideas that clog the ability to understand the process of writing a research paper, students can feel confused about it.

One important point to remember here is that there are many stops and starts and curving lines on the path to any new knowledge—a straight line is very rarely involved, and the "eureka" moment (which often passes by the learner unnoticed) may be preceded by a mix of head-scratching, returning to old and comfortable ways, and plain giving up. This idea will be expanded upon in Chapter 4. For faculty, students, and librarians, what motivating factors would convince them to explore their preconceived attitudes toward a task? A response might be that reevaluating one's ideas or considering the idea of unlearning is not the type of task normally associated with doing a research paper. But this crucial step needs to occur, and it may be the purview of librarians to be the ones to make this happen.

Mindfulness can be achieved with dedicated effort, and even small mindful changes brought to daily life can be impactful. For example, a simple clearing of the mind and a restful focus on the task at hand can initiate calmer, more pleasant experiences. Mark Williams, professor of clinical psychology at the Oxford Mindfulness Centre, calls mindfulness a "direct knowing of what is going on inside and outside ourselves, moment by moment."[4] This self-awareness and connectedness ripples out into all aspects of life. According to U.S. Representative Tim Ryan (D-OH), "The goal of mindfulness is to make you more focused and aware, so your mind and body can be in the same place at the same time."[5] Aligning mental and physical modes helps to see life anew and can lead to a sense of hyper-consciousness. This objective to inhabit our actions with more than rote habits is not easy to achieve, and the desire to "get this off my plate and move on to the next more important and pressing event" is difficult to overcome.

From the start, there should be a discussion with students about some mindful strategies for taking a relaxed attitude when approaching the task. These could include breathing exercises or any other related approach. One of the main aims afterward would be to help the students see the

[4] Mindfulness: a beginner's guide. Available from: <http://www.theguardian.com/lifeand-style/shortcuts/201four/jan/07/mindfulness-beginners-guide-meditation-technique-treatment-depression>
[5] Sole-Smith, V., 2015, January 09. The no. 1 health-booster in 2015. Available from: <http://parade.com/36four863/virginiasolesmith/the-no-1-health-booster-in-2015/>

research paper as a journey, with important stages that can be done in a mindful manner. Perhaps the most significant idea would be one of pacing through the project in a steady and consistently mindful way. In essence, working too quickly does more to add to a mindless pursuit than anything else. As Lao Tzu stated, "Nature does not hurry, yet everything is accomplished." [6] The first step is a critical one when considering pace. What is the first step of writing a research paper? In many cases, as it is in all writing tasks, it is attempting to find a direction for the writing. For students, this is often the choice of a topic. This crucial first step or initial approach is so vital to the research paper endeavor that the effort expended on the choice of a topic (or direction) can be a key indicator of a good, mindful creation or a bad, unmindful one chiefly characterized by elements of haste or lack of interest.

Although it is developed through practice, mindfulness requires a small moment of enlightenment early on that sets its course for each person and shows its value. Becoming mindful means developing a new, different, or hyperaware state of mind. Asking questions about how to approach a task becomes much more important than having the skill set to do the task or bulling through the required checklist of how it is done. In Chapter 6 from *The Mindful Way to Study Dancing with Your Books*, authors Jake J. Gibbs and Roddy O. Gibbs state that "seeing things differently or exploring a new perspective is often the first step in doing things differently. It is frequently the most important step." [7] Perhaps the greatest challenge for both teacher and learner is changing entrenched habits and applying the concept of beginner's mind (a concept mentioned in several places throughout this book). In addition to a general lack of enthusiasm about the research paper by the average student (especially first-year students), there are anxieties about the numerous components associated with this type of assignment, such as choosing the topic, writing, researching, synthesizing, and citing. Confronted with these issues, and possibly lacking the confidence to put these disparate parts together to make a collective whole, do not necessarily lead to a mindful environment. Yet the teacher (and the librarian) have opportunities to calm fears, bolster confidence, and create a nonjudgmental setting that might allow the student to flourish. In addition to providing individual strategies for creating this situation,

[6] Baubata, L., 2010, January 28. How not to hurry [web log post]. Available from: <http://zenhabits.net/no-hurry/>

[7] Gibbs, J.J., Gibbs, R.O., 2013. The Mindful Way to Study. Dancing with Your Books. O'Connor Press, Chicago, IL, p. 37.

a goal for librarians and instructors should be to consider combining efforts to pace students through research to develop habits of mindfulness that lead to lifelong mindful learning. In a blog post that could apply to working through the paces of a research paper, Leo Babauta sums up this development nicely:

> *Practice this. Every action you take today, no matter how little … give it weight. Put some space around it. Start it intentionally, with the intention to be mindful, to inhabit that action fully, to notice with all your senses the entire moment. When the action is done, don't just rush to the next one, but take half a second to appreciate what you just experienced. Then move to the next with equal weight and space.*[8]

THE MINDFUL APPROACH

From a practical perspective, there needs to be a concerted effort by both the mindful faculty member and librarian to inspire a student to take a more focused approach to writing a research paper, especially if mindfulness is a novel idea to that student. Therefore, a great deal of communication and planning would need to occur to fully realize a comprehensive mindful research paper. This high-level and consistent type of collaboration may not always be possible. One tactic that could be applied here, however, would be to scaffold some of the research paper components and take on each one in a separate, mindful manner. For example, the aforementioned importance of choosing the direction or topic of the paper can be considered in a more mindful way than in the past. In essence, this usual first step to composing the research paper (or any endeavor) sets the tone for almost all that follows. Taking some extra time to add a mindful motivating factor that propels the work forward cannot be underestimated. Being attentive to this choice is a "make or break" moment, and it can dictate much more about what is come than is generally thought.

Let us examine in detail a positive mindful topic selection process versus one that is not. Making a mindful topic choice is such an important aspect of writing a research paper (and, more important, feeling a sense of ownership toward it), and yet somehow, it is frequently glossed over by students. A certain gage about where a student falls on the interested scale is their approach to this first rung of the process. It can be a clear sign of success or failure due to the impact that it creates moving forward. How, then, can

[8] Baubata, L., 2010, January 28. Inhabit the moment [web log post]. Available from: <http://zenhabits.net/inhabit/>

one get students to take some time when choosing a topic and be more mindful about this crucial step? Perhaps a separate assignment for students to contemplate their choice of topic in a mindful way could help. Personal reflection by students on what motivates them to want to do research may be much more constructive than simply going through the motions with a topic they are not interested in. In addition to the mindful techniques previously discussed, such as breathing and paying attention to the present, asking questions such as "What aspects of this topic would create motivation and enthusiasm for you?" can mindfully move a student past a potential stopping point, bring out the importance of investing in a topic for future projects, and create a sense of investment in the remainder of the research assignment.

One of the threshold concepts of the Framework for Information Literacy for Higher Education (discussed further in Chapter 4) is that scholarship is a conversation. The core of this idea is that once a person understands that research is a multilogue that progresses forward, then that person can enter into it in a more meaningful way. Yet students are often introduced to this conversation without their own voice, or with someone else's in place of theirs. When students are told that they must do research on a specific assigned topic that they have no interest in, how are they to understand scholarship as a conversation without a voice? If students are assigned or pick a topic that they have no real interest in finding more information about, why would they be motivated to research it? The faculty member can set the mindful tone for an assignment that helps to nudge students in ways that create more connection to the task at hand. Adding some information to a class lecture or to an assignment of the importance of "owning" a topic and on the way that research leads to discussions, as well as that a student's voice needs to be part of that conversation, may turn on a lightbulb. A fire may be set within a formerly disinterested student's mind when he or she realizes the value of personal investment in a research project, and that will make this person move away from the habit of slogging through a rote activity.

A research paper written mindfully would not only produce a more viable work, but would offer the creator a more rewarding experience. This makes it worth examining what a mindful approach is and how it is accomplished. A mindful methodology has been mapped for other elements of librarianship throughout this book, and many of these techniques can be applied to tactics here. For example, in Chapter 5, it is pointed out that the value of being present in more ways than the simple physical sense when doing reference work creates a better experience for both student and librarian. It is added there that increased awareness and focus on the part of the reference librarian sends a clear sign that approachability and willingness to help are priorities. In a similar manner for the student working on an assignment, the mindful strategy of being at ease and developing a sense of increased awareness can help with scholarly work. Making a conscious effort to make the research experience "different this time" gives students a chance to open up to new possibilities.

The emotional component of the information seeker was brought to the forefront by Carol Kuhlthau, Professor Emerita of Library and Information Science at Rutgers University, as she mapped out the stages and experiences for the student researcher. Her six stages of the information search process were developed in the 1980s, revised in the 1990s, and reevaluated again in 2008. One of the breaks from former information use studies was her focus on how the information seeker is affected by the research process, and a pivotal discovery was how much uncertainty factors into the search process. This uncertainty could be diminished by human or technological intervention. A mindful tactic here could be to teach strategies for acceptance and comfort with apprehension and doubt. Although that sounds counterintuitive, it is exactly what mindfulness attempts to achieve. Understanding that there will be challenges and reacting to them in a measured manner diminishes their control over us.

The mindful researcher is aware that there will be times when they are "stuck," and that they may also have a difficult time starting their project. The nonjudgmental facet of mindfulness that leads toward self-acceptance allows a student to recognize that these stoppages are a natural part of the research process. This awareness takes time to develop, and eventually, one becomes accustomed to embedded difficulties and comes to regard them as normal in some way, even to the point where it would seem unusual *not* to have them occur. Adjacent to this idea is the thought that the challenging and demanding features of a task are what make it rewarding or encourage progress by the learner. Without these, the act is fruitless, and our focus should be on how we react to these tribulations. What mindfulness teaches us is an acceptance of both good and bad events and its ability to fine-tune our reactions to all that we experience. In essence, the mindful student would be armed with the knowledge that the research process is a series of highs and lows that can take an emotional toll if reacted to disproportionately. Overreactions to the highs and lows can cause unrealistic expectations, and not being able to grasp the idea that frustrations and complications are part of the process can lead to abandoned projects and poor experiences in the future. Mindfulness helps to create an even-keeled route.

A rewarding side effect that occurs when developing mindfulness is how focused habits can be applied to an extraordinarily wide range of behavior. Although we are discussing the research process in an academic setting, once one develops a mindful state and cultivates mindful habits, his or her world opens up to a new way of dealing with all elements of life. That is to say that the ability to become present in time, reacting in an accepting manner to both positive and negative experiences and openly embracing the challenges in life as an opportunity for growth and existential awareness, filters out to a great number of experiences. Once developed, mindfulness helps one deal positively with daily events such as traffic, busy schedules, health issues, and difficult personal interactions. It helps one find a type of balance for dealing with larger life events too. To apply this train of thought to this topic, mindfulness can help when researching for a new smart phone, writing a research paper, or writing a chapter in a book. Related to this rippling effect, once mindful habits are taken up, it becomes imperative to share the idea of mindfulness with others.

It can also be advantageous to keep in mind that the majority of the advice given for the research process can be applied to a wide variety of creative work. Of course, that idea comes with a rather large caveat. There are certainly creative acts that do not appear to have mindful associations at all, such as artistic work done in haste that might be said to have more emotional resonance but is still regarded as fine achievement, such as Automatism in the Surrealist Movement or abstract expressionist works. One overlooked mindful aspect embedded within work that has a high emotional component (versus a more intellectual flavor) would be the intense devotion that generally accompanies it. This intensity of purpose equates nicely with the idea of being focused and in the present moment, so even though the speed at which something is created is important, something made quickly does not inherently void its ability to have mindful attributes.

This type of ambiguity that might initially seem inconsistent frequently gives pause to newcomers to the concept of mindfulness. Yet the overarching idea of mindful acceptance toward uncertainty trumps this apprehension in those who understand how embracing troublesome ideas can be enlightening. This idea is discussed in more detail in Chapter 4, which explores threshold concepts. For now, keeping in mind that elements of mindfulness that can be considered to be contradictory stem from its Buddhist roots and developing the ability to be comfortable with this paradoxical nature can be beneficial. Armed with the knowledge that mindfulness can be accepting of both focused and detached positions, work done slowly and quickly, prepared, and spontaneous, a level of non-judgmental acceptance is always at the ready.

More recently, survey findings from the Project Information Literacy (PIL) progress report from 2010 entitled *Truth Be Told: How College Students Evaluate and Use Information in the Digital Age* bear out the continuing relevance of Kuhlthau's findings on challenges that students have when conducting research. This survey reported, "For over three fourths (84%) of the students surveyed, the most difficult step of the course-related research process was getting started."[9] and "....half of the students in our sample reported nagging uncertainties with concluding and assessing the quality of their own research efforts. Have I done a good job? How do I sort through all that I've found to find what I need? How do I know when to stop looking?"[10] Again, motivation and uncertainty rear their ugly heads. Cultivated mindfulness helps to address these concerns in two specific ways: first by learning to accept dispositions such as uncertainty as part of the process rather than impediments; and second, in a related manner, not evaluating whether or not a "good job" has been done, but rather feeling a sense of accomplishment that a focused effort was put into the process and it is up to others to judge the results. Finally, as pointed out earlier in relation to the idea that students have many research needs outside the classroom and that they may not necessarily continue their careers in academia, it should always be remembered that this mindful approach should be nurtured for all activities, not just the research paper or project of the moment.

The student who is confronted with the research assignment created by faculty and the librarian will hopefully be interested in receiving personal assistance. The librarian generally helps the student with tasks such as topic choice, narrowing a topic, finding reliable evidence, and citation. Often overlooked is how the librarian can help the faculty with assignment creation. An individualized (yet connected) look at each of their perspectives will follow, with the intent of showing how mindfulness improves the experience of each one individually, as well as the process collectively.

---

[9] Head, A.J., Eisenberg, M., 2010. Truth be told how college students evaluate and use information in the digital age. Washington, DC: Information School, University of Washington.

[10] Ibid.

THE STUDENT PERSPECTIVE

It can be the case that first-year students do not view a research assignment as having the same amount of value that faculty may wish them to. For a student, there is a great deal of anxiety, trepidation, hand-wringing, procrastination, and possibly hatred directed toward the research assignment, which tends to cloud the potential positives. An excellent resource that gives a good overview of the specific stress associated with academic writing and also provides some resources that try to reduce the apprehension is Marsi G. Wisniewski's *Writing Anxiety and the Undergraduate Experience: An Annotated Bibliography*.[11] Consternation about doing research is also well documented. A 2009 PIL progress report entitled "What Today's College Students Say about Conducting Research in the Digital Age" found that students used terms such as "angst, tired, dread, fear, anxious, annoyed, stressed, disgusted, intrigued, excited, confused, and overwhelmed"[12] when describing their feelings about course research. Many student remarks about the research paper reveal that the stress associated with it is at the forefront of their minds. Is there an opportunity here for both student and teacher to take some time and reevaluate the presentation and the design of the research paper so that it can be done in a more mindful manner?

There may also be additional apprehension for the student associated with the burden of completing an assignment that requires, among other tasks, finding a topic, developing a research question, proposing a hypothesis, locating sources, synthesizing information, writing, revising, and editing. In addition, there may be the issue of a student's lack of confidence about the ability to do any and all of these tasks well. All of these realizations about how students view the research assignment indicate how hard it is to change their approach and general aptitude toward it. Despite this, the mindful approach and stance are propitious and offer excellent return on input. Convincing a student to develop an open approach and gain a greater awareness of the value of an assignment may create a more

[11] Wisniewski, M.G., 2009, May. Writing anxiety and the undergraduate experience: an annotated bibliography. Available from: <https://www.plymouth.edu/office/writing-center/online-resources/writing-anxiety-and-the-undergraduate-experience-an-annotated-bibliography/>

[12] Head, A.J., Eisenberg, M.B., Finding context. What today's college students say about conducting research in the digital age. Available from: <http://files.eric.ed.gov/fulltext/ED535161.pdf>

enjoyable research experience. However, it does not necessarily constitute a magical cure for all ills or guarantee an excellent grade. A student's attachment to preconceptions about the elements of a good research paper, combined with worry about grades, also hampers the ability to be nonjudgmental. What the mindful approach outlined here can comfort students with is the calming knowledge that a resolute effort is its own reward.

Another hindrance that mindfulness can help alleviate is the harried mentality and rushed approach that one may take, carelessly speeding through a task. To reiterate an earlier point, pacing oneself through scaffolded steps may be a much clearer path here. But, once again, a significant reevaluation of one's approach may be in order. In some cases, students may feel as though they work better in a pressured state of mind and past achievement and even good grades may have reinforced this idea. Therefore, all of the benefits listed, and even proof of the scientific evidence of the value of mindfulness, may not be enough to convince someone to bring mindful habits to a research assignment.

Tangential to rushing through an assignment is the oft-heard lament of faculty that "students do not read the assignment requirements." Mindful students, pacing themselves, would consider an understanding of prerequisites to be a natural step in the process. Even more than putting a minimal effort into topic choice, mindlessly ignoring what is required dooms the research assignment (and almost all tasks) to a poor outcome. Although it may seem as if mindfulness does not have a direct connection to following requirements, British Theravada Buddhist monk Ajahn Brahmavamso points out that "mindfulness is not just being aware, being awake, or being fully conscious of what's occurring around you. There is also that aspect of mindfulness that guides the awareness on to specific areas, remembers the instructions and initiates a response."[13] There is a discipline to mindfulness that often gets obscured by the layperson's misguided focus on the "laissez-faire" aspect that is often propagated. Certainly, it takes a great deal of focus and dedication to meditate. In fact, some of the mental discipline associated with becoming mindful and maintaining mindfulness makes that process quite rigorous.

The main concern here is the research portion of the assignment, and thinking about why students struggle specifically with it can lead to mindful recommendations. Is there something in particular about the research

---

[13] Brahmavamso, A., 2001, July. The quality of mindfulness. Available from: <http://www.budsas.org/ebud/ebmed070.htm>

aspect of a paper that appears to put it at the forefront of a student's complaints about writing such a paper? Or is it just one in a long line of grievances? PIL continues to delve into this problem and, in addition to their aforementioned 2010 study, they have listed the aspects of a research assignment that students struggle with the most. Taking each and applying mindful principles can prove valuable.

The PIL study reveals that the hardest part of research for students is getting started, which makes sense when approach to an activity is considered. As pointed out earlier, developing a mindful approach can minimize the emotional roadblocks that make starting a project difficult. Fostering an open mindset that breaks through the hypercritical and creates an accepting attitude also helps here. Subsets of this difficulty include defining and narrowing a topic. It seems as if the research assignment step that should be the most mindful is often the one that has the least focus placed upon it—that is, choosing a topic. Again, the tone that it sets for the entire research endeavor is usually greatly underestimated by students (and sometimes by faculty and librarians as well). A type of solution was offered earlier in this chapter for faculty improvement here; yet how does a student get started on a dreaded assignment? In addition to taking a considerably more time thinking about what topic to choose, simple methods adopted by students such as taking the time to breathe and developing careful reflection can help solve some of these problems.

Mindfulness is greatly concerned with developing awareness and education purports to broaden the knowledge base of students. But self-direction and a deeper understanding of society along with how one fits into the world are also goals. A greater sense of the direction of one's own education and life means that an enlarged awareness of purpose is also at stake here. These are some of the ideas at the foundation of critical pedagogy, a concept that is concerned with giving individuals the knowledge to create social change, but also has an aspect that connects to social responsibility and personal growth. Becoming an intentional agent is a large step for a student to take, but the attention placed upon the move across that threshold can be helped with the use of mindfulness. This idea is discussed in further detail in Chapter 4. The point here is that once students realize that they are more responsible for their own development, smaller decisions such as educational choices and topic choices become much easier to grapple with.

Perhaps a larger consideration here that expands much further out from this discussion is moving away from the focus on just one type of assignment: the "classic" research paper. A mindful approach to all activities in general can potentially create a more rewarding and efficient experience. One of the reasons that a mindful mental mode is so helpful in this case is that the specific elements that make up the research paper lend themselves well to a mindful approach. For example, the care taken to find and evaluate sources takes time, and when done mindfully, improvements will be noticed. Developing the mindful habit of verifying that an author is found (and, even more important, assessing the writer's credentials) when using a web site article as a source can improve the quality of a paper, simple as that may seem. Taking time to proof papers was considered by students in the past to be a given part of turning in an assignment, but not so much today. This careful proofing and editing now needs to be mindfully added by current undergraduates.

Two other obstacles that students can encounter when confronted with a research assignment are a general dislike for that particular type of work and distractions from the task at hand. For those who have a negative view or find this type of schoolwork unappealing, the nonjudgmental aspect of mindfulness can be helpful. A great deal of distraction takes place in our technologically enhanced environment and there are numerous studies that point out how multitasking affects performance. What of the conundrum that current students are mostly concerned and react to what is happening right now when creating an instant text response to the latest social media update, but have a difficult time bridging to the current moment when looking at a blank computer screen when they have to begin writing a research paper? One solution advanced in response to this phenomenon is writing prompts. Another may be the focus that meditation strengthens. Interestingly, Gibbs and Gibbs (2013) point out how we so often tell students to "pay attention," yet we do not teach them how to do this.

Finally, the health benefits of mindfulness, as documented elsewhere in this book (particularly the MBSR benefits in Chapter 1), can establish a great baseline for students to deal with stress in general. Without the energy to face the challenges presented here (which are just a small portion of those encountered on a college campus), all of the mindful insights are for naught. As we shall see, faculty, librarians, and anyone who moves toward mindful behavior finds ways to meet life's peaks and valleys with wise and balanced responses.

As can be seen from this overview of the challenges that may occur for a student when faced with a research assignment, it can be quite helpful to take each specific aspect and apply mindful assistance to it. An even better approach, however, as put forth earlier, is to develop an all-encompassing mindful nature and apply it as needed. A student may find it less important to contemplate how to approach the research assignment than adopting strategies for contending with it when faced with the undertaking. Like a student procrastinating with starting to work on the task, it may be enjoyable, even enlightening, to theorize and ruminate, but the actual work still needs to be produced. So, where does mindfulness move to where the real work happens? For the mindful expert, there is a continuum here, and mindful practice is put to real use. For the novice who sees mindfulness as strictly contemplative, there is room for the excuse that the mindful ideas are too theoretical. In this space, the mindful faculty and librarian can both be an aid. Reviewing the preceding mindful approach as a process, one needs to develop the discipline to begin work in the present moment and continue in a mindful manner. With this perspective in mind, it is easy to see a student with mindful skills rising up to any challenge, much less a research assignment.

Dr Howard Slutzky on Conquering Procrastination

There are numerous factors that may undermine a student's success when writing a research paper, but one that is often overlooked is procrastination. Many students struggle with this, particularly on tasks (such as a writing a research paper) that are time consuming and daunting. Procrastinators often fall into one of two categories. The first are those who ultimately get the job done and suffer no overt consequences (i.e., a student who ultimately submits the paper on time and earns an "A"). On the surface, this may seem like an acceptable outcome, and those engaging in this type of procrastination are likely to have little or no motivation to alter their behavior. If we look beneath the surface, however, we can identify several possible consequences, including increased stress, decreased sleep, a finished product that is less than it could have been, and a decrease in personal satisfaction during the process of completing the paper. The second category of procrastinators are those who either miss the due date or submit a paper that is incomplete, of poor quality, and/or full of careless mistakes. But what individuals in both of these categories share in common is that they oftentimes have little to no insight into the factors contributing to their behavior. Without this insight, change is unlikely. So the "mindful researcher" is one who has become aware of internal and external factors that may be undermining their success.

In the field of clinical psychology, one key feature of mindfulness is gaining insight into underlying forces that are negatively impacting our psychological and behavioral functioning. Sigmund Freud believed that the unconscious mind consists of motivations, beliefs, and emotions that occur automatically and under the radar of introspection. This makes the unconscious more dangerous and influential. Freud believed that it is aspects of our unconscious that contribute to our emotional and behavioral dysfunction, and that shedding light on the unconscious was the primary curative factor for his patients. I am not recommending psychotherapy to "treat" procrastination, but some form of intervention or resource may certainly be warranted. Unfortunately, for those with little or no motivation for change, it is unlikely they will seek out such resources on their own.

While some argue that procrastination is largely due to a fear of success, others (myself included) have found that it is oftentimes reflecting a fear of failure. Students who lack confidence (or experience) in writing are likely to experience a lot of apprehension. If we examine this fear, we will likely identify several underlying beliefs such as "I'm not a good writer," "I'm going to fail," "I have no idea where to start," "I'm stupid," or "I can't do this." Again, these beliefs are often below the surface. What rises to the surface may range from mild discomfort to a full-blown panic attack. Since is human nature to avoid that which is dangerous or threatening, those experiencing this discomfort are likely to "run" as far as they can from the perceived threat. And consistent with Freud's theory, one way this is done is by keeping these fears and insecurities tucked safely in our unconscious mind.

I was recently preparing a PowerPoint presentation for a time-management workshop and came across the term "productive procrastination." While I was familiar with the concept, I had never heard it labeled as such. One of the ways cope with the discomfort associated with our unconscious fear of failure is engage in productive activities that seem necessary or important. Procrastinators often find themselves straightening up their house or engaging in household projects or chores instead of working on the most pressing task (i.e., the research paper). This is a convenient way to dupe oneself into feeling productive while masking the avoidance that is truly occurring.[14]

So in addition to instructing students on writing skills, proper referencing, and appropriate grammar, procrastination should be a topic of equal importance. Incorporating graded deadlines prior to the final project (i.e., submitting an outline, submitting a reference section for preliminary resources, submitting a rough draft) can be highly effective in undermining procrastination. Additionally, there are numerous self-help books available on this topic, as well as resources such as campus writing centers and counseling services. Whatever resource or strategy used, it is important to assist students gaining insight and awareness into the factors underlying their procrastination. Doing so will significantly increase their likelihood of "recovery."

---

[14] Kassel, K., 2007. Productive procrastination: make it work for you, not against you. Laurel, MD: Echelon Press.

THE FACULTY PERSPECTIVE

Being mindful is often associated with increased awareness. Would an improved attentiveness by teaching faculty to a student's research assignment experience bring about different results? The foremost consideration here would be motivating students to think differently about their specific approach to the research paper and then embed mindful habits in them when working on future projects. Yet a secondary benefit for faculty might be a new mindful method when designing research assignments and a renewed focus on helping students through the research portion (preferably in conjunction with a librarian). In reference to the subject at hand (namely, the research paper as written by first-year students in an English composition class), some exploration of the rationale behind this type of assignment (from a faculty perspective) can shed some light on how to apply mindful aspects to it.

Before discussing how a mindful faculty approach to a research paper assignment can help both student and teacher, it may be valuable to get a more appropriate definition of "the research paper" that this chapter is discussing. A rudimentary definition was offered at the beginning of this text, but it is beneficial to explore some other ideas here. It can be quite difficult to parse out what common concrete elements of research papers are universal, and doing that is not the goal of this exploration. It is, however, interesting to review the literature and some contemporary ideas on what connotes the research paper and additionally examine some of the inquiries into its format, current status, and potential future.

Despite the innumerable efforts of many, an untold number of research papers each year are written by first-year (and later) undergraduates who do not understand why they are writing them. This lack of understanding leads to patched-together, incoherent documents that do not even begin to present personal ideas using supporting evidence or take the time to analyze perspectives. Is there something inherent within the research paper itself that creates a type of disconnect for current students? Has the pervasive nature of technology created an academic environment that has superseded the research paper? Are there other types of assignments that achieve the effects normally associated with research papers that may embed similar outcomes and present value to students more readily? These are the types of mindful questions that arise when considering improvements or changes to this traditional model.

The research paper as it is being discussed here had its start over 150 years ago. As Howard and Jamieson review its chronology:

> *Late nineteenth-century U.S. higher education was powerfully influenced by the German model of "rigorous 'scientific' philology and historical criticism", and Russell explains that this influence caused research papers to become part of FYW (First Year Writing) in the 1860s and 1870s (79–80). In a 1955 study, 33 percent of 1,309 courses surveyed assigned "documented papers" ranging from one thousand to five thousand words. The majority of these 433 courses were junior-and senior-level writing courses (CCCC, "writing").*
>
> *That rate subsequently increased, and the research paper increasingly became a staple of FYW, not just advanced courses. Of the 171 colleges' surveyed in 1961, 83 percent required a research paper in the first year (Manning), and that rate held steady thereafter. Of 397 institutions surveyed in 1982, 84 percent included a first-year research paper, and 78 percent required it (Fodr, Rees, and Ward). Of 166 respondents to a 2010 survey on the listserv **WPA-L**, **86** percent reported giving some sort of researched assignment in FYW (Hood).[15]*

The authors go on to point out how the initial drive to learn research skills bridged to the teaching of information literacy in the library and note that alternative forms are on the rise, including adding multimedia to the research assignment.

The 2010 survey referenced by Howard and Jamieson here, which led to Carra Leah Hood's *Ways of Research: The Status of the Traditional Research Paper Assignment in First-Year Writing/Composition Courses*, pointed out how the research paper is not designed consistently and showed a move toward more alternative research assignments versus ones defined as traditional. The distinction in the study between traditional (an informational or explanatory piece of writing that reviews a prescribed number of sources[16]) and alternative (projects such as ethnographies, i-search papers, profiles, or brochures[17]) helps to show how faculty are reflecting on research assignment outcomes and reevaluating design. Hood concludes that "the traditional assignment has become one assignment type among others offered to students taking first-year writing/composition courses."[18] One reason put forth for this change is connected to the learning outcome priorities shifting. Hood and others, such as Dunn, Pappas, and Dirk address this.

---

[15] Tate, G., Taggart, A.R., Schick, K., 2001. A Guide to Composition Pedagogies. Oxford University Press, New York, NY.

[16] Hood, C.L., 2010, Summer. Ways of research: the status of the traditional research paper assignment in first-year writing/composition courses. Available from: <http://compositionforum.com/issue/22/ways-of-research.php>

[17] Ibid.

[18] Ibid.

Perhaps the most mindful action that an instructor could take would be to evaluate their own motivation behind adding a research element to an assignment. Apart from the need to fulfill an academic requirement, what deep goal or information-related skill or outcome is sought by faculty when adding comments such as "This paper requires three reliable sources" to their syllabi? Is there deep reflection occurring when copying requirements from one term to another, or just rote mechanics? Each new class offers the transformative opportunity to review what the student (and faculty) experience will contain as it relates to a research assignment. Will it be another academic year of confused students turning in cobbled-together, unoriginal "research" facsimiles, or could mindful changes to the assignment itself or added student participation about improvements to the research assignment significantly improve this experience?

One question for a faculty member to ask at the outset is, "What is the purpose behind the research requirement in this type of assignment?" It often appears to be self-evident that the writing component serves some purpose, although that aspect has also been under a great deal of scrutiny. Bruce Ballenger weighs in with his assessment of the research assignment: "It seems to encourage a very closed process of inquiry. Come up with a thesis quickly, hunt down evidence to support it, and wrap it up—all the while focusing less on learning something than on getting it right: the right number of pages, the right citations, the right margins."[19] The move from a focus on "getting it right" versus responding to student need and capability is a topic of discussion that continues to gain momentum.

For both the instructor and the librarian, it can be helpful to cultivate the mindful element of patience in students because the disciplinary nature of pacing through any project can lead to a focused effort rather than a "race to the finish" ideology. In addition to pointing out that rushing quickly into a research assignment might commit one to a topic that cannot yield good (or even any) information sources, it is good to reinforce that the research process is difficult, more work intensive, and different from finding information by using a search engine. Also, envisioning so-called perfection or ideal scenarios is anathema to mindfulness. Therefore, an English composition research paper assignment in which the professor takes time (working with the mindful librarian) to explain to students why this research work is being requested and performed may be in order. As information use specialists, instruction librarians spend a great

[19] Ballenger, B., 2015. The Curious Researcher. Pearson, Boston, MA.

deal of time contemplating ways to help students understand the value of research (rather than simply pointing them to resources and creating a codependent situation).

A group of English composition students passionately describing their deep devotion to their topic and eager to find out everything they can about it may not suddenly happen in a class. Patience is needed by all parties. Note that it is not just undergraduates that deal with the rollercoaster research experience. Dr Inger Mewburn, director of research training at the Australian National University, edits a blog called *The Thesis Whisperer.* A post entitled "The ups and downs of PhD research,"[20] by guest blogger Nilam Ashra-McGrath, details the emotional and physical toll that stress can take on the lifelong learner. As we have seen, the improvement of mindful capabilities can help here in numerous ways.

Historically, and until recently, there was not an overt need to explain to students the purpose or value of writing a research paper or the importance of finding high-quality information to support evidence for claims. Most faculty in the past most likely did not reflect upon their decision to assign a research project, often offering tradition or academic requirements as a rationale. However, as just one factor, the advent of instant access to a preponderance of information has changed how current students view such a project. Perhaps it is time to become more mindful of these changes and both consider more deeply and put more effort into how to present the research paper assignment to students rather than focusing on the content that it contains. Librarians have been wrestling with a shift from "how to" to "why" for some time now. As a direct strategy to alleviate anxiety, frustration, and confusion, mindfully discussing the background logic for requiring the research component may help students develop a more mindful stance toward it. In the next section, a focus on the need for librarians to work toward a relationship with students that implies a sense of empathy creates a passageway to mindful student encounters. In a similar path, faculty reflection upon the research experience of current students can lend perspective and open a gateway to more mindful insights when developing, teaching, and grading research projects.

The development of mindfulness can often be accompanied by the epiphany associated with experiencing beginner's mind as well.

[20] Ashra-McGrath, N., 2013, November 05. The ups and downs of PhD research [web log post]. Available from: <http://thesiswhisperer.com/2013/11/06/the-ups-and-downs-of-phd-research-2/>

As discussed in Chapter 5, this concept helps us to open up to ideas and experiences that we have become so accustomed to that we miss out on their full impact and meaning. It means "experiencing people and situations as though for the first time, without the filter of history and established beliefs."[21] Often, we forget that we are all still students in some form or another and must revisit our own research experiences to gain a greater connection to current scholars.

THE LIBRARIAN PERSPECTIVE

In the beginning of this chapter, it was mentioned that the librarian may be the agent who needs to step forward and begin the process with faculty and students to "unlearn" the traditional approaches and conceptions about the research process. Chapter 4 deals with this responsibility in a more detailed manner, but for now, it is important to note the unique position that the librarian is in. In the times in which all three interact with each other students, faculty, and librarians often have little time to consider each other's roles in detail. This is the rationale behind the structure of this chapter, and hopefully it enforces the mindful link to empathy. It is important to realize how mindful practices developed by all three of the agents involved here (students, faculty, and librarians) apply in all the interactions between each. That is to say that any mindful idea or action mentioned as beneficial for one relationship works for all. Therefore, when a mindful benefit is presented from librarian to student, it would be just as beneficial from a librarian to a faculty member, and this works in all permutations. This concept shows how mindfulness and mindful collaboration can be transmissible, expansive, and transformative.

To the student, and often to the instructor as well, the librarian may play a curious role in relation to the research assignment. Although for many years, and through great effort, librarians have attempted to show their worth as a valuable ally to both students and teachers, librarian research services are not actively sought out as a general rule. The chagrin felt by librarians about this situation creates a sense of disappointment and distress for them. The book *College Libraries and Student Culture: What We Now Know* contains a chapter entitled "Why Don't Students Ask Librarians for Help: Undergraduate Help-Seeking Behavior in Three

---

[21] Roberts, S., 2015. Beginner's mind for mindfulness in everyday life. Available from: <http://mindspaceclinic.com/beginners-mind-for-mindfulness-in-everyday-life/>

Academic Libraries." In it, the authors conclude, "Students will seek help from those with whom they have established relationships."[22] This advice can be heeded by librarians in a mindful way by self-assessing their own daily interactions with students and making dedicated efforts to forge connections. In a daily encounter, sensing that someone is not paying attention or is distracted can be quite off-putting. Conversely, mindfully paying attention to someone's situation and their request for help creates an empathetic meeting. To initiate that linkage, there may be a simple mindful habit that academic librarians could develop to improve relations with students.

As far back as 1986, Joan Durrance pointed out, "In most professions, those who interact directly with the client are known by name."[23] She goes on to state that students will regularly use librarians who they know by name and will return to them. Perhaps this is one reason for the recent success of personal librarian programs. Despite the fact that this study is almost 30 years old, the idea that knowing someone by name creates a good environment for seeking and offering help may offer an opportunity for mindfulness here. It can be a rewarding experience for the librarian to see a student who frequents the library pass by and exchange greetings using first names. It may seem to be minor, even trite, but doesn't mindfulness reveal to us how small acts can enlarge us? From a practical point of view, and in preparation for making these types of connections, a loving kindness meditation can set a tone of compassion for the mindful librarian to reach out to all who enter their sphere.

Becoming a mindful listener and embracing a warmer, approachable nature with students is proposed in Chapter 5 as one way to bring focus and the atmosphere of kindness to the reference desk. Perhaps by reaching out and introducing ourselves by name to frequently seen students, librarians can create a less nerve-racking collegial experience. A connection to at least one person on campus could provide a great deal of resonance and provide some affirmation to a lonely, stressed-out student. As it pertains specifically to doing research, librarians are generally quite familiar with library anxiety and can be the first ones to initiate a sense of calm reassurance in students by getting to know them.

[22] Duke, L.M., Asher, A.D., 2012. Why don't students ask librarians for help: undergraduate help-seeking behavior in three academic libraries. In: College Libraries and Student Culture: What We Now Know. American Library Association, Chicago, IL.
[23] Durrance, J., 1986. The influence of reference practices on the client–librarian relationship. College Res. Librar. 47 (1), 57–67.

Another consideration that may be more difficult to address is how librarians are perceived. Librarian stereotypes and perceptions around the profession is a subject unto itself. As one example, librarians have been portrayed as having introverted tendencies and have been shown historically as stodgy perfectionists. Another seemingly negative image is the impatient (sometimes presented as elitist) or standoffish librarian dealing with the "public." In reaction to this and other concerns, such as the aforementioned underutilization of assistance, it is the responsibility of the profession to change perceptions and increase awareness of what librarians can do to support students. Librarians themselves seem most sensitive to how they present and are considered, and they should mindfully detach from an obsession with self-conscious judgment. Librarians could also take a more detached attitude to their representation or embrace negative stereotypes to defuse their strength. K.R. Roberto mindfully responds to the view of the librarian in his afterword to *The Librarian Stereotype: Deconstructing Perceptions and Presentations of Information Work*, "We can and will worry about externally projected stereotypes of library workers all we'd like, but the ones we project upon each other are ultimately most concerning."[24]

One avenue for librarians to help students is through face-to-face, focused appointments or research consultations. There are many advantages that these meetings have over reference desk interactions and library instruction, some of which can be considered to be mindful. Of course, the most obvious of these is the ability for both parties to be more focused on the work at hand and on each other as well. But these opportunities, which seem to occur sparsely, also afford the librarian a great chance to create a nonjudgmental zone that alleviates stress and creates confidences for the student. Mindfulness has been proven to lead to the improvement of listening skills and other habits. In an often overlooked way, mindfulness allows us to listen more to ourselves as we speak since we are in tune with the moment. So then, mindful librarians become more aware of not only their own thoughts and feelings, but also their ideas and statements and the effect of their words. Listening attentively is a vital competency for a librarian, especially when considering the important task of helping a student (or anyone else) who might be struggling with research.

[24] Rigby, M.E., Pagowsky, N., 2014. The Librarian Stereotype: Deconstructing Perceptions and Presentations of Information Work. Association of College and Research Libraries, a Division of the American Library Association, Chicago, IL, p. 283.

The compassionate characteristic of mindfulness also comes into play with librarian and student interactions. Occasionally, overt efforts to ease a student's workload can be met with faculty reactions such as charges of coddling or codependency. Service-driven librarians often find themselves leaning in that direction. While there is always a line to be drawn and students may request help from a librarian beyond norms (such as a request to construct numerous citations), a librarian can be a valuable and reliable ally. For example, the librarian is sometimes in an advantageous position as one who does not grade, and older adult students often rely on the librarian's help with newer technologies or what has changed relative to their educational experience in the intervening years for that student. Mindfully compassionate and empathic librarians can take these opportunities for student interactions and realize another core tenet of mindfulness.

As the next step to defining information use and helping students understand the research process, ACRL's Framework for Information Literacy is discussed in more detail in the next chapter. As it becomes adopted by more librarians (and, hopefully, more faculty and others as well), it will shed light on a conundrum that has plagued instruction librarians. That is, how do they help students with a current need (finding resources for their research assignments) and also satisfy the librarian's desire to put larger information literacy concepts in front of students for lifelong learning? A mindful librarian realizes that working within the present moment alleviates anxiety about the future and sees that they will need to embed the framework in a practical way. Additionally, because the framework is more conceptual in nature than the earlier standards, librarians will need to become much more mindful about the intent of their instruction if they are interested in moving to the framework. Looking at these challenges, the librarian can disconnect from future concerns, concentrate on the here and now, and feel empowered by the idea that information literacy affects each concurrent moment for a student. In a related note, a current topic in the library instruction literature is the realization that "solving information problems" is a much larger need moving forward for student lifelong learning than "doing research."[25]

There are many opportunities for the librarian to be mindful in interactions with students and faculty. As mentioned previously, mindfulness resonates and radiates from a central change of consciousness. Although

[25] What can we learn from students about information literacy? Available from: <http://www.slideshare.net/mvanhoeck/bridgewater-keynote>

a litany of mindful tactics can be listed and reviewed, once mindful habits are formed, all thoughts and acts have elements of mindfulness embedded in them. The mindful librarian becomes acutely aware, and each interaction benefits from a balanced point of reaction. Working in close tandem with mindful students and faculty communally improves the research paper writing experience.

CONCLUSION: BRINGING IT ALL TOGETHER IN A MINDFUL WAY

In January 2015, Mindful Nation UK produced the interim report of the Mindfulness All-Party Parliamentary Group (MAPPG). The report has recommendations for the criminal justice system, the workplace, health, and education. In it, the group states:

> We recommend making mindfulness in schools a priority for development and research. Mindfulness programmes are popular with children and teachers, and research has shown promising potential, with an impact on a wide range of measures, including wellbeing, executive function (attention, focus), emotional self-regulation and improved relationships.[26]

The inclusion of improved relationships is a key focal point for our discussion in this chapter. The mindful need to connect humanely during important moments that make up our own lives and the lives of others seems to be ever present. The crucial need to find a way to coexist with the overtly expeditious times that we live in requires a thoughtful response. The reports summarize mindfulness in this way: It leads to a deeper understanding of life and how to respond wisely.

There is a surprising amount of ways to perform research. Each authentic researcher brings his or her own subjective strategy. In a typically Zen way, it is futile to feel as though you should feel compelled to *always* do research mindfully. Like the general practice of mindfulness, it cannot be forced. This lesson appears at first to be self-contradictory, and yet it is within the mindful mindset to react to its lack of consistency with a shrug of the shoulders. Stranger still, the mindful practitioner welcomes the troublesome and ambiguous as just another thought, event, or idea in the queue.

---

[26] Inquiry Held: May–December 201. (n.d.). Mindful Nation UK. Available from: <http://oxfordmindfulness.org/wp-content/uploads/mindful-nation-uk-interim-report-of-the-mindfulness-all-party-parliamentary-group-january-2015.pdf> (accessed 08.03.15.).

For faculty and students, understanding mindfulness, becoming an adherent, and using it as an approach in their daily lives can offer many rewards. Faculty can benefit by being open, attentive, nonjudgmental, and calm in the classroom. Students can develop their capabilities to show more attention in class, become more open to new ideas, and decrease anxiety about their workload and other stressful events and experiences. As for librarians, it can be interesting to think about the ways in which S.R. Ranganathan's laws of library science coincide with mindful librarianship. Many of the core tenets of mindfulness seem to align with some of his laws, and therefore, some of the larger goals of librarianship: namely, sharing (books are for use), helping, and in an ideal way, reacting in a balanced way to the changes that seem to consistently occur in life (the library is a growing organism).

RECOMMENDED RESOURCES

Ballenger, B., 2015. The Curious Researcher. Pearson, Boston, MA.
Duke, L.M., Asher, A.D., 2012. College Libraries and Student Culture: What We Now Know. American Library Association, Chicago, IL.
Gibbs, J.J., Gibbs, R.O, 2013. The Mindful Way to Study: Dancing With Your Books. O'Connor Press, Chicago, IL.
Pagowsky, N, Rigby, M.E., 2014. The Librarian Stereotype: Deconstructing Perceptions and Presentations of Information Work. Association of College and Research Libraries, A Division of the American Library Association, Chicago, IL.
Tate, G., Taggart, A.R., Schick, K., 2001. A Guide to Composition Pedagogies. Oxford University Press, New York, NY.

BIBLIOGRAPHY

Ashra-McGrath, N., (2013. November 05). The ups and downs of PhD research. Available from: <http://thesiswhisperer.com/2013/11/06/the-ups-and-downs-of-phd-research-2/> (accessed 09.03.15.).
Ballenger, B., 2015. The Curious Researcher. Pearson, Boston, MA.
Baubata, L., 2010, January 28. Zen Habits: breathe. Retrieved from: <http://zenhabits.net/no-hurry/> (accessed 09.03.15.).
Brahmavamso, A., 2001, July. The Quality of Mindfulness. Available from: <http://www.budsas.org/ebud/ebmed070.htm>.
Duke, L.M., Asher, A.D., 2012. College Libraries and Student Culture: What We Now Know. American Library Association, Chicago, IL.
Durrance, J., 1986. The influence of reference practices on the client–librarian relationship. College Res. Libr. 47 (1), 57–67.
Gibbs, J., Gibbs, R., 2013. The Mindful Way to Study: Dancing with Your Books. O'Connor Press, Chicago, IL.
Head, A.J., Eisenberg, M., 2009. Finding Context: What Today's College Students Say About Conducting Research in the Digital Age. Information School, University of Washington, Washington, DC.

Head, A.J., Eisenberg, M., 2010. Truth Be Told: How College Students Evaluate and Use Information in the Digital Age. Information School, University of Washington, Washington, DC.

Henley, J., 2014, January 07. Mindfulness: a beginner's guide. Available from: <http://www.theguardian.com/lifeandstyle/shortcuts/2014/jan/07/mindfulness-beginners-guide-meditation-technique-treatment-depression> (accessed 09.03.15.).

Hood, C.L., 2010, Summer. Ways of research: the status of the traditional research paper assignment in first-year writing/composition courses. Available from: <http://compositionforum.com/issue/22/ways-of-research.php> (accessed 09.03.15.).

Inquiry Held: May–December 2015. Mindful Nation UK. Available from: <http://oxford-mindfulness.org/wp-content/uploads/mindful-nation-uk-interim-report-of-the-mindfulness-all-party-parliamentary-group-january-2015.pdf> (accessed 09.03.15.).

Kassel, K., 2007. Productive Procrastination: Make it Work for You, Not Against You. Echelon Press, Laurel, MD.

Pagowsky, N., Rigby, M.E., 2014. The Librarian Stereotype: Deconstructing Perceptions and Presentations of Information Work. ACRL, Chicago, IL.

Sole-Smith, V., 2015, January 09. The no. 1 health-booster in 2015. Available from: <http://parade.com/36four863/virginiasolesmith/the-no-1-health-booster-in-2015/> (accessed 09.03.15.).

Tate, G., Taggart, A.R., Schick, K., 2001. A Guide to Composition Pedagogies. Oxford University Press, New York, NY.

Van Hoeck, M., 2014, October 17. What can we learn from students about information literacy? Keynote. Available from: <http://www.slideshare.net/mvanhoeck/bridgewater-Keynote> (accessed 09.03.15.).

Wisniewski, M.G., 2009, May. Writing Center. Available from: <https://www.plymouth.edu/office/writing-center/online-resources/writing-anxiety-and-the-undergraduate-experience-an-annotated-bibliography/> (accessed 22.09.14.).

CHAPTER 4

The Association of College and Research Libraries Framework for Information Literacy: Connecting to Mindfulness

Joe Eshleman and Howard Slutzky

THE ACRL FRAMEWORK

In the United States, the Framework for Information Literacy for Higher Education[1] (henceforth referred to in this chapter as the "ACRL Framework") began development in March 2013 and went through a number of iterations. It was advanced in response to the ever-growing changes to the information landscape that information seekers must traverse. In addition, from its proponent's point of view, some of the design deficiencies in the Information Literacy Competency Standards for Higher Education[2] (ACRL Standards) from the year 2000 needed to be addressed. For example, the ACRL Standards have been considered to be rigid in structure and take a somewhat-closed path to what defines someone as being information literate. The ACRL Standards are composed of Standards, Performance Indicators, and Outcomes, while the ACRL Framework has Frames based on Threshold Concepts, Knowledge Practices, and Dispositions. The driving force behind both documents is the Association of College and Research Libraries (ACRL). Other similar information literacy standards went through updates recently, including the Seven Pillars of Information Literacy, from the Society of College, National, and University Library (SCONUL).

In addition, ACRL and SCONUL were not alone in their recent focus on revising ideas about information literacy. As Justine Martin pointed out

---

[1] Framework for Information Literacy for Higher Education, 2015, February 2. Available from: <http://www.ala.org/acrl/standards/ilframework> (accessed 10.04.15.).

[2] Information Literacy Competency Standards for Higher Education, 2000. Available from: <http://www.ala.org/acrl/standards/informationliteracycompetency> (accessed 28.04.15.).

in 2013, "Four groups in the United Kingdom recently produced new or revised models to articulate the developmental needs of the information literate in higher education. These models are: A New Curriculum for Information Literacy (ANCIL), Society of College, National, and University Libraries' Seven Pillars of Information Literacy (SCONUL), National Information Literacy Framework Scotland (Scottish framework) and the Information Literacy Framework for Wales (Welsh framework)."[3] She concluded the following:

> The four recent models from the United Kingdom—ANCIL, SCONUL, Scottish, and Welsh frameworks—provide innovative guidelines for practitioners to promote and incorporate information literacy holistically into learning processes. Not only do these models address emerging technological changes and publication modes, but they also incorporate new educational approaches to address weaknesses of previous models. Model authors view information literacy as holistic, contextual and emerging out of an individual's information experiences...... In the end, the authors of the four models view their work as a continuous process of assessing and improving information literacy guidelines. Information literacy is an evolving concept and, as such, professionals will continue to adapt guidelines to meet the needs of today's information users.[4]

The new educational approaches here can also be seen in the ACRL Framework. The movement from information literacy models that are considered to be less connected to an individual's information-seeking process and focus on an all-encompassing integrated experience can be mapped to mindfulness. A possible foundation for the ACRL Framework is evident within the ideas that Susan Langer associated with mindfulness. Christine E. Sherretz points out that "Langer (1989) stated that mindfulness is a process in which an individual views one situation from several perspectives. Instead of moving in a linear fashion from question to answer, the mindful individual seeks out other vantage points to view the problem. This in turn may raise additional questions and scenarios."[5] It is not difficult to see a contrast here between the linear ACRL Standards and the "many viewpoints" position developed in the ACRL Framework, which is influenced by mindful ideas. This chapter will show how the ACRL Framework authors are concerned with the same elements of the four European models that Martin references, which are "holistic, contextual, and emerging out of an individual's information experiences."

[3] Martin, J., 2013. Refreshing information literacy. Commun. Info. Liter. 7 (2), 114–127.
[4] Martin, J., 2013. Refreshing information literacy. Commun. Info. Liter. 7 (2), 124.
[5] Sherretz, C.E., 2011. Mindfulness in education: case studies of mindful teachers and their teaching practices. J. Thought 46 (3–4), 80.

In 2015, The ACRL board of directors took the official action of filing the ACRL Framework document, and ACRL continues to foster its intended flexibility and future potential. Through its transparency and shared nature, which allows feedback from anyone interested in the document (mostly librarians), it will continue to be reedited, added to, and revised, and it will go through numerous changes as time goes on. The open design of the document has allowed for continued feedback, and many of the ideas and suggestions put forth from its creation, design, and implementation took a great deal of collaborative effort. It can be stated that there is a presence of mindfulness attached to its open progress. The focused intent of trying to create a dynamic document that has the ability to change (or even transform) as time passes was a crucial concern as it was being created, and this ideal will continue moving forward. A guideline document that allows for flexibility helps to encourage openness and far-reaching application, two tangential properties of mindfulness. In the same way that it can be helpful to consider the library as a growing organism, the ACRL Framework has a conceptual foundation that allows it to adapt to the "ever present change" that we have grown accustomed to and that appears to be part of our future. While at first, the phrase "ever present change" appears to be an oxymoron, it does make sense when applied to technological change.

In a chapter of the book *Mindfulness: Diverse Perspectives on Its Meaning, Origins, and Applications*, edited by J. Mark G. Williams and Jon Kabat-Zinn, Mirabai Bush does excellent work relaying all of the various ways in which "Mindfulness in Higher Education"[6] has taken hold. Mindful ways to react to technological change continues to be a subject of great concern for higher education, and interacting with the digital world is sometimes overlooked as an aspect of information literacy. Bush gives an example of a course that mindfully explores this topic and offers practical mindful habits:

> Many educators are concerned about the effects of technology and multitasking on their students. At the University of Washington, David Levy uses contemplative practices as a lens to observe and critique information practices, and in particular to investigate problems of information overload, the fragmentation of attention, and the busyness and speed of everyday life. The basic practice of the course is mindfulness: mindful sitting (attention to the breath) and walking (attention to the feet). Students then mindfully observed an information practice like texting or emailing, documented what they observed, and reflected on what they documented. They discovered, for example, that they tended to check email when they were anxious or bored and that reading email only exacerbated their anxiety.

[6] Bush, M., 2013. Mindfulness in higher education. In: Williams, J.M.G., Kabat-Zinn, J. (Eds.), Mindfulness: Diverse Perspectives on Its Meaning, Origins and Applications. Routledge, London.

Their practice became:

1. *Observe your own patterns of behavior, bringing attention to body, breath, emotions, etc.*
2. *Decide which dimensions of your experience you want to cultivate or minimize (clarity of attention, fatigue, anxiety, etc.)*
3. *Make conscious choices in order to cultivate some states and minimize others.*[7]

What is important to note here is not only the flexible capability to apply mindful practice to information studies, but also the significance of reflection and the examination of dispositions in this approach. Interestingly, the ACRL Framework pays less specific attention to technology than do the ACRL Standards, possibly in part due to the concern that focusing on current technologies may limit the flexibility of the current guidelines. Dispositions, as we shall see, are extremely important components of the ACRL Framework and can provide clues about the connections to mindfulness underlying it. Another example from Mirabai Bush's chapter from *Mindfulness: Diverse Perspectives on Its Meaning, Origins, and Applications* comes from an art class and puts forth once again how the more straightforward "checklist" attributes of the ACRL Standards are expanded upon in the more holistic ACRL Framework. Professor of Studio Art at State University of New York (SUNY) at New Paltz is interested in using mindfulness in contemplative education "to tap the intuitive creative functions of the right brain: to think in complex images rather than in sequential order, to see the whole as well as the parts, to grasp interconnections, correspondences, resemblances and nuances rather than the bits and pieces and linear, logical patterns."[8] It is this move from a reliance on a more regulated way to define and teach information literacy, which did not connect as well to mindful practice, to a more expansive and dimensional framework, which is more closely aligned to mindfulness, that is the core of the ideas in this chapter.

THE ACRL FRAMEWORK AND DISPOSITIONS

One interesting aspect of the updated ACRL Framework is the stress given to the dispositions and attitudes that accompany the task of finding information. Dispositions correspond nicely to mindfulness. Defined as inherent qualities of mind and character, one's disposition obviously has a great impact on daily life and therefore, information-seeking experiences. Another definition of the word that aligns more closely to mindfulness

[7] Ibid., 193.
[8] Ibid., 189.

is "a tendency to think or act in a particular way."[9] The importance of disposition to information seeking and research has continued to move to the forefront of concern when evaluating a student's information literacy strategies. These affective aspects play a significant role in the ways in which students and others approach research and information seeking. Looking at more than the cognitive elements and focusing on influences "such as attitude, stance, and motivation"[10] help to lend a more holistic view to assessing how one seeks information. As Meredith Farkas states in in her blog post about the framework, "How much of being good at research is about being persistent? Tolerating frustration? Asking for help? Being curious? Looking at things with a critical eye?"[11] The role that many factors, including mindfulness, play in the research process was examined in Chapter 3, and this same approach can be taken when examining the ACRL Framework. It is important to note that within the current ACRL Framework document itself, the discussion of dispositions has a footnote that refers to "To Be or Not to Be (Mindful)," a paper presented at the 1994 meeting of the American Educational Research Association (AERA) by Israeli educational psychologist Gavriel Salomon.[12]

A close reading of how Salomon considered the word *mindful* and a fuller understanding of the concept, as used in this book, does show some slight but noteworthy semantic differences of the term's usage. There does not seem to be as much of a connection to meditative practices and the earlier Buddhist foundation as Salomon uses the word *mindfulness*. Often, psychological and cognitive studies tend to focus less on the ancient spiritual connections to mindfulness and may put more emphasis on the scientific ties. Both Salomon and David Perkins commented on the troublesome nature of achieving "mindful or high road transfer,"[13] adding

---

[9] Definition of Disposition, 2015. Available from: <http://www.merriam-webster.com/dictionary/disposition> (accessed 28.04.15.).

[10] Kuhlthau, C.C., 1991. Inside the search process: information seeking from the user's perspective. J. Am. Soc. Info. Sci. 42 (5), 361–371.

[11] Farkas, M., 2014, March 03. Getting into the gray areas with the draft framework for information literacy for higher education [web log post]. Available from: <http://meredith.wolfwater.com/wordpress/2014/03/03/getting-into-the-gray-areas-with-the-draft-framework-for-information-literacy-for-higher-education/> (accessed 28.04.15.).

[12] Framework for Information Literacy for Higher Education, 2015, February 2. Available from: <http://www.ala.org/acrl/standards/ilframework> (accessed 10.04.15.).

[13] Salomon, G., 1994. Interaction of Media, Cognition, and Learning. L. Erlbaum, Hillsdale, NJ, p. 17.

that attaining it includes "a positive attitude towards ambiguous and complex situations, a preference for novelty and incongruity, and an intention to seek out such situations, or even shape situations in a way that makes them fit the preference"[14] Salomon's work also has dealt with thinking dispositions; therefore, it is not difficult to see the influence that he could have on the ACRL Framework. Perhaps the best linkage to the ACRL Framework and mindfulness is the importance placed on attitudes toward difficult ideas or those that challenge and create trouble for the student but offer growth opportunities as expressed with threshold concepts. These will be discussed in more detail later in this chapter.

Salomon's ideas on mindfulness are often joined with those of Ellen Langer, who has uses the term *mindful* in numerous psychological studies and has explored how mindfulness applies to learning. She has focused on the importance of different perspectives to highlight how mindfulness can create more openness. Langer uses the term *mindlessness* often as a way to show how we can easily move to a type of automatic pilot in our thinking. She states that it "is characterized by an entrapment in old categories, by automatic behavior that precludes to attending to new signals; and by action that operates from a single perspective."[15] To express another point on how mindfulness has influenced the thoughts that have led to the multiperspective ACRL Framework, Langer's web site sums up her position on the difference between mindfulness and mindlessness as follows: "To be mindful, she notes, stressing process over outcome, allows free rein to intuition and creativity and opens us to new information and perspectives."[16]

Others focus on the importance of dispositions as well. Shari Tishman posits that dispositions are core elements of good thinking. With Eileen Jay and D. N. Perkins, she argues that "Good thinking dispositions—the ones that normally describe productive intellectual behavior—can be characterized as consisting of seven broad but key intellectual tendencies."[17] Mindfully connected keywords such as *alertness, focus,* and

[14] Ibid., 22.

[15] Langer, E.J., 1997. The Power of Mindful Learning. Addison-Wesley, Reading, MA, p. 4.

[16] Langer, E.J., 2009. Ellen Langer. Available from: <http://www.ellenlanger.com/books/3/mindfulness> (accessed 19.04.15.).

[17] Tishman, S., Jay, E., Perkins, D.N., 1993. Teaching thinking dispositions: from transmission to enculturation. Theory Pract. 32 (3), 148.

reflective are sprinkled among the seven dispositions. The focus on these affective attributes that influence cognitive decisions seems to grow more important as time passes, perhaps as a movement toward a greater empathetic understanding of students and all information seekers. The ACRL Framework supports this need to be aware of the diverse viewpoints of information seekers and the ability for librarians (and others) to take note of their dispositions as they move them forward in their lifelong research capabilities.

Connecting mindfulness to many of the conceptual underpinnings of the ACRL Framework is not difficult, for several reasons. The primary reason is that a case could be made that the ACRL Framework is based upon mindfulness (or, at minimum, it is one of its largest influences). The examples given here show a direct connection to the mindful position in the ACRL Framework that corresponds to Jon Kabat-Zinn's definition: "Mindfulness is an awareness, cultivated by paying attention in a sustained and particular way: on purpose, in the present moment, and non-judgmentally."[18] The need to be much more aware of the many nuanced aspects of information seeking and research pushes information literacy into a more dimensional experience for students; the ACRL Framework moves from "how" to be information literate to "why" to be information literate, and mindfulness can be used as both a starting point and a bridge to this development. Being aware (and sustaining attention with the idea) that there are a number of processes and deeper conceptual understandings, as well as dispositional attitudes that affect information literacy, can foster a greater awakening to what is available and a superior grasp of how to approach the "information ecosystem" (in the words of the ACRL Framework).[19]

The ACRL Framework was designed to use information literacy threshold concepts, which are designated as "frames." Bolstering each of the initial six frames are a set of knowledge practices, and a set of dispositions. There are a total of 38 dispositions divided among the frames. A cursory look at the frames reveals the repetitive use of words such as *mind, open, awareness, maintain,* and *ambiguity*—all keywords that can be associated

[18] Kabat-Zinn, J., 2012. Mindfulness for Beginners: Reclaiming the Present Moment—and Your Life. Sounds True, Boulder, CO, p. 25.
[19] Framework for Information Literacy for Higher Education, 2015, February 2. Available from: <http://www.ala.org/acrl/standards/ilframework> (accessed 10.04.15.).

with mindfulness. In the first draft of the ACRL Framework, from a February 2014 iteration, the dispositions are even more emphasized:

Students and others learn best when they use more than their cognitive faculties. It is important that they be open to the experience and substance of what they are learning. This is particularly true with threshold concepts, which, by definition, are troublesome. The Dispositions section provides a guide that will assist instructors and learners alike. While it is provided for instructors to design learning experiences that will encourage students to consider their attitudes and feelings about the new concepts, it might also, in appropriate situations, be shared directly with students to promote self-reflection.[20]

The importance of creating learning experiences that advance a disposition toward mindfulness past the point of introduction and short-term goals drives the main thesis of the article, "Life in the Mindful Classroom: Nurturing the Disposition of Mindfulness" (Ritchhart & Perkins, 2000). In response to the question "Is mindfulness a worthwhile educational goal?" the authors state, "Mindfulness is a facilitative state that promotes increased creativity, flexibility, and use of information, as well as memory and retention… Consequently, the real education potential of mindfulness lies not in raising test scores but in addressing some of the other intractable problems of education, such as the flexible transfer of skills and knowledge to new contexts, the development of deep understanding, student motivation and engagement, the ability to think critically and creatively, and the development of more self-directed learners."[21] As a way to get students to develop mindfulness, three high-level practices (looking closely, exploring possibilities and perspectives, and introducing ambiguity) are put forth. All of these practices can also be seen as connecting to the ACRL Framework and will be explored in more detail later in this chapter as threshold concepts and frames are reviewed.

While dispositions are important, threshold concepts play an even larger part in the ACRL Framework. Before moving on to a discussion of what they are and how they connect to mindfulness, it is helpful to make a few final points about dispositions. A dispositional aspect of mindfulness that is often overlooked is resiliency. It can be quite easy to fall into the trap of hearing about mindfulness and thinking it is a good idea, and then halfheartedly attempting to adopt its ideas. Mindfulness must be

[20] Framework for Information Literacy for Higher Education, First Draft, 2014, February. Available from: <http://www.ala.org/acrl/standards/ilframework> (accessed 14.04.15.).
[21] Ritchhart, R., Perkins, D.N., 2000. Life in the mindful classroom: nurturing the disposition of mindfulness. J. Social Issues 56 (1): 27.

developed thorough disciplined habits and attentiveness to its principles. When practiced correctly with diligence, consistent meditation and the development of mindful habits, mindfulness can benefit health (physical and mental), relationships, cognitive abilities, parenting, and more. One of the health benefits of mindfulness is the ability to increase resiliency and what is important for this discussion is a student's (or any information seeker's) ability to maintain a type of consistent pliability to work through the process of stops and starts that can occur when researching. As pointed out in Chapter 3, students have many more challenges navigating the current information landscape than in the past, and the ability to approach it in a mindful way can help them to overcome these hurdles. As we will see later when examining the "frames" of the ACRL Framework, the ability to value persistence is mentioned in relation to a disposition. While persistence (continuing a course action despite difficulty) and resiliency (the ability to return to the original form) are different attributes, they both are enhanced by mindful habits.

THE ACRL FRAMEWORK AND THRESHOLD CONCEPTS

Threshold concepts are core tenets of the framework. They were developed in the United Kingdom by Jan Meyer and Ray Land in the early 2000s, who were initially concerned with applying them to the discipline of economics. Meyer and Land summarize the idea this way: "A threshold concept can be considered as akin to a portal, opening up a new and previously inaccessible way of thinking about something."[22] A threshold concept "gives a name to points in new learning that mark a departure from old ways of viewing the world and entrance into new ways that may be counterintuitive and thus upsetting ("troublesome"), and yet they are ways that must be grasped in order to go forward in learning."[23] An important aspect of a threshold concept is that it must adjust or alter your way of thinking about a certain subject, and there is a type of change or growth involved. In essence, if there is no change in your thought or behavior when you are confronted by a threshold concept, then you have not crossed over or advanced. But more important, as we look to bring in

[22] Meyer, J., Land, R., 2006. Overcoming Barriers to Student Understanding: Threshold Concepts and Troublesome Knowledge. Routledge, New York, NY, p. 1.

[23] Rhem, J., 2013, November 6. Before and after students "get it": threshold concepts. Available from: <https://teachingcommons.stanford.edu/teaching-talk/and-after-students-get-it-threshold-concepts>.

concepts of mindfulness to threshold concepts and the framework, is the idea that threshold concepts can change not only how one sees ideas, but also how one sees oneself.

Perhaps the best way to grasp a threshold concept is to give one as an example. Later in this chapter, a number of threshold concepts are put forth within the ACRL Framework, which can also help to illuminate how they work. Meyer and Land posit a threshold concept in the field of cooking, the idea of heat transfer:

> *Imagine that you have just poured two identical hot cups of tea (i.e. they are at the same temperature) and you have milk to add. You want to cool down one cup of tea as quickly as possible because you are in a hurry to drink it. You add the milk to the first cup immediately, wait a few minutes and then add an equal quantity of milk to the second cup. At this point which cup of tea will be cooler, and why? (The answer is the second cup, because in the initial stages of cooling it is hotter than the first cup with the milk in it and it therefore loses more heat because of the steeper temperature gradient.) When the physics of heat transfer is thus basically grasped by people in terms of things specific to what goes on the kitchen, it will fundamentally alter how they perceive this aspect of cooking, and they might consequently even filter out what to look for (the signified!) when they watch the better class of television cookery programmes; for example, a focus on the pots and pans that are selected by the chef in context (the heat source in relation to the cooking process to be applied as a function of time and its regulation to the ingredients) rather than simply on the ingredients and, superficially, the "method". So it could be said that, as a stand-alone example, heat transfer or, more precisely, controlling the rate of heat transfer, is a threshold concept in cookery because it alters the way in which you think about cooking.[24]*

Other examples from a slideshow presented by Ray Land in 2008 include opportunity cost from economics, metabolism from exercise physiology, evolution from biology, and "the state" from politics.[25] Because threshold concepts come from the ideas that surrounded troublesome knowledge, they can be difficult at first to fully comprehend, and it is not always easy to state discipline specific examples. Furthermore, someone well versed in his or her specialized knowledge field, having passed through several threshold concepts, would be hard pressed to separate them out

[24] Meyer, J., Land, R., 2006. Overcoming Barriers to Student Understanding: Threshold Concepts and Troublesome Knowledge. Routledge, New York, NY, pp. 3–4.

[25] Land, R., 2008. Threshold concepts and troublesome knowledge: a transformational model of learning [PowerPoint slides]. Available from: <http://www.sddu.leeds.ac.uk/uploaded/learning-teaching-docs/teachtalk/5-12-2008/ray_land_presentation.pdf>.

from their current understanding. As Meyer and Land put it: "Respondents within our study the difficulty experienced by expert practitioners looking back across thresholds they have personally long since crossed and attempting to understand (from their own transformed perspective) the difficulties faced from (untransformed) student perspectives."[26] This is where the mindful concept of beginner's mind can be of some use.

The type of openness that coincides with beginner's mind sheds light on how this approach can help one to see things afresh and become more prepared to fail and grow. There is an associated feeling of "letting go of" or "setting aside" preconceived notions and embedded ideas that is part of this position begun as "Shoshin" in Zen Buddhism. A child or one with beginner's mind has the capacity to see life anew. They are more willing to admit their lack of knowledge and consequently are more open to asking questions. Shuntyu Suzuki succinctly summarizes, "In the beginner's mind there are many possibilities, but in the expert's there are few."[27] This mindful manner of seeing ideas afresh can lead to more opportunities to perceive threshold concepts, and the ability to question can lead to more agency for the questioner and a better sense of the need to continually learn. Awareness of the need for lifelong learning and an awareness of threshold concept leads to openness and motivation. Tapping into beginner's mind can also help us to understand how threshold concepts work because an openness to new ideas is a prerequisite for crossing knowledge barriers.

Note that, in the heat transfer example given here, there is a type of process happening that describes the event and the understanding that comes with it. This metacognitive element is usually present, and once the idea of a threshold concept is understood, there is sometimes awareness on the part of the learner when the threshold is being crossed. But that is not always the case. In most instances, there is an "in-between" experience defined as a "liminal space," which accompanies the crossing of a threshold concept. A cursory look at liminal spaces and liminality reveals that they can coincide in an interesting way with beginner's mind. A *liminal space* is the state of moving from one stage to another, and it is occasionally compared to the feeling of adolescence; these spaces have their roots in anthropology and describe the middle stage of rituals wherein one is

---

[26] Meyer, J., Land, R., 2006. Overcoming Barriers to Student Understanding: Threshold Concepts and Troublesome Knowledge. Routledge, New York, NY, p. 7.
[27] Suzuki, S., 2011. Zen Mind, Beginner's Mind. Shambhala, Boston, MA, p. 1.

in the process of transforming. Liminality, which draws from the Latin word *līmen*, which means "threshold," is therefore related to Meyer and Land's ideas, as they make this connection (Meyer, Land, & Baillie, 2010): "Difficulty in understanding threshold concepts may leave the learner in a state of 'liminality,' a suspended state of partial understanding, or 'stuck place,' in which understanding approximates to a kind of 'mimicry' or lack of authenticity. Insights gained by learners as they cross thresholds can be exhilarating but might also be unsettling, requiring an uncomfortable shift in identity, or, paradoxically, a sense of loss."[28]

How could mindfulness and liminality coincide? Perhaps when developing mindfulness, there is a prethreshold period of entering a liminal state when it could be said that practitioners are copying what they think they know about mindful behavior before becoming more fully aware. Regarding some of the ACRL Framework threshold concepts, there can be places where an instruction librarian can see these liminal places up close. Seeing students struggle with attempts to move away from quick fallback "finding information" strategies using a search engine and moving to exploring a topic that they are more engaged with and spending more mindful time understanding the research process is a core goal of the ACRL Framework. Patch writing, while often deemed plagiarism, can also amount to mimicry of what a student thinks research should be and is another example of liminality. The ambiguity and indeterminacy that is associated with liminal spaces and thresholds also juxtaposes nicely with similar concepts in the Zen roots of mindfulness.

Many who first encounter the ideas expressed in mindfulness come away with a type of reaction that can be described as "Is that all there is?" The initial simplicity of the concept of mindfulness can sometimes take the neophyte aback. Ideas such as "paying attention" and "maintaining a moment by moment focus on our lives" can at first appear trite or unworthy of pursuit. Yet throughout this book, time and again, it is shown that adopting mindful habits cannot only be its own reward, but there is more than first meets the eye about mindfulness; it takes dedicated effort and is fulfilling on many levels. The adjacency of mindfulness and threshold concepts can be thought provoking to contemplate because not only is mindfulness a threshold concept, but also the interweaving threads of supporting suppositions underlying them lead to personal growth.

[28] Land, R., Meyer, J., Baillie, C., 2010. Editors' preface: threshold concepts and transformational learning. In: Land, R., Meyer, J.H.F., Baillie, C. (Eds.), Threshold Concepts and Transformational Learning. Sense Publishers, Rotterdam, p. 9.

Meyer and Land put forth five characteristics of threshold concepts in their 2003 report, "Threshold Concepts and Troublesome Knowledge: Linkages to Ways of Thinking and Practising within the Disciplines":

- *Transformative*, in that once understood, its potential effect on student learning and behavior, is to occasion a significant shift in the perception of a subject
- Probably *irreversible*, in that the change of perspective occasioned by acquisition of a threshold concept is unlikely to be forgotten, or will be unlearned only by considerable effort
- *Integrative*; that is, it exposes the previously hidden interrelatedness of something
- Possibly often (though not necessarily) *bounded*, in that any conceptual space will have terminal frontiers, bordering with thresholds into new conceptual areas
- Potentially (and possibly inherently) *troublesome* (defined as counterintuitive, alien, or incoherent)[29]

These aspects of threshold concepts help to shed light on their understanding and can also be considered dispositional for those experiencing them, at least in the case of transformative, irreversible, and troublesome. As we shall see shortly, regarding the criteria that help to define threshold concepts, mindfulness shows traits for each. In some cases, there is a more obvious or pronounced connection; in others, it can take some discussion to find the links.

Mindfulness Is Transformative

As transformative ideas, threshold concepts are closely related to the idea of perspective transformation as developed by Jack Mezirow. For Mezirow, perspective transformation is "the process of becoming critically aware of our assumptions and ways of viewing the world."[30] Certainly this definition could stand in as a goal of mindfulness. Concerned with how adults learn, Mezirow "mentions that one of the most important areas of learning for adults is that which frees them from their habitual ways of thinking and acting."[31] Mindfulness also removes us from habits of thought and action by asking us to reflect and be more conscious of what we are doing.

---

[29] Meyer, J., Land, R., 2003. Threshold concepts and troublesome knowledge: linkages to ways of thinking and practising within the disciplines. ETL Project Occasional Report. Available from: <http://www.colorado.edu/ftep/documents/ETLreport4-1.pdf>.

[30] Mezirow, J., Taylor, E.W., 2009. Transformative Learning in Practice: Insights from Community, Workplace, and Higher Education. Jossey-Bass, San Francisco, CA, p. 18.

[31] Ibid., 19.

A thorough understanding of mindfulness is not necessary to see how it is transformative. In fact, it is difficult to see how one could become more mindful without being transformed in some way. Mindfulness, in this sense, is closest to this threshold concept characteristic. As Meyer and Land go on to explain the threshold concept type of transformation, they shift to a higher plane:

> In certain powerful instances, such as the comprehension of specific politico-philosophical insights (for example, aspects of Marxist, feminist or post-structuralist analysis) the shift in perspective may lead to a transformation of personal identity, a reconstruction of subjectivity. In such instances a transformed perspective is likely to involve an affective component—a shift in values, feeling or attitude.[32]

Mindfulness can have similar effects. When taking time to meditate or reflect in a focused way, we can transform our ideas about who we are as we transform our reactions to life. As mentioned previously with liminal states, developing and mastering mindfulness can create an identity change (and loss from previous identifications). The beginner's mind aspect of Zen is particularly helpful here once more because it allows us to be transformed. Being comfortable with stating "I don't know" entertains an open world of possibilities and allows for change to occur. Thích Nhất Hạnh states, "There's a seed of anger in every one of us. There is also a seed of fear, a seed of despair. And when the seed of anger or fear, we should be able to recognize it, to embrace it tenderly, and to transform it. And the agent of transformation and healing is called mindfulness."[33]

The transformative power of mindfulness also coincides with the academic discipline growth that occurs with threshold concepts. When passing through the threshold concepts associated within one's field, the identity shifts occur from novice, to "thinking like a philosopher" or "thinking like a librarian," and then to expertise. Mindful practitioners also go through stages and identity shifts. As introduced by Jon Kabat-Zinn in *Mindfulness for Beginners*, "Welcome to the practice of mindfulness. You may not know it, but if you are coming to the systematic cultivation of mindfulness for the first time, you may very well be on the threshold of

---

[32] Meyer, J., Land, R., 2003. Threshold concepts and troublesome knowledge: linkages to ways of thinking and practising within the disciplines. ETL Project Occasional Report. Available from: <http://www.colorado.edu/ftep/documents/ETLreport4-1.pdf>.

[33] Jaksch, M., 2012, April 05. How mindfulness transforms ordinary into extraordinary. Available from: <http://goodlifezen.com/how-mindfulness-transforms-ordinary-into-extraordinary/> (accessed 28.04.15.).

a momentous shift in your life, something subtle and, at the same time, potentially huge and important, which just might change your life."[34]

Mindfulness Is Irreversible

It would appear at first that once you begin mindful practice and continue to progress toward a state of mindfulness, that the process could be considered irreversible. Still, a deeper look at what is meant by the term *irreversible* may provide more understanding here. In reference to a threshold concept, the term is used to reinforce the idea of progress and growth. Meyer and Land extrapolate irreversible ideas as those that cannot be undone: "the change of perspective occasioned by acquisition of a threshold concept is unlikely to be forgotten, or will be unlearned only by considerable effort."[35] How could someone possibly "unlearn" mindfulness? One might abandon mindful habits, meditate less frequently or not at all, and even perhaps lapse back into a state of "unmindfulness" (or better still, mindlessness), and yet the core idea itself would most likely be retained. Technically, this idea of retention does not fully correlate to irreversibility. In this case, it appears as if irreversible is more closely associated with the inability to "return to an earlier state."

And it is an inherent characteristic of mindfulness itself to become less mindful on occasion. Mindfulness allows all types of behavior. It is the awareness and attention given to what is occurring that is most important. That is to say that a mindful person can be angry, upset, anxious, or stressed out and they can still be said to be mindful. Therefore, once mindful habits are developed, in an interesting conundrum, mindfulness once more would be needed to "unlearn" or move back to a premindful state, if that is even possible. The concept of irreversibility itself is quite troublesome itself, because returning to an earlier state is counterintuitive, would appear to be quite difficult to do consciously, and does not seem to present much benefit. Yet, connecting back to the earlier discussion of the value of beginner's mind and the ability to relate to the experience of a novice can prove to be very advantageous for the instruction and reference librarian. That is to say that having the capability to reverse your own state to empathize with a student who is just beginning to do research may create important links. Abandoning expertise, taking note of preconceived ideas, and having an

[34] Kabat-Zinn, J., 2012. Mindfulness for Beginners: Reclaiming the Present Moment—and Your Life. Sounds True, Boulder, CO, p. 12.

[35] Meyer, J., Land, R., 2006. Overcoming Barriers to Student Understanding: Threshold Concepts and Troublesome. Routledge, New York, NY, p. 7.

awareness of when discipline specific jargon creates misunderstandings can be beneficial when working with younger researchers. The ability to reverse course and tap into that experience can help to bridge educational chasms.

Mindfulness Is Integrative

The idea of bringing together separate concepts into a unified whole can also be applied to mindfulness. Meyer and Land state that an integrative idea "exposes the previously hidden interrelatedness of something."[36] The way in which mindfulness connects to various aspects of our lives (and different facets of librarianship) has been pointed out throughout this book. And mindfulness can be shown to seep into unexpected places. Mindfulness has been shown to reduce anxiety, decrease loneliness, affect the motivation to exercise, reduce neural activity in the craving-related region of the brain, and curtail distress and enhance mental health, physical health, and behavioral regulation, among other benefits. The idea that mindful behavior has various far-reaching consequences and benefits has been proven in numerous studies: chronic pain,[37] tolerance of pain,[38] parenting,[39] depression, anxiety, and stress.[40]

The first draft of the ACRL Framework from February 2014 mentions the integrative learning taking place in campus programs that rely on interdisciplinarity, and also in learning communities.[41] Librarians often have unique opportunities on campuses to impart a wide range of information about what is happening in numerous areas and with many different groups. This can be even more the case when the librarian gets out

---

[36] Meyer, J., L and, R., 2003. Threshold concepts and troublesome knowledge: linkages to ways of thinking and practising within the disciplines. ETL Project Occasional Report. Available from: <http://www.colorado.edu/ftep/documents/ETLreport4-1.pdf>.

[37] la Cour, P., Petersen, M., 2015. Effects of mindfulness meditation on chronic pain: a randomized controlled trial. Pain Med. 16 (4), 641–652.

[38] Liu, X., Wang, S., Chang, S., Chen, W., Si, M., 2013. Effect of brief mindfulness intervention on tolerance and distress of pain induced by cold-pressor task. Stress Health J. Int. Soc. Investig. Stress 29 (3), 199–204.

[39] Douglas Coatsworth, J., Duncan, L.G., Nix, R.L., Greenberg, M.T., Gayles, J.G., Bamberger, K.T., Berrena, E., Ann Demi, M., 2015. Integrating mindfulness with parent training: effects of the mindfulness-enhanced strengthening families program. Dev. Psychol. 51 (1), 26.

[40] Song, Y., Lindquist, R., 2015. Effects of mindfulness-based stress reduction on depression, anxiety, stress and mindfulness in Korean nursing students. Nurse Educat. Today 35 (1), 86–90.

[41] Framework for Information Literacy for Higher Education, First Draft, 2014, February. Available from: <http://www.ala.org/acrl/standards/ilframework> (accessed 14.04.15.).

of the library and tries to engage with faculty, staff, and students. From this point of view, a mindful librarian can become a linchpin who is able to create connections. For example, a librarian could be involved as a club advisor, attend and volunteer to help with campus events, serve as a liaison, teach library instruction, join committees, and support other campus initiatives (first-year programs, orientation, and financial literacy). The librarian who spends a great deal of time with as many different groups as possible can act as an integrated information conduit to each. But there does need to be focused awareness on the interrelatedness aspect here and how to see connections that others may miss.

Turning away from the concept of an integrated librarian let's look again at how mindfulness itself can be united into different aspects of life and more specifically, how it has been integrated into education. Shapiro, Brown, and Astin posit three major reasons for the incorporation of meditation in higher education: (i) the enhancement of cognitive and academic performance, (ii) management of academic-related stress, and (iii) the development of the "whole person."[42] Groups such as the Association for Mindfulness in Education, the Mindfulness in Education Network, Mindfulness in Schools, and the Association for Contemplative Mind in Higher Education attempt to provide examples and leadership on mindfulness and education. As time passes, the growing need for students to attain and retain focus will continue to be needed, and the application of mindfulness will most likely be at the forefront of that necessity.

Finally, common Western thought has a history of mind/body dualism that extends to thoughts and emotions. However, from a mindful point of view, the connectedness of these ideas greatly diminishes the aspects of their polarity and opposition. Jon Kabat-Zinn points to seven attitudinal factors that should be cultivated to help us open ourselves up to mindfulness: nonjudging, patience, beginner's mind, trust, nonstriving, acceptance, and letting go.[43] These factors have a small cohesive theme of detachment beneath them, and yet there is also the interrelatedness among them of cultivating the awareness of impermanence and the ephemeral nature of life. The ability to unearth and make connections moves understanding forward with mindfulness and advances knowledge of threshold concepts.

[42] Shapiro, S.L., Brown, K.W., Astin, J., 2011. Toward the integration of meditation into higher education: a review of research evidence. Teachers College Record 113 (3), 493–528.

[43] Kabat-Zinn, J., 2004. Full Catastrophe Living: How to Cope with Stress, Pain and Illness Using Mindfulness Meditation. Piatkus, London.

Mindfulness Is Bounded

This threshold concept characteristic could be considered to be the hardest to comprehend and has the least flexibility to be used outside of academia. The notion here that an idea is bounded is associated with discipline borders, demarcations between fields of study that help to define and draw distinctions between them. For students, the boundedness of an idea can help to create a clearer focus about what separates their discipline with another. For example, deconstruction is considered a threshold concept in literature and philosophy, but it rarely ventures away from these disciplines. It fits other threshold concept criteria; it is transformative because it changes the way that literary texts are interpreted, it is irreversible because it is difficult to read literature in the same manner once you understand how to look for deeper hidden meaning, and it is certainly troublesome to many because it is considered to be negative and destroys meaning. The way in which deconstruction could be said to be bounded is that this concept would not be applicable in the same way or have as a great of an impact in another discipline.

Could mindfulness be said to be "bounded"? At first, it would appear that the many applications and the far-reaching effects of mindful behavior would seem to make mindfulness less limited or without boundaries. Despite this, it has been pointed out that there is a great deal of discipline needed to become mindful, and in the same way that one could go into "mindlessness autopilot," there needs to be an awareness of the consistent and concentrated effort that goes into being mindful. So, while there are limitations to what mindfulness can affect, as a holistic approach, there appears to be very little that would limit it to a specific area—at least, in relation to the boundaries of ideas within academic disciplines. One other facet of this threshold concept characteristic is that the language associated with a specific field also differentiates it among others. Therefore, the terms and communication styles in medicine may be so different from those in architecture or librarianship that the boundaries are evident. While there is language that might be said to be closely associated with mindfulness, it is not exclusively within its domain. It is interesting to note that being "bounded" is the least referenced and fully realized threshold concept trait that is employed by the ACRL Framework.

Mindfulness Is Troublesome

Similar to the idea that mindfulness is irreversible, it can take some unpacking to figure out what is meant here about troublesome ideas. Often the terms *difficult* and *counterintuitive* are used as synonyms or substitutes for *troublesome* when this threshold criteria is discussed. Mindfulness can appear to be troublesome to the novice for several reasons. Initially, there are often readjustments to be made when meditating. Often, it is thought that mediation is being done incorrectly and nonmindful frustrations accompany the forced notion that "I am not being mindful right now." Not only is this troublesome feature of mediation a stumbling block to newcomers, but there is the added enigma that the common Zen answer is that there is no trouble inherent in the problem; rather, the meditator is creating the problem. That is to say that there are events that occur almost as if within a vacuum, and our reactions define them. Mindfulness in its simplest form is focused attention—nothing less, nothing more—and in another nod to Zen, there is a type of disciplined focus to it, and yet it cannot be forced.

It was the concern that students have with troublesome knowledge that led Meyer and Land to develop threshold concepts. David Perkins initiated the conversation around troublesome knowledge, and he uses terms such as "counter-intuitive, alien … or incoherent"[44] in his descriptions. Troublesome knowledge might be an affront to some students because it can test ingrained thoughts or beliefs, act as a challenge to a student's worldview or comfort zone, and directly target shallow thinking or confirmation bias. Students may also be aware of the changes needed to move forward and, and there may a great deal of trepidation about letting go of stability. Again, mindfulness and the aforementioned attitudinal factors (particularly acceptance) can minimize this impact.

Glynis Cousin states that the difficulty with threshold concepts involves more than just being able to move past accepted ideas and behaviors: "From this view, mastery of a threshold concept can be inhibited by the prevalence of a 'common sense' or intuitive understanding of it. Getting students to reverse their intuitive understandings is also troublesome because the reversal can involve an uncomfortable, emotional repositioning."[45] The idea of "being stuck" is referenced numerous times in the work of Meyer and Land; this harks back to the notion that valuable knowledge does not come easy. The difficulties that students encounter when seeking information and researching is detailed in Chapter 3. The ACRL Framework is attempting to give researchers a greater awareness

---

[44] Panke, S., 2015, January 12. Threshold concepts for learning—AACE. Available from: <http://blog.aace.org/2015/01/12/threshold-concepts/> (accessed 28.04.15.).

[45] Cousin, G., 2006. An introduction to threshold concepts. Planet 17. Available from: <http://www.et.kent.edu/fpdc-db/files/DD%2002-threshold.pdf> (accessed 28.04.15.).

and a deeper understanding of the research process, which leads to a more mindful experience. Moving past cognitive "stuck" moments can be more easily accomplished when mindfulness is employed because heightened awareness allows openness and acceptance of not only new ideas, but more important, of new identities as well.

These identity shifts are often very uncomfortable. Mindfulness helps with awareness of self. Whole body or body-scan meditations allow for deep connections to all parts of the body. Beginning in a similar fashion as many types of mediation, with a concentration on breathing, the body scan works its way from head to toe and gives the meditator the opportunity to unite closely with physical sensation. Kabat-Zinn points out that when we mediate on how we breathe, "we are learning right from the start to get comfortable with change."[46]

Dr Howard Slutzky on Mindset, Confirmation Bias, and Self-Fulfilling Prophecy

There are several psychological phenomena that pose a threat to this chapter's idea of the threshold concept. One such threat is what Carol S. Dweck, PhD, refers to as a "fixed mindset." In her book *Mindset: The New Psychology of Success*, Dweck describes a fixed mindset as being characterized by an assumption that our personality, intelligence, and creativity are largely unalterable. This mindset undermines growth not because the individual is unable to change, but because they falsely *believe* that these things are unchangeable. For instance, a student who does poorly on a test may have the belief that he is a bad test-taker. With this belief, he is unlikely to attempt any new approach in test preparation, as doing so is seen as futile. Thus, his fixed mindset remains intact. On the contrary, a "growth mindset" reflects a belief that our personality, intelligence, and creativity are malleable and subject to intentional and voluntary efforts to further develop them. Within this mindset, failure is seen as a learning opportunity. This sentiment is probably best captured in a quote by Thomas Edison regarding his persistence in his efforts to invent the lightbulb: "I have not failed. I've just found 10,000 ways that won't work." Gaining insight into one's mindset is a crucial prerequisite to the full experience of a threshold concept. A fixed mindset is the enemy of change and growth as it vehemently protects one's current belief system. Dweck's book is a useful tool, as it thoroughly describes the concept of mindset, it explains the

---

[46] Kabat-Zinn, J., 1991. Full Catastrophe Living: Using the Wisdom of Your Body and Mind to Face Stress, Pain, and Illness. Bantam Doubleday, New York, NY.

shortcomings of a fixed mindset, and it provides strategies for shifting to a mindset characterized by curiosity, openness, and growth. Ironically, those who would most benefit from reading Dweck's book are probably the least likely to do so on their own. It is, therefore, the responsibility of educators to introduce this concept to students and to offer various resources to assist them in the transition from a fixed to a growth mindset.[47]

Social psychology describes two additional factors that also inhibit insight and growth. The first, confirmation bias, refers to the tendency to reach conclusions that are consistent with our preexisting beliefs and expectations. That is, we tend to seek out information that confirms our preconceptions, and we tend to overlook, dismiss, invalidate, or even attack any information (or source of information) that challenges these beliefs. We can see this in the areas of religion, politics, relationships, and self-reflection, and in both professional and personal settings. Consider the simple example of conducting an online search. If I am interested in researching information regarding veganism (I have been a vegetarian for almost 20 years and a vegan for almost 1 year), I am likely to exclusively search for "the benefits of a vegan diet." Searching in this manner inadvertently excludes most if not all evidence that may suggest some shortcomings of this dietary lifestyle.

I'll borrow another illustration from my clinical work with couples. I have worked with couples in which one partner is struggling with issues of jealousy and insecurity. While there are certainly circumstances when such concerns are founded, I often see them as residual wounds from previous relationships. Nevertheless, those plagued with these issues will search for evidence that their current partner is also cheating. Due to the subjectivity of perception, they are certain to find it. They are also likely to ignore or dismiss any evidence to the contrary.

The second factor, closely related to confirmation bias, is what social psychologists refer to as the "self-fulfilling prophecy." This concept was first articulated by sociologist Robert Merton in his 1948 article "The Self-Fulfilling Prophecy." While confirmation bias involves the maintenance of our distorted beliefs and expectations, the self-fulfilling prophecy occurs when our distorted beliefs and expectations inadvertently cause their own fulfillment.[48] This reminds me of a colleague who had just been hired to teach an Introduction to Sociology class at the university where I had been working for a year. Having had some challenging, disrespectful, and unmotivated students at previous institutions, she approached this new position with an attitude that she believed would prevent these same issues from resurfacing. She informed me that on the first day of class, she intended to "lay down the law." She told her students

[47] Dweck, C., 2006. Mindset. Ballantine Books, New York, NY.
[48] Merton, R., 1948. The self-fulfilling prophecy. Antioch Rev. 8 (2), 193–210.

that she didn't care if they showed up, nor did she care if they succeeded. She told them: "I get paid either way." Subsequently, her students revolted. They were aggressive and disrespectful. They were argumentative in class, and their performance was substandard. She saw their behavior as clear evidence that her preconceptions were accurate. Ultimately, a group of students from her class approached our department chair to complain. Our cubicles were in the same area of office space, so she regularly vented to me regarding this situation as it unfolded. I ultimately shared with her my opinion regarding the reason for her negative experience. I pointed out the likelihood that this was a prime example of the self-fulfilling prophecy. I explained that the aggressive and dismissive approach that this instructor took with her students at the beginning of the term most likely led to the very behavior she had hoped to prevent. Fortunately, she was given an opportunity try a different approach the following term. This time, she approached her students in a supportive and encouraging manner, without compromising an appropriate level of assertiveness and boundaries. Her experience this second term was a sharp contrast from the previous. Students *loved* her, they enjoyed the subject, and the majority made a concerted effort to succeed. So, the confirmation bias and the self-fulfilling prophecy both represent distortions that undermine insight and growth. Therefore, identifying and addressing these distortions is a necessary prerequisite to the full experience of a threshold concept.

THE ACRL FRAMEWORK AND THE FRAMES

As a way to integrate threshold concepts that apply to information literacy into the ACRL Framework, the concept of "frames" was employed, which can be considered to coincide with the idea of information literacy threshold concepts. Currently, there are six frames:
* Authority Is Constructed and Contextual.
* Information Creation as a Process.
* Information Has Value.
* Research as Inquiry.
* Scholarship as Conversation.
* Searching as Strategic Exploration.

For the purposes of discussing these frames and mindfulness, each section that follows lists the frame and the ACRL Framework description of it, and will list at least two of the dispositions for each frame that can be connected to mindfulness (there are more dispositions for each frame in the ACRL Framework). One of the principal ideas to keep in mind is that the previous ACRL Standards focused on the qualities that helped to define the information literate, whereas the ACRL Framework has two goals: (i) a better understanding of how the research process works and (ii) a more holistic approach to the development of the information seeker.

Authority Is Constructed and Contextual

Information resources reflect their creators' expertise and credibility, and are evaluated based on the information need and the context in which the information will be used. Authority is constructed in that various communities may recognize different types of authority. It is contextual in that the information need may help to determine the level of authority required.

Dispositions

Learners who are developing their information literate abilities do the following:

- *Develop and maintain an open mind when encountering varied and sometimes conflicting perspectives.*
- *Develop awareness of the importance of assessing content with a skeptical stance and with a self-awareness of their own biases and worldview.*[49]

Most of the threshold concepts associated with the frames can be linked in some way to the original ACRL Standards, even in an oblique manner. Not only that, but there does seem to be a conceptual consistency behind the ACRL Standards–ACRL Frame mapping. For example, "Information Has Value" idea aligns with ACRL Standard Five ("The information literate student understands many of the economic, legal, and social issues surrounding the use of information and accesses and uses information ethically and legally."[50]). This first frame of the ACRL Framework, however, does appear to not only update ACRL Standard Three and some of its underlying tenets ("The information literate student evaluates information and its sources critically and incorporates selected information into his or her knowledge base and value system."[51]), but it also extends these ideas to a great degree. One of the breaks from the ACRL Standards is the emphasis here on "different types of authority," which opens up the possibility of taking a much deeper look at how authority is constructed. In the majority of cases outlined in this book, mindfulness has been used as a way to focus attention and elevate the ability to react nonjudgmentally. A somewhat lesser known aspect of mindfulness is the development of loving-kindness meditation, which helps to advance feelings of goodwill, kindness, and warmth toward others.

---

[49] Framework for Information Literacy for Higher Education. Available from: <http://www.ala.org/acrl/standards/ilframework>.

[50] Information Literacy Competency for Higher Education. Available from: <http://www.ala.org/acrl/standards/informationliteracycompetency>.

[51] Ibid.

Increasing empathy and decreasing bias are worthy goals, and there are studies that show that mindfulness helps with each of these.[52] The growing awareness of critical pedagogy and the move toward becoming active agents that support its ideals in librarianship continue to grow. Educating students to become more active social agents and recognizing how knowledge advances them and others in society are core concepts of the type of teaching espoused by Paulo Friere.[53] Rather than thinking of themselves as docile and empty "buckets" to be filled by a teacher's wisdom, students in a class based on critical pedagogy learn to bring a more subjective and personally representative mindset to learning. Combined with this and a more dimensional understanding of how personal motivation and knowledge affect one's place in the social strata, students are able to become much more engaged with their own learning and understand how education connects to personal agency.

There is an element of mindfulness here when considering how focus and attention is needed to move toward a deeper understanding of the embedded inequalities in society. A closer look at the dispositions shows how mindfulness can be brought to bear when assessing the credentials and backgrounds of resource creators. The two dispositions listed for this frame highlight openness, awareness, and ambiguity, all concepts associated with mindfulness. Terms such as "open mind," "self-awareness," and "varied and conflicting" show how mindfulness can be helpful when assessing authority.

Information Creation as a Process

Information in any format is produced to convey a message and is shared via a selected delivery method. The iterative processes of researching, creating, revising, and disseminating information vary, and the resulting product reflects these differences.

Learners who are developing their information literate abilities do the following:
- *Are inclined to seek out characteristics of information products that indicate the underlying creation process*
- *Accept the ambiguity surrounding the potential value of information creation expressed in emerging formats or modes[54]*

---

[52] Greason, P.B., Cashwell, C.S., 2009. Mindfulness and counseling self-efficacy: the mediating role of attention and empathy. Counselor Edu. Superv. 49, 2–19; Kang, Y., Gray, J.R., Dovidio, J.F., 2014. The nondiscriminating heart: lovingkindness meditation training decreases implicit intergroup bias. J. Exp. Psychol. Gen. 143 (3), 1306; Lueke, A., Gibson, B., 2014. Mindfulness meditation reduces implicit age and race bias the role of reduced automaticity of responding. Soc. Psychol. Personal. Sci. 1948550614559651.

[53] Freire, P., 2000. Pedagogy of the Oppressed. Continuum, New York, NY.

[54] Framework for Information Literacy for Higher Education. Available from: <http://www.ala.org/acrl/standards/ilframework>.

An understanding of process implies mindful practice. As pointed out in Chapter 3, taking the time to understand how something works and why you are taking an action can be equally if not more important than understanding the content of an idea. One of the dispositions for this threshold concept frame is "Accept the ambiguity surrounding the potential value of information creation expressed in emerging formats or modes."[55] The first noticeable connection to mindfulness is acceptance, which can imply a nonjudgmental attitude. The ability to embrace the uncertainty of the potential value of information is an interesting quality of mind to foster. Unpacking this idea a bit, one implication here is an understanding that information processes and packages are not static, and that either of these at face value do not confer automatic quality over another. For example, taking some mindful steps to assess the information within a nontraditional resource may allow students to explore not only how information is created, but also how authority is constructed. One other insight could be that there is not necessarily an "answer" to a research question, but rather that there can be an exploration of ideas about it. And finally, being comfortable with the feeling that there is not a distinct answer is connected directly to the nonjudgmental aspect of mindfulness and how that ambiguity can be embraced instead of being feared.

Similar to the "Authority Is Constructed and Contextual" frame, this frame and its associated dispositions involve enlarging the ideas about what constitutes acceptable research. The proliferation of emerging information formats adds to the researcher's ability to access more types of information, which of course can create difficulty. But there needs to be an awareness of the numerous information formats available, and the other disposition focuses on knowing how they were created. As stated in the ACRL Framework, information literate learners "are inclined to seek out characteristics of information products that indicate the underlying creation process"[56] could be a nod to an increasing push to support open-access materials and promote more ownership and access to academic research.

Information Has Value
  Information possesses several dimensions of value, including as a commodity, as a means of education, as a means to influence, and as a means of negotiating and understanding the world. Legal and socioeconomic interests influence information production and dissemination.

[55] Ibid.
[56] Ibid.

Dispositions

Learners who are developing their information literate abilities do the following:

- *See themselves as contributors to the information marketplace rather than only consumers of it.*
- *Are inclined to examine their own information privilege.[57]*

The dispositions for this frame take on a decidedly active stance and can map to the mindful attribute of becoming more fully aware. Admittedly, mindfulness is usually associated with raising awareness of how you live your life and react to events and others. But that does not mean that we cannot extend that awareness out to others and their situations. Remembering that mindfulness is integrative and that loving-kindness meditations allow us to build empathy, we can become more mindful about the ideas of others and be more reflective about our own position in society.

Again, the disposition for this frame that most aligns with a striving for social justice is "Are inclined to examine their own information privilege."[58] There would be a number of personal attributes that would help those pre-disposed to looking deeply at themselves and the strata of society, and those attributes would then allow them to determine if they have any special rights granted to them when they access information. Certainly, an under-standing of how people from a myriad of backgrounds and social positions access information and what is available to them would be necessary to understand authority.

Research as Inquiry

Research is iterative and depends upon asking increasingly complex or new questions whose answers in turn develop additional questions or lines of inquiry in any field.

Dispositions

Learners who are developing their information-literate abilities do the following:

- *Consider research as open-ended exploration and engagement with information.*
- *Maintain an open mind and a critical stance.*
- *Value persistence, adaptability, and flexibility and recognize that ambiguity can benefit the research process.*
- *Seek multiple perspectives during information gathering and assessment*
- *Seek appropriate help when needed.*
- *Demonstrate intellectual humility (i.e., recognize their own intellectual or experiential limitations).[59]*

[57] Ibid.
[58] Ibid.
[59] Ibid.

Mindfulness helps one become more comfortable with open-ended ideas and learn to accept abstruse concepts. Dispositions such as "Maintain an open mind and a critical stance," "Value persistence, adaptability, and flexibility and recognize that ambiguity can benefit the research process," and "Demonstrate intellectual humility (i.e., recognize their own intellectual or experiential limitations)"[60] show links to mindful tenets. This is similar to the way that a disposition in the frame "Information Creation as a Process" shows that there is not necessarily an "answer" to a research question, but rather that there can be an exploration of ideas about it. "Research as Inquiry" reinforces the idea that research questions can take many forms and can lead to open spaces rather than closure.

In Chapter 3, which aims to show how mindfulness can help during the research process, it was pointed out that the nonjudgmental nature of mindfulness can help to alleviate frustration and stopping points when students work on research papers and projects. This frame helps to clarify the types of hurdles that occur when doing research, and most important, states that persistence is a key disposition. In their study, "The effects of mindfulness and self-consciousness on persistence," D.R. Evans, R.A. Baer, and S.C. Segerstrom point out that "the theory of metacognitive awareness (Teasdale, Segal, & Williams, 1995) suggests that judgmental and reactive thoughts triggered by a difficult task lead to less persistence because they promote self-criticism, frustration, and impulsive decisions to stop, whereas mindfulness promotes acknowledging self-critical thoughts or frustration and allowing these experiences to dissipate."[61] The philosopher Martin Heidegger believed that true being and meditative thinking "flourish only through persistent, courageous thinking."[62] Persistence combined with adaptability is an adage connected to mindfulness.

Scholarship as Conversation
Communities of scholars, researchers, or professionals engage in sustained discourse with new insights and discoveries occurring over time as a result of varied perspectives and interpretations.
Dispositions
Learners who are developing their information literate abilities do the following:
- *Recognize they are often entering into an ongoing scholarly conversation and not a finished conversation*

---

[60] Ibid.
[61] Evans, D.R., Baer, R.A., Segerstrom, S.C., 2009. The effects of mindfulness and self-consciousness on persistence. Personal. Indiv. Differ. 47 (4), 379–382.
[62] Heidegger, M., 1966. Discourse on thinking: a translation of "Gelassenheit" by John M. Anderson and E. Hans Freund, 56.

- *See themselves as contributors to scholarship rather than only consumers of it*
- *Suspend judgment on the value of a particular piece of scholarship until the larger context for the scholarly conversation is better understood*
- *Recognize that systems privilege authorities and that not having a fluency in the language and process of a discipline disempowers their ability to participate and engage.[63]*

It is here that we also see a distinct opportunity to bring mindfulness into the conversation. This enlarged understanding that answers the question "Why do I need to do research?" can illuminate the importance of student motivation and ownership for an instruction librarian. Echoing the earlier idea of beginner's mind, many librarians might not see the need to ask a question like this because they passed through this portal of understanding long ago and do not remember the need to connect to these dispositions.

A disposition that connects directly to the bounded language nature of threshold concepts is "Recognize that systems privilege authorities and that not having a fluency in the language and process of a discipline disempowers their ability to participate and engage."[64] This would appear to be another recognition that aligns with previous recognitions of information privilege and information hierarchies. And agency again is alluded to when self-reflecting on one's role as an information creator, as well as an information consumer. The ability to show mindful patience when recognizing ongoing conversations and suspending judgment (or being nonjudgmental) are also needed here.

Searching as Strategic Exploration

Searching for information is often nonlinear and iterative, requiring the evaluation of a range of information sources and the mental flexibility to pursue alternate avenues as new understanding develops.

Dispositions

Learners who are developing their information-literate abilities do the following:

- *Exhibit mental flexibility and creativity.*
- *Understand that first attempts at searching do not always produce adequate results.*
- *Seek guidance from experts, such as librarians, researchers, and professionals.*
- *Recognize the value of browsing and other serendipitous methods of information gathering.*
- *Persist in the face of search challenges, and know when enough information completes the information task.[65]*

---

[63] Framework for Information Literacy for Higher Education. Available from: <http://www.ala.org/acrl/standards/ilframework>.

[64] Ibid.

[65] Ibid.

"Mental flexibility" is an interesting phrase. Mindfulness is not rigid, and there are no strict requirements or standard ways to be mindful. That is not to say that mindfulness has no procedures or goals, or that it lacks development. In fact, a revision of this that says "mindfulness as strategic exploration" could be in order. The resiliency and persistence touched upon earlier come into play here, and the ability to mindfully peruse information and not quickly feel obligated to conform to preconceived notions is also evident here. Although strategy implies planning and taking a tactical position, the combination of steady back-and-forth processes without "settling" or "satisficing" fits in nicely with mindful focus and direction united with acceptance and nonjudgment. Even more connected is the awareness of knowing "when enough information completes the information task," coinciding with the perspective leaden and balanced reactions associated with mindfulness.

An interesting disposition here for librarians is, of course, "Seek guidance from experts, such as librarians, researchers, and professionals."[66] Although there is not a direct correlation to mindfulness here, the agency that comes with this disposition (and also the disposition "Seek appropriate help when needed"[67] from the frame "Research as Inquiry") is worth pointing out. Asking questions and seeking help show a great deal of self-directed motivation and participation in one's own learning process. Students who ask questions are not afraid to admit that they do not know or they are engaging with the material and show a much greater ability to interact with experts who can help them. Because a greater awareness of the research process is a goal of the ACRL Framework, an excellent mission for librarians is to promote an increased understanding of their role. The discussion and teaching of the ACRL Framework provides an excellent opportunity for librarians to move to the forefront of students' minds when seeking information guidance.

BRINGING IT ALL TOGETHER—MINDFUL LIBRARIANS AND THE ACRL FRAMEWORK

How can librarians take the ACRL Framework and use it to improve their daily work and enrich their lives? With a better understanding of how mindfulness informs the ACRL Framework, librarians should work toward fostering conversations with students about ideas such as threshold

[66] Ibid.
[67] Ibid.

concepts. Mindful instruction librarians should take steps to talk about how mindfulness helps to create dispositions that push them past information literacy thresholds. Librarians can discuss liminality with faculty and work with them to recognize discipline specific threshold concepts. They also have an opportunity to become helping hands for the students who are in liminal spaces, recognizing what that feeling of uncertainty can be like and mindfully guiding students through it. In their article, which examines undergraduate students learning about leadership, Hawkins and Edwards (2015) define the role that leadership educators can play: "Anthropologists have noted that liminal rituals require the presence of a 'master of ceremonies,' who supports the liminal subjects in their passage through liminal space and whose role is to 'maintain order once the stabilities of everyday life are dissolved in the separation' (Horvath and Thomassen, 2008: 13). From the students' perspective, the leadership educator is the permanent occupant or 'host' of the liminal space, who provides the conditions and support, that make learning possible, and who thereby facilitates a potential transformation in how the student sees himself or herself and the world around them."[68]

As a way to connect more fully with threshold concepts, a helpful exercise for librarians would be to attempt to come up with some examples from the field of librarianship. What threshold concepts are within librarianship as a whole, or even in selected roles? For instruction librarians, ideas such as library anxiety and critical pedagogy may come to mind. A theme (besides mindfulness) that continues to gain prominence, as was evident in the dispositions, is increasing awareness and recognition of ingrained societal power structures and how these affect information design, access, and authoritative structure. These ideas that spring from critical pedagogy are directly stated in three frames and tangentially in the others. Mindful librarians should begin to take steps to cross the threshold and understand how critical pedagogy was formulated and why it is pivotal to the ACRL Framework and how it informs librarianship today and will in the future. Its concern with how people are viewed and treated will continue to also be a topic as technology becomes more pervasive in society.

The ACRL Framework, like any document of standards or adherence, has philosophical underpinnings. While there has been some criticism about consistent evidence for certainty when a threshold concept has been

[68] Edwards, G., Hawkins, B., 2015. Managing the monsters of doubt: liminality, threshold concepts, and leadership learning. Manage. Learn. 46 (1), 27.

attained and the potentially unlimited and indistinct definitions of threshold concepts, the general consensus for most librarians at this point appears to be excitement for a new way to define and teach information literacy. The elasticity of the ACRL Framework portends a more lasting document than the ACRL Standards, and the inclusion of the ideas of Meyer and Land from the United Kingdom into this document may also lead to more global information literacy initiatives as time passes. The application of the ACRL Framework and its wide range of ideas and concepts from many sources, its relative transparency, and the potential for adapting it over time based on feedback is a leap forward from ACRL's older and more static Standards.

In the same way that the ACRL Framework requires an identity shift, librarians must be willing to make their own changes and alter their ideas. Although traditions should not be abandoned, the openness of the ACRL Framework allows for agency for librarians. It creates a conversation that positions librarians as creators and is forward thinking. Because mindfulness may be so readily connected to the foundations of the ACRL Framework, it would be helpful for more librarians to study and adopt mindful habits. Mindful librarians should be able to see how the ACRL Framework can be integrated with many of the basic tenets of mindfulness and use those points to help students gain a much more nuanced and holistic understanding of how information can be used to improve their experience in school and in life.

RECOMMENDED RESOURCES

Framework for Information Literacy for Higher Education, 2015, February 02. Association of College and Research Libraries.

Information Literacy Competency Standards for Higher Education, 2000, January 18. Association of College and Research Libraries.

Kabat-Zinn, J., 1991. Full Catastrophe Living: Using the Wisdom of Your Body and Mind to Face Stress, Pain, and Illness. Bantam Doubleday, New York, NY.

Meyer, J., Land, R., 2006. Overcoming Barriers to Student Understanding: Threshold Concepts and Troublesome Knowledge. Routledge, New York, NY.

Tishman, S., Andrade, A., 1996. Thinking Dispositions: A Review of Current Theories, Practices, and Issues. Project Zero, Harvard University, Cambridge, MA.

BIBLIOGRAPHY

Bush, M., 2013. Mindfulness in higher education. In: Williams, J.M., Kabat-Zinn, J. (Eds.) Mindfulness: Diverse Perspectives on Its Meaning, Origins and Applications, Routledge, London.

Coatsworth, J.D., Duncan, L.G., Nix, R.L., Greenberg, M.T., Gayles, J.G., Bamberger, K.T., et al., 2015. Integrating mindfulness with parent training: effects of the mindfulness-enhanced strengthening families program. Dev. Psychol. 51 (1), 26.

Cousin, G., 2006. An introduction to threshold concepts. Planet 17 Available from: <http://www.et.kent.edu/fpdc-db/files/DD%2002-threshold.pdf> (accessed 28.04.15.)

Edwards, G., Hawkins, B., 2015. Managing the monsters of doubt: liminality, threshold concepts and leadership learning. Manage. Learn. 46 (1), 27.

Evans, D.R., Baer, R.A., Segerstrom, S.C., 2009. The effects of mindfulness and self-consciousness on persistence. Pers. Indiv. Differ. 47 (4), 379–382.

Facione, P.A., 2000. The disposition toward critical thinking: its character, measurement, and relationship to critical thinking skill. Informal Logic 20 (1), 61–84.

Farkas, M., 2014, March 03. Getting into the gray areas with the draft framework for information literacy for higher education [web log post].

Framework for Information Literacy for Higher Education, 2015, February 02. Available from: <http://www.ala.org/acrl/standards/ilframework> (accessed 10.04.15.).

Giancarlo, C.A., Facione, P.A., 2001. A look across four years at the disposition toward critical thinking among undergraduate students. J. Gen. Edu. 50 (1), 29–55.

Greason, P.B., Cashwell, C.S., 2009. Mindfulness and counseling self-efficacy: the mediating role of attention and empathy. Couns. Edu. Superv. 49, 2–19.

Heidegger, M., 1966. Discourse on thinking: a translation of "Gelassenheit" by John M. Anderson and E. Hans Freund.

Jaksch, M., 2012, April 05. How mindfulness transforms ordinary into extraordinary. Available from: <http://goodlifezen.com/how-mindfulness-transforms-ordinary-into-extraordinary/> (accessed 28.04.15.).

Kang, Y., Gray, J.R., Dovidio, J.F., 2014. The nondiscriminating heart: lovingkindness meditation training decreases implicit intergroup bias. J. Exp. Psychol. Gen. 143 (3), 1306.

Kuhlthau, C.C., 1991. Inside the search process: information seeking from the user's perspective. J. Am. Soc. Inf. Sci. 42 (5), 361–371.

Kuhlthau, C.C., 2004. Seeking Meaning: A Process Approach to Library and Information Services. Libraries Unlimited, Westport, CT.

la Cour, P., Petersen, M., 2015. Effects of mindfulness meditation on chronic pain: a randomized controlled trial. Pain Med. 16 (4), 641–652.

Land, R., 2008. Threshold concepts and troublesome knowledge: a transformational model of learning [PowerPoint slides]. Available from: <http://www.sddu.leeds.ac.uk/uploaded/learning-teaching-docs/teachtalk/5-12-2008/ray_land_presentation.pdf>.

Langer, E.J., 1997. The Power of Mindful Learning. Addison-Wesley, Reading, MA.

Langer, E., 2009. Ellen Langer. Available from: <http://www.ellenlanger.com/books/3/mindfulness> (accessed 19.04.15.).

Liu, X., Wang, S., Chang, S., Chen, W., Si, M., 2013. Effect of brief mindfulness intervention on tolerance and distress of pain induced by cold-pressor task. Stress Health J. Int. Soc. Invest. Stress 29 (3), 199–204.

Lueke, A., Gibson, B., 2014. Mindfulness meditation reduces implicit age and race bias the role of reduced automaticity of responding. Soc. Psychol. Pers. Sci. 1948550614559651.

Martin, J., 2013. Refreshing information literacy. Commun. Inf. Lit. 7 (2), 114–127.

Meyer, J., Land, R., 2003. Threshold concepts and troublesome knowledge: linkages to ways of thinking and practising within the disciplines. ETL Project Occasional Report. Available from: <http://www.colorado.edu/ftep/documents/ETLreport4-1.pdf>.

Meyer, J., Land, R., 2006. Overcoming Barriers to Student Understanding: Threshold Concepts and Troublesome Knowledge. Routledge, New York, NY.

Meyer, J.H.F., Land, R., Baillie, C. (Eds.), 2010. Threshold Concepts and Transformational Learning, Sense Publishers, Rotterdam.

Mezirow, J., Taylor, E.W., 2009. Transformative Learning in Practice: Insights from Community, Workplace, and Higher Education. Jossey-Bass, San Francisco, CA.

Panke, S., 2015, January 12. Threshold concepts for learning—AACE. Available from: <http://blog.aace.org/2015/01/12/threshold-concepts/> (accessed 28.04.15.).

Perkins, D.N., Jay, E., Tishman, S., 1993. Beyond abilities: a dispositional theory of thinking. Merrill Palmer Q., 1–21.

Rhem, J., 2013, November 06. Before and after students "get it": threshold concepts. Available from: <https://teachingcommons.stanford.edu/teaching-talk/and-after-students-get-it-threshold-concepts>.

Ritchhart, R., Perkins, D.N., 2000. Life in the mindful classroom: nurturing the disposition of mindfulness. J. Soc. Issues 56 (1), 27–47.

Salomon, G., 1994. Interaction of Media, Cognition, and Learning. L. Erlbaum, Hillsdale, NJ.

Shapiro, S.L., Brown, K.W., Astin, J., 2011. Toward the integration of meditation into higher education: a review of research evidence. Teach. Coll. Rec. 113 (3), 493–528.

Sherretz, C.E., 2011. Mindfulness in education: case studies of mindful teachers and their teaching practices. J. Thought 46 (3–4), 79–96.

Song, Y., Lindquist, R., 2015. Effects of mindfulness-based stress reduction on depression, anxiety, stress and mindfulness in korean nursing students. Nurse Educ. Today 35 (1), 86–90.

Standards for the 21st-Century Learner in Action, 2009. Available from: <http://www.ala.org/aasl/standards-guidelines/in-action>.

Suzuki, S., 2011. Zen Mind, Beginner's Mind. Shambhala, Boston, MA, p. 1.

Teasdale, J.D., Segal, Z.V., Williams, M.G., 1995. How does cognitive therapy prevent depressive relapse and why should attentional control (mindfulness training) help? Behav. Res. Ther. 33, 25–39.

Tishman, S., Andrade, A., 1996. Thinking Dispositions: A Review of Current Theories, Practices, and Issues. Project Zero, Harvard University, Cambridge, MA.

Tishman, S., Jay, E., Perkins, D.N., 1993. Teaching thinking dispositions: from transmission to enculturation. Theory Pract. 32 (3), 147–153.

CHAPTER 5

Mindful Reference Service

Richard Moniz and Howard Slutzky

HISTORY AND INTRODUCTION: THE DEVELOPMENT OF GUIDELINES

According to Liya Deng, the term *reference service*, as we commonly understand it, dates back to 1876.[1] Other authors concur that the approach to modern reference service finds its roots in the late nineteenth century. For example, as early as 1892, Providence Public Library in Rhode Island had hired a full-time reference librarian position, the duties of which closely resembled the job duties of a modern–day reference librarian.[2] These services in most libraries were very basic in the times before librarianship really existed as a true profession. Samuel Rothstein looked back at the years 1850–1900 to discover the origin of reference services. He notes that, even in the 1950s, "consideration of foreign library practices would show that reference work is still by no means universally regarded as a fundamental element of library services." He goes on to note "that even in the United States, reference was not always an integral part of the library order."[3] So, reference service was fairly inconsistent from one library to the next.

In 1953, Rothstein set out to explore reference service origins using three fundamental questions: "1. What are the distinctive features of reference service? 2. In what form were these features originally conceived? 3. By what process of development did these features come to be merged into the present concept of reference service?"[4] One reason given for the delay in the adoption of modern reference service was the view of perception of the librarian's role as a caretaker of books. Another factor that delayed the development of reference service was the lack of professional

---

[1] Deng, L. 2014. The evolution of library reference services: from general to special, 1876–1920s, Libri 64 (3), 254.

[2] Ibid., 15.

[3] Rothstein, S., 1953. The development of the concept of reference service in American libraries, 1850–1900. Libr. Q. 23 (1), 1.

[4] Ibid., 1.

education for those working at the library reference desk. According to Rothstein, Samuel Green, a librarian who served at the Worcester Free Public Library from 1871 to 1909, first advocated for something more like modern-day reference service as a norm within the profession. Rothstein claims, like the example of the Providence Public Library, that public libraries actually led the way as they sought avenues of demonstrating their worth to their local community.[5] According to Rothstein, "The librarian should make himself accessible to the readers and extend to them a cordial reception. He should encourage them to make their difficulties known to him and be willing to assist them."[6] This philosophy begins to capture the need for developing interpersonal relationships with patrons and active listening, two important elements of mindfulness practice as it is understood today. It would not be long before reference service in the United States and beyond would emerge as a fundamentally important facet of library services.

According to Deng, while the lobbying and the work of John Dewey was critical in the transformation of reference service, it was the Industrial Revolution and the development of special libraries that focused on personalized library services. This, coupled with the aforementioned efforts made by public libraries, resulted in the idea of modern reference services. "In their daily activities special librarians were able to push the boundaries of research and reference farther out…."[7] By providing detailed, one-on-one service that involved the establishment of relationships and a deep understanding of user needs, reference services reached a new level of professionalism.

It was in the latter half of the twentieth century that the Reference and User Services Association (RUSA) established formal standards by which reference work was to be judged and measured. According to the American Library Association (ALA), the Reference and Adult Services Division dates back to 1972, when it was formed from the Adult Services Division and Reference Services Division, which had in turn been created in 1956. ALA's first RUSA Bylaws, first drafted in 1972, have since been revised many times. Article II of RUSA's current bylaws, revised in 2012, states:

> **Section 1.** The Reference and User Services Association is responsible for stimulating and supporting excellence in the delivery of general library services and materials, and the provision of reference and

---

[5] Ibid., 4.
[6] Ibid., 5.
[7] Deng, L., The evolution of library reference services, 260.

information services, readers' advisory, collections development, and resource sharing for all ages, in every type of library. This involves facilitating the development and conduct of direct service to library users, the development of programs and guidelines for service to meet the needs of these users, and assisting libraries in reaching potential users.

Section 2. The responsibilities of RUSA are:

    a. Conduct of activities and projects within the division's areas of responsibility;

    b. Encouragement of the development of librarians engaged in these activities, and stimulation of participation by members of appropriate type-of-library divisions;

    c. Synthesis of the activities of all units within the American Library Association that have a bearing on the type of activities represented by the division;

    d. Re-presentation and interpretation of the division's activities in contacts outside the profession;

    e. Planning and development of programs of study and research in these areas for the total profession; and for continuous study and review of the division's activities.[8]

RUSA has created a number of very detailed and useful guidelines for the provision of services. Most important for our purposes here are the *Guidelines for Behavioral Performance of Reference and Information Service Providers*. In the United States, any librarian who acquires a degree from an ALA-accredited institution must be familiar with these. They are:

1. Visibility and approachability

2. Interest

3. Listening and Inquiring

4. Searching

5. Follow-up.[9]

From a broader international perspective the International Federation of Library Associations (IFLA) also has guidelines. While IFLA's guidelines emphasize digital or virtual references more than RUSA's standards do, there is considerable overlap. In fact, IFLA refers directly to RUSA's

---

[8] Reference and User Services Association, Bylaws. Available from: <http://www.ala.org/rusa/about/bylaws>.

[9] Reference and User Services Association, Guidelines for behavioral performance of reference and information service providers. Available from: <http://www.ala.org/rusa/resources/guidelines/guidelinesbehavioral>.

Guidelines for Behavioral Performance of Reference and Information Service Providers:

Digital reference services must meet the same standards as traditional reference services. Participants should:

* Be committed to providing the most effective assistance.
* Show professional courtesy and respect when answering questions.
* Uphold the principles of intellectual freedom.
* Acknowledge receipt of patron question. Provide patrons with responses as quickly as possible. Letters and other forms of communication should be answered promptly and courteously.
* Create and adhere to stated response turnaround policy.
* Comply with contractual licensing agreements, for both electronic and print materials, as well as specific restrictions of use, and any copyright laws governing the materials in question.
* Practice good search strategies.
* (**See RUSA document: Guidelines for Behavioral Performance of Reference and Information Services Professionals**.) [bold added]…
* Respond to 100% of questions that are assigned, if only to say, *"I'm sorry I don't know, but you can try…"*[10]

While IFLA's guidelines provide guidance in additional areas, such as intellectual freedom, the interpersonal components seem to reiterate those espoused by RUSA.

Some studies have explored the effectiveness of both IFLA and RUSA guidelines across campuses and countries. Pnina Shachaf and Sarah Horowitz, for example, conducted an analysis of 324 virtual reference transactions from 54 libraries and applied both IFLA and RUSA standards to determine the effectiveness of transactions. According to the authors, "these two sets of guidelines suggest [ideal] behaviors for librarians."[11] Citing an earlier study, they state that "the best predictor of user satisfaction was the librarian's behavior."[12] Like other researchers before them,

[10] International Federation of Library Associations, IFLA digital reference guidelines. Available from: <http://www.ifla.org/files/assets/reference-and-information-services/publications/ifla-digital-reference-guidelines-en.pdf>.

[11] Shachaf, P., Horowitz, S., 2008. Virtual reference service evaluation: adherence to RUSA behavioral guidelines and IFLA digital reference guidelines. Libr. Inf. Sci. Res. 30 (2), 124.

[12] Ibid., 3.

they discovered mixed results regarding the successful application of the guidelines. Other studies have examined reference interactions across cultures and countries as well. Laurence Olszewski and Paula Rumbaugh examined reference transactions in 10 different countries and found greater differences between graduate and undergraduate students than between countries. Graduate students seemed to go back to a stage of needing help finding resources. Perhaps this is due to increased research demands.[13]

Laura Saunders and her fellow researchers did notice some subtle differences when exploring reference services across countries. They state, "Education in Anglo-American countries such as the United States, the United Kingdom, and Australia emphasizes critical thinking, analysis, and independent learning. As a result, patrons of academic libraries in these cultures are often expected to be self-directed, and the role of the librarian is as a facilitator and guide. In cultures which focus on memorization and rote learning, patrons might view librarians as authoritative and expect them to offer definitive answers to questions, rather than assistance in the information process." They go on to emphasize, however, that "the generalizability of competencies for the reference profession regardless of culture, supporting the idea that these skills be integrated into library science education across geographic borders to ensure graduates are properly prepared for employment wherever they go to work."[14] Among the behaviors observed, they made special note of the importance of the librarian having excellent communication and listening skills and demonstrating approachability. This is in straight alignment with RUSA's guidelines. Again, they state that "core reference services span national boundaries, and that academic reference librarians share many of the same values and expectations for provision of services."[15] As such, we will consider each step in the *Guidelines for Behavioral Performance of Reference and Information Service Providers* and how mindfulness can, by improving each step or component, create more successful interactions between librarians and the patrons they serve.

[13] Olszewski, L., Rumbaugh, P., 2010. An international comparison of virtual reference services. Ref. User Serv. Q. 49 (4), 360–368.
[14] Saunders, L., Kurbanoglu, S., Jordan, M.W., Boustany, J., Chawner, B., Filas, M., et al., 2013. Culture and competencies: a multi-country examination of reference service competencies. Libri: Int. J. Libr. Inf. Ser. 63 (1), 41.
[15] Ibid., 43.

CONNECTING RUSA'S GUIDELINES AND MINDFUL PRACTICE

Approachability

The first step in the *Guidelines for Behavioral Performance of Reference and Information Service Providers* is approachability. This element can be considered from slightly different angles if one is focused on a virtual reference desk or services, as opposed to being physically in the library. It is taken as a given at this point in time that in the latter situation, the desk should be situated in a clearly visible location and that the librarian should be positioned to greet individuals as they pass by. Likewise, in an online setting, one would consider the necessity of having a link to a chat box that is obvious, overt, and easy to navigate to. What is being explored, however, are commonalities across both physical and virtual reference as they relate to mindful practice. One facet, and possibly the central tenet of mindfulness, is the need to be mentally present. Susan Smalley and Diana Winston state, "Mindfulness encourages you to be present, without shame or blame or fear, to what is truly happening."[16] In terms of working in an educational setting, Donald McCown, Diane Reibel, and Marc Micozzi state that "the teacher's presence is deemed central to how the class learns."[17] It is practical to consider that this holds true for reference librarians as well—that they be as *mentally* present as possible. While the library literature on mindfulness is sparse, Alexandra Delgado, in her exploration of mindfulness applied to law libraries, makes it clear that being a practitioner of mindfulness plays a critical role in making her a more effective reference librarian. She quotes Jon Kabbat-Zinn in stating, "We learn how to drop in ourselves, visit, and hang out in awareness."[18] According to Delgado, this ability to be totally aware is at the forefront of great reference service.

So, how does one get started? How do reference librarians make themselves more mentally present, and thus approachable? What are the challenges faced by reference librarians in being fully approachable and present? All librarians bring different experiences and, more important,

---

[16] Smalley, S.L., Winston, D., 2010. Fully Present: The Science, Art, and Practice of Mindfulness. Da Capo Lifelong, Cambridge, MA, p. 113.

[17] McCown, D., Reibel, D., Micozzi, M.S., 2011. Teaching Mindfulness: A Practical Guide for Clinicians and Educators. Springer, New York, NY, p. 27.

[18] Delgado, A.L., 2013. One percent: a new definition: practicing mindfulness in the law library. AALL Spectrum 18, 27.

personal issues and concerns into the workplace, and consequently to duties at the reference desk or in the provision of reference service. Practicing mindfulness addresses one's tendency to focus on mindlessly running through a to-do list for the day, something that happened at home, or something that is of concern in the near or distant future, either at work or at home. Mindfulness teaches an individual not to be imprisoned by such thoughts or concerns, but rather to accept them, acknowledge them, and let them go, focusing instead on the task at hand or the patron in need of immediate assistance. While the intellectual understanding of this concept of "readiness for reference" is of critical importance, it is through *practice* that one is able to make it happen.

In order to be more approachable at the reference desk, one should meditate, or at least take a few moments to breathe and reflect on the work that needs to be done or the potential needs that patrons may bring to the desk. Part of the excitement and interest that reference librarians have in working at the reference desk may include the idea that one never really knows what is going to be needed during a given shift.

Students may come with a range of questions that are difficult or easy. Students may also have varying feelings when approaching the librarian and asking for help. According to Nahyun Kown et al., "Library anxiety, a term originally coined by Constance Mellon, refers to recurring fear and the feeling of being lost among students who use an academic library for their research."[19] They go on to claim that 75–80% of college students are affected by this anxiety. This is a truly significant barrier that reference librarians must overcome. According to author Lesley Brown, "In order to gain a better understanding of the issue, it must be recognized as a real dilemma for some, and before librarians can be empathetic to users that suffer from library anxiety, librarians themselves must be better informed on the issue."[20] To illustrate that this is an issue across national boundaries, a recent study in the United Kingdom by Robinson and Reid (2007) will suffice. They concluded, among other findings, that students were confused over seemingly easy issues regarding library equipment and that resultant "hesitance to use library equipment illustrates a

---

[19] Kown, N., Onwuegbuzie, A.J., Alexander, L., 2007. Critical thinking disposition and library anxiety: affective domains on the space of information seeking and use in academic libraries. Coll. Res. Libr. 68 (3), 270.

[20] Brown, L.J., 2011. Trending now-reference librarians: how reference librarians work to prevent library anxiety. J. Libr. Admin. 51 (3), 316.

wider ranging anxiety and lack of confidence about the library."[21] Some have suggested that anxiety issues may be a bit less of a concern in the online setting, but it remains a concern in general when working with undergraduates. There also appears to be differences in anxiety based on year of study. Interestingly, students experience the greatest anxiety in their freshman and sophomore years, experience less library anxiety in their junior year, and then became more anxious again in their senior year. Anxiety can also spike based on the specific ebb and flow of a particular program or course.[22] Because of this, reference librarians must go out of their way to look approachable. Library anxiety is not going away. Reference librarians need to acknowledge this fact and mitigate its consequences to whatever degree possible. One way to do this is to ensure that one is fully in the present moment. This can be achieved in many ways, but perhaps the best would be to engage in a brief meditation before taking the desk. By doing so, one can calm the mind and perhaps even generate an aura of calm and approachability that students or other library patrons can recognize.

In their book *Buddha's Brain: The Practical Neuroscience of Happiness, Love, and Wisdom*, authors Rick Hanson and Richard Mendius offer many recommendations that can be applied to the goal of being more approachable as reference librarians. Reference librarians are frequently in a hurry and often jump to conclusions as to what a patron needs. According to Branson and Mendius, one element of mindful interaction entails slowing down.[23] It seems obvious, but how many reference librarians plow through to the answer quickly, before a patron has even finished speaking? This may occur only in the librarian's mind. It is not that the librarian necessarily verbally interrupts the patron but simply may have rushed through the listening process and is ready to share a solution before hearing the full question. This will be discussed further in this chapter when considering mindful listening, but being conscious about slowing down certainly has a place in approachability as well.

Another of Branson and Mendius's suggestions is to do one thing at a time.[24] This is a special challenge as it relates to approachability and the

---

[21] Robinson, C.M., Reid, P., 2007. Do academic enquiry services scare students? Ref. Ser. Rev. 35 (3), 420.

[22] Platt, J., Platt, T., 2013. Library anxiety among undergraduates enrolled in a research methods in psychology course. Behav. Soc. Sci. Libr. 32 (4), 242–244.

[23] Hanson, R., Mendius, R., 2009. Buddha's Brain: The Practical Neuroscience of Happiness, Love & Wisdom. New Harbinger Publications, Oakland, CA, p. 184.

[24] Ibid., 184.

reference desk. At most institutions, reference questions ebb and flow. There are times when one sees a regular stream of patrons, and other times are less busy, so the reference librarian tends to focus on other activities. These activities could be anything from skimming research articles, cataloging materials, or engaging in collection development. It is critically important for the success of the reference interaction that the librarian be able to shift and fully focus on the patron's request, especially if it is a question or concern that is more involved. A special awareness of one's mind and body language is required to convey approachability. Most librarians would admit that they are inconsistent or not as aware as they could be on some days. What mindful practice does, however, is increase the chances that a reference librarian will be able to make that transition to becoming fully present with the person who is looking for assistance.

Julie Has an Opportunity

Julie goes out to the reference desk in a hurry. She is running late, having argued with her son that morning about putting on his jacket and hat before going to school in freezing weather. She is thinking about all the tasks to be done today. She has to develop the new information literacy quiz, meet with two faculty members about resources for their classes, meet with a student one on one about her research paper, teach an instruction session for an English course, and attend a campus wellness meeting. A student approaches and the dialogue goes as follows:

Not Mindful

Student:	Can you help me to find a book for my class?
Julie (looking stressed and a little bit frantic):	Yes, we have a list of textbooks here.
Student:	I am not sure it's a textbook.
Julie (hurrying and facing somewhat away from the patron):	Just tell me the title.
Student:	It's called *The Ancestor's Tale*.
Julie (typing in the catalog rather than teaching the student how to search):	Here it is. (*She proceeds to write down the call number and hand it to the student.*)
Student (looking confused):	OK? I guess I will go and try to find this.

Mindful

Before approaching the desk, Julie notices that her heart is racing and she feels stressed. She takes a moment to compose herself, grab a cup of herbal tea and take a few deep breaths. She is able to calm herself fairly quickly as she reflects back on the peaceful feeling she experienced when doing a 10-min meditation that morning before waking her son. She knows she has a lot to do today, but she has her day well planned and will get everything accomplished, one task at a time.

Student:	Can you help me to find a book for my class?
Julie (looking at the student and smiling):	Hello, yes, I can help you. What is the book you are looking for?
Student (relaxed):	It's called *The Ancestor's Tale*.
Julie:	Oh, by Richard Dawkins?
Student:	Yes, I think that's the author.
Julie:	That's a great book. I have read it myself. Here, let's see if we can find it. (*Julie turns the screen of her computer so that the student can see her search.*). First, we go to the library home page, and then we click here for books and type "ancestors tale." There it is. This is the call number (*pointing*), and the information here next to it (*pointing*) tells us that it is available. (*Julie writes down the call number.*). Come on. Let's go find it. (*She leads the student to the shelf, stating out loud the call number and drawing the student's attention to how the shelves are organized. She pulls the book and hands it to the student.*)
Student (smiling):	Thanks!
Julie (smiling back):	Be sure to come back if you need anything else. We always have someone at the reference desk like myself who can assist you.

Questions:

How do these interactions differ? How does the application of mindfulness help the librarian with approachability in this circumstance?

Dr Howard Slutzky's Thoughts on Approachability

One key feature of this chapter is approachability. Approachability reflects the degree to which one is perceived by others as being friendly, receptive, and welcoming. In some respects, our approachability is a function of others' perceptions, which are oftentimes influenced by their past experiences (and are not always accurate). However, approachability also refers to one's ability to foster skills, behaviors, and attitudes that convey a friendly, inviting, and respectful aura. Oftentimes, it is difficult to assess our own level of approachability, but to consult the opinion of others can be quite threatening. We might find out that others' perception of our approachability is inconsistent with our own perception. For some who are willing to take the risk, they may consult others who are will sing their praises, giving only positive feedback. While this approach is highly effective at preserving and protecting our oftentimes fragile sense of self, it offers a false sense of security, and precludes insight and growth. Certainly, feedback will be most effective when it is communicated in a supportive and respectful manner, and in a safe environment.

So, mindfulness in this area of approachability and feedback entails a willingness to recognize not only our insecurities, but our defensive strategies for self-protection as well. One of the best ways of assessing how others perceive us is to simply ask them. For library staff, this means asking for feedback from the very students they are serving. This can most easily be done with comment cards or surveys. They are best done anonymously, as this will generate the most honest feedback. Colleagues and supervisors can be valuable sources of feedback as well.

A common term used in this scenario is "constructive criticism." This, however, carries with it a very negative and potentially threatening connotation. While the intention of the one giving feedback, and the manner in which they offer it, are key features, so are the perceptions of the one receiving the feedback. The language we use reflects aspects of our belief system. The belief that feedback is a criticism understandably invokes fear in most people. There are several reflexive reactions when we are feeling threatened in this manner. One such reaction is to "shoot the messenger." If we attack or invalidate the messenger, we can protect our sense of self from the potentially damaging message. For instance, we may look for mistakes they've made or any areas of imperfection about them. Another reaction is to invalidate the message itself. Perhaps we tell ourselves that they have misperceived us, that they are uninformed, or that they are simply mistaken. A third protective strategy that is commonly implemented is to consult our "yes man" or "yes woman," who will always be on our side, to tell us how wonderful and perfect we are and how anyone suggesting otherwise is obviously wrong. Therefore, instead of the word "criticism," a term I prefer to use instead is "constructive feedback."

So mindfulness in this section pertains to developing the skill of recognizing not only our insecurities and fears of inadequacy, but also the defensive strategies we employ in the name of self-preservation. Again, we can only evolve when taking an approach of self-reflection, openness, and vulnerability. An area of weakness doesn't improve or strengthen by hiding, protecting, or favoring it. Instead, growth and healing come from recognizing the vulnerable areas and gradually strengthening them in a safe, supportive, and constructive manner. Sigmund Freud identified numerous "defense mechanisms" that people use for the purpose of self-protection. Specifically, he argued that part of our psyche (the ego) activates a series of unconscious defense mechanisms to protect us from our needs, urges, desires, and fears that are too threatening to handle on a conscious level. So a key feature of our defense strategies is that we engage in them automatically and without conscious awareness. That is the genius and danger of our defense mechanisms. They work so well because we aren't even aware that we are engaging them. Our lack of conscious awareness is precisely how and why they work so well.[25] To borrow a famous line spoken by Jack Nicholson during a military trial in *A Few Good Men*, our defense mechanisms are in place because we "can't handle the truth!"[26] One of these defense mechanism is projection, which involves disowning aspects of ourselves that we find unacceptable and seeing them (and typically criticizing them) in someone else instead. For instance, someone who struggles with feelings of inadequacy and insecurity might look for and criticize the insecurities and inadequacies of others. Again, such individuals have little to no insight into their own feelings of inadequacy or the true reason that they are criticizing others. Yes, defense mechanisms help protect us from that which is threatening to our sense of self. But in addition to often acting them out at the expense of those around us, the cost is that these defense mechanisms preclude any insight, healing, and growth. With an approach of mindfulness that includes vulnerability, compassion, and motivation toward insight and growth, we can gradually identify our use of defense mechanisms and finally access and address that which we have been so vehemently protecting.

---

[25] Freud, A., 1937. The Ego and the Mechanisms of Defense. Hogarth Press, London.
[26] *A Few Good Men*. Directed by Rob Reiner. Sony Home Pictures, 2002. DVD.

Interest

The next criterion presented by the *Guidelines for Behavioral Performance of Reference and Information Service Providers* involves showing interest. Body language is of central importance for face-to-face interaction. Even in an online environment such as chat reference, one can still be affected by personal body language. Mindfulness teaches one to become aware of the body. Two common and helpful practices relating to body awareness are body-scan meditation and yoga. Both teach awareness in a way that affects how we interact with others throughout the day. Body scan does this through meditation that focuses on each part of the body in turn, and yoga does this through mindful movement connected to breathing. In order to show interest in others, one must first be aware of his or her posture and physical disposition. Actually practicing yoga or body-scan meditation helps build one's reserve when serving at the reference desk.

Simply paying attention is key. Beyond this, being mentally present is also critical. In making oneself approachable by focusing on the present moment, one should then be able to transition that focused awareness to consider the challenge at hand. While multitasking seems to be the norm in our society, it is only by giving full, undivided attention that the librarian can attend to a patron's needs to the degree that is expected in the profession.

Reference librarians often choose this profession because they enjoy assisting others in their intellectual or research endeavors. Some topics may be of greater personal interest than others. A deep sense of caring and concern for patrons in general can help one to not just fake, but actually have, greater interest in someone's information needs. Once again, mindfulness is inclusive of many practices, and one effective practice is loving kindness meditation.

This type of meditation, described in more detail next, focuses on caring for both oneself and others. In an earlier chapter, it was mentioned that teachers engaging in contemplative practice sometimes meditate about their students in order to develop a deeper sense of concern and caring about their needs. Reference librarians likewise could meditate about students occasionally, while away from the desk, and thus become better prepared to express real kindness and compassion when it comes to showing interest. It is important for librarians to regularly reflect on just how anxious or intimidated our students are by research, the library, or even the librarians.

Another concept related to mindfulness can also be especially help-ful: the beginner's mind. When practitioners of mindfulness talk about the beginner's mind, they are speaking of the need to take a step back and "unclutter" our thoughts and habits, of which we are sometimes unaware. As one meditates, the application of this concept of beginner's mind helps facilitate a greater space between a stimulus and how one responds. This, in turn, encourages one to explore more creative solutions to a given problem or challenge. According to Kristen Mastel and Genevieve Innes, "The seasoned professional might find it more challenging to walk in the shoes of these students who are learning research skills or to use the library for the first time. The benefit of a beginner's mind, if one can culti-vate and achieve it, is that one will then look at the world from fresh eyes, and can rediscover the joy of learning something new, of finding just the right article or book, the deep satisfaction of having a question or curios-ity answered, a curiosity-sated—experiences which excited one and first drew him into the profession."[27] This is a profound statement that points to the possibility of not just a positive interaction, but rediscovery of the joy in the work that reference librarians perform every day.

Here We Go Again

John had been at the reference desk for the past 2 h. In that time, several students had approached asking for books about sustainability. Initially, he spent some time with them helping them not only in finding materials, but also in determining a focused research question. Another student is about to approach him concerning the same research assignment.

Not Mindful

Student (anxious look on her face):	Can you help me? I have to do a paper on sustainability.
John (slightly distracted and tired):	Sure. The books on sustainability are over here (*He leads the student to a space in the stacks and points to them.*) If there is anything else you need, please let us know.
Student:	Thanks!

[27] Mastel, K., Innes, G., 2013. Insights and practical tips on practicing mindful librarianship to manage stress. LIBRES: Libr. Inf. Sci. Res. Electron. J. 23 (1), 5.

Mindful

Having practiced a loving kindness meditation that morning, John is determined to treat every student with kindness and respect. He reminds himself that just because he has heard a question or research problem many times, for a given student, it may be his or her first time. He also keeps in mind that students can be very anxious, especially when doing research papers as undergraduates.

Student (anxious look on his face):	Can you help me? I have to do a paper on sustainability.
John (tired but smiling):	I would love to help you. Have you considered an aspect of sustainability that you would like to explore?
Student:	I had heard something about sustainable homes. My mother told me she read an article about it in *The New York Times* recently.
John:	Interesting. Yes, this is a hot topic. Let's look in *The New York Times* and see if we can find the article your mother mentioned. (*John proceeds to turn his screen toward the student and demonstrate how someone can search a specific newspaper using the library databases.*) There—is this it?
Student (looking at the screen):	Yes, I believe so.
John:	Let me print that for you. I could also show you to the general books about sustainability, but I sense that you need more specific information. This article gives me some ideas. (*John then shows the student two other databases, how to conduct searches in each, and how to narrow the search, and then he prints several articles and hands them to the student.*) After you have done some more reading, you may decide to choose a different direction in terms of research. Just remember we are always here to help (*smiling*).
Student:	Thanks so much for all this. I think I am ready to get started!

Questions:

What went right in the first scenario (even if the interaction was not as ideally mindful as possible)? How did John apply mindfulness to enhance the reference interaction in the mindful condition? How can mindfulness help librarians when it comes to showing interest?

Listening

Listening is the third component identified by the *Guidelines for Behavioral Performance of Reference and Information Service Providers* as needing our attention. Again, there is a natural fit between how reference librarians have viewed the need to listen with focused intent and how mindfulness seeks to enhance this very skill. Susan Smalley and Diane Winston suggest practicing mindful listening with a friend or colleague.[28] While related to traditional listening skills, which involve asking clarifying questions and repeating back at times what is said by the other person, mindful listening goes a step further. The practice of mindful listening incorporates everything that is occurring at that moment. One needs to be mindful of one's own personal thoughts, posture, and disposition. In addition to listening to what the other person is saying, mindful listening involves noting subtle cues in body language or tone that may affect the interaction or point toward the true nature of a given reference question. More tips on mindful listening are provided in Chapter 7. Obviously, chat reference can be extremely limited in this regard in terms of the information the librarian has about who they are helping. Still, the librarian can monitor his or her own disposition and "listen" by reading carefully through the dialogue with an online patron.

The importance of listening is critical and not always easily applied. In her article "Zen and the Art of Dealing with the Difficult Patron," Louisa Toot discusses how her daily practice of mindfulness helps her gain greater patience and calm in interacting with challenging patrons of various kinds. According to Toot compassion for others is key.[29] Clearly, patience and empathy are central components working alongside application of the beginner's mind.

Mary Hurries Along

Not Mindful

Student:	Do you have the book for the English class?
Mary (typing a report, looks up):	Yes, the *Bedford Guide*. It's right here. (*She reaches back and hands it to the student.*)
Student:	Thanks!

---

[28] Smalley, S.L., Winston, D., Fully Present, p. 216.

[29] Toot, L., 2002. Zen and the art of dealing with the difficult patron. Ref. Libr. 36 (75–76), 217–233.

5 min later…

Student (looking confused):	Something doesn't seem right about this book. I thought I was supposed to read something about the Vietnam War.
Mary (stopping what she was doing and giving the student full attention for the first time):	What class is this for? Do you know who the instructor is?
Student:	It's a literature class taught by Dr Smith.
Mary (suddenly coming to a realization):	Dr Smith! Oh, he's having you read *The Things They Carried*, by Tim O'Brien. Let me get that for you. (*Mary reaches back, grabs the book, and hands it to the student.*) Let me know if you need anything else.

Mindful

Mary had just returned from her lunch break when doing yoga at the YMCA. She has a lot on her mind, but she feels very relaxed as she sits behind the desk.

Student:	Do you have the book for the English class?
Mary (stops typing and smiles at the student):	Which class is it?
Student:	It's an English class.
Mary (calm and sympathetic):	Can you tell me a bit more? Is it a textbook? Who is the instructor?
Student (confused):	He, Dr Smith, said it was required reading. It had something to do with Vietnam.
Mary:	Is it *The Things They Carried* by Tim O'Brien?
Student:	Yes, that's it!
Mary (smiling):	Great (*handing it to the student*)! If you need anything else, please don't hesitate to ask.

Searching

Searching is the next component in the *Guidelines for Behavioral Performance of Reference and Information Service Providers*. Searching is where specific skills as librarians are most critical, especially in the context of respective institutions. For example, it is interesting to note that many of the other skills would be central to good teaching. Finding information is the special purview of the reference librarian. Mindfulness can usefully be considered on a couple of levels. First, searching that is connected to the mindful listening, as previously mentioned, is critical. The reference librarian should be searching based on the needs of the patron, so it is important to seek continual clarification. Second, one needs to be aware of what sources of information exist for solving a given patron's need. Mindfulness in this sense can really encompass a great deal. It relates to one's willingness to learn about sources and be familiar with a wide variety of them for solving patrons' needs.

It is not uncommon for an enthusiastic undergraduate studying history to want to know "all there is to know" about a given period of history. Given the depth of research and knowledge about just about any period or aspect of history, however, even the most accomplished historian will still have gaps. One can never know all there is to know in any discipline. Furthermore, current librarians are at a disadvantage from the reference librarian 50 years ago, who could memorize certain key sources and rely on them throughout his or her career. Now, everything changes so rapidly that no librarian could possibly be expected to know it all. Thus, one must be thoughtful in balancing our time to consider what one knows and in trying to explore new sources.

Master of Library and Information Science (MLIS) students taking courses related to electronic resources, as well as librarians in the field, have come to realize that, even over a short period of time, a substantial amount of change has occurred in terms of what databases are available, how databases have merged or changed, and how the way that we access information has shifted. Just think of discovery services and the way that they blend what were once isolated material types such as books and periodicals. Librarians have also seen dramatic shifts and change in what MLIS students bring into the classroom regarding comfort and experience with online resources or tools. Being mindful in the search process requires considering all of this at once, listening, clarification and understanding, and the need to stay abreast of changes in resources. It is a daunting task, but one for which librarians are uniquely prepared.

Rhonda Thinks it Through

Rhonda is an experienced reference librarian who has been at Smith University for 12 years. She has been having a bad day and is wondering if she left the coffeepot on at home. She is also thinking about the weekend, as she has a long trip planned but hasn't packed or made any other preparations for it. Suddenly, a student approaches the desk.

Not Mindful

Student:	Hello, I need some books about German cakes.
Rhonda:	(*Not looking up and appearing exceptionally preoccupied*) OK. (*Rhonda then types "German cakes" into the online catalog and gets a hit. She writes down the call number for the book and hands it to the student.*) Do you know how to find this? (*She makes eye contact with the student when asking.*)
Student:	Yes, I think so. I will come back if I have any trouble.
Rhonda (smiling):	OK. Remember that we are always here to help.

Mindful

Rhonda rushes out to her desk and recognizes that she has a lot on her mind. She reassures herself that it will all get done in good time. She thinks about the loving kindness meditation she did that morning and goes to the desk with the thought, "If I can help even one person today…"

Student:	Hello, I need some books about German cakes.
Rhonda (smiling and making eye contact right away with the student):	Good morning. I can help you find what you need. What is it that you need the books for?
Student:	My teacher wants us to do a paper about German cakes that includes something about German culture and also has some recipes for cakes.

Rhonda (maintaining eye contact):	OK. I think there may be a few things that can help you. We will try to locate some books about German history. These will give you some of the cultural information you need. German history is pretty interesting and especially its food history. Next, we will look for books that have German cake recipes. We may have to go into some books on either German cuisine or cakes in general to find this. I will walk you through each step. (*Rhonda proceeds to turn on her computer so the patron can see it more clearly, demonstrates the use of the catalog to find books in the areas mentioned, jotting down call numbers as she goes and pointing out to the student various useful features of the catalog. She then gets up. Together, they walk to the stacks where Rhonda pulls the books, and as she is pulling each one, she explains what aspect of the research each source could best be used to address. She also notes the use of the index in the back of each one and how useful it is to help find targeted information. Smiling at the student, she then closes the interaction.*). This should get you started, but if you need anything else, please let me know.
Student (smiling):	Thank you.
Rhonda:	(*Rhonda then walks over to Joe, who serves as academic liaison to the culinary department, and mentions the question to see if she has covered all her bases. Joe points out an additional great source for German cake recipes which Rhonda pulls and brings it to the student.*). Sorry to bother you, but a colleague of mine who specializes in this area suggested this book as well. When you are finished with all these, you can leave them here and we will pick them up; or, if you need to take them out, our circulation staff can check you out. (*points to the circulation desk*)
Student:	Thanks again.

Questions:

What were some of the good and bad elements in each of these exchanges? How did mindfulness applied in the second iteration improve upon the ideals for searching as interpreted by RUSA's *Guidelines for Behavioral Performance of Reference and Information Service Provider?*

Follow-up

The last criterion from the *Guidelines for Behavioral Performance of Reference and Information Service Providers* is the need to conduct follow-up. This layer is more straightforward than the other layers. It simply requires that reference librarians interact with patrons after assisting them to see if their needs have been met. It also requires that librarians make it obvious to patrons that they can come back for additional reference assistance as needed. This latter piece is frequently left out but is of great importance. The last thing a reference librarian wants is for a patron to think is that he or she "already bothered the librarian once." Mindfulness can be applied here as well. In addition to elements such as empathizing with the patron, it is critical to slow down and finish the reference transaction in its entirety, but leave the door open for the patron to return.

Melanie Juggles at the Reference Desk

It's a busy afternoon, and a lot of students are coming by the reference desk asking for assistance. No sooner does Melanie help one student than another appears. She knows that she must find a way to help everyone even though the library is short-staffed today. As she finishes assisting a patron, three more approach, forming a line.

Not Mindful

Student #1:	Can you help me find a book for my class? It's a textbook for English Composition.
Melanie:	Yes, it's the *Bedford Guide*, (She *hands it to the student and smiles*.)
Student #1 (smiling):	Thanks!
Student #2:	I need some articles on gun control.
Melanie (smiling, making eye contact with the student, and turning her screen so that the student can see):	This is the Opposing Viewpoints database. It's a great resource for any controversial issues like the one you are exploring. You can get there from here (*showing the student the link*). Next, just type "gun control" and you will find lots of resources.
Student #2 (looking worried):	Thanks!
Student #3:	Hi, my teacher placed a video on reserve here. I believe the title is *The Happiness Advantage*.

Melanie (smiling again and making eye contact with the student):	Yes, it's right here (*reaches around and hands the video to the student*).
Student #3:	Thanks!
Melanie:	You're welcome. (*As she wipes the sweat from her brow, another group of students approaches.*)

Mindful

It's busy, but Melanie knows that things will be slower later in the afternoon. She also knows that tomorrow, they should have more help at the reference desk.

Student #1:	Can you help me find a book for my class? It's a textbook for English Composition.
Melanie:	Yes, it's the Bedford Guide (*hands it to the student and smiles*).
Student #1 (smiling):	Thanks!
Melanie (smiling):	Is this it? (*Student nods.*) If you need anything else, please let us know.
Student #2:	I need some articles on gun control.
Melanie (smiling, making eye contact with the student, and turning her screen so that the student can see):	This is Opposing Viewpoints. It's a great resource for any controversial issues like the one you are exploring. You can get there from here (*showing the student the link*). Next, just type "gun control" and you will find lots of resources. Do you feel comfortable getting started? I can check on your progress is a little while, when things slow down here at the desk. Would that be OK?
Student #2 (smiling):	Yes. Thanks!
Student #3:	Hi, my teacher placed a video on reserve here. I believe the title is *The Happiness Advantage.*
Melanie (smiling again and making eye contact with the student):	Yes, it's right here (*reaches around and hands the video to the student*).
Student #3:	Thanks!

Melanie:	You're welcome. (*She wipes the sweat from her brow, and as she sees another group of students approaching, she calmly takes a deep breath to relax. She then looks back up at the student she has just helped.*). Come see us if you need any help playing this on one of the PCs or have any other questions.

45 minutes later, when things slow down...

Melanie (to Student #2, who is at a study carrel):	Did you find what you needed?
Student #2:	I think I have what I need for now to start reading and get a better understanding of the topic.
Melanie:	I have some time tomorrow afternoon when I am not on the desk. Would you like to schedule an appointment? We could sit down together and look at your research topic further to make sure you have what you need.
Student #2:	That would be great. I get out of class at 1:40 tomorrow.
Melanie:	Perfect, I will see you then. My office is located on the second floor of the library, but if you want to ask for me at the reference desk, I could come out and get you as well. Here is my card (*hands her a business card with contact information*). Feel free to email me as well beforehand or any time if I can be of help.

Questions:

Melanie is obviously limited to what one person can do. What things has she been doing well in handling the situation in both the fully mindful as well as not mindful conditions? How was she more mindful in the relationship to follow-up in the second example (especially with Student #2)?

CONCLUSION

In closing, a couple of additional points need to be addressed that are connected to RUSA's overall mission, the *Guidelines for Behavioral Performance of Reference and Information Service Providers*, and the overall importance of reference librarians being happy, even joyful, as they do their work. Obviously loving one's work and being satisfied with one's lot in life will affect how one interacts with others, and librarians are no exception. According to Marie Landry, "The life satisfaction of librarians and the possible consequences of job satisfaction in library settings are new areas of study in the field of library and information science."[30] She goes on to state that her experiment was the "only study conducted to investigate the life satisfaction of librarians"[31] and that it showed a strong reciprocal relationship between the two areas, one's personal life, and one's work life. In the Western way of thinking, there is sometimes an unrealistic expectation that we are able to keep personal and professional lives rigidly separated. The two are interconnected whether management or administration wishes to recognize this or not. Perhaps this is why studies show that managers who concern themselves with the personal well-being of their staff are also more effective. This has significant meaning for those who are responsible for managing library staff, as discussed further in Chapter 7. Mindfulness-based programs do not just affect one's work, but one's life in general. Thus, encouragement from senior library administrators to participate in mindfulness-based activities can have the twofold impact of making library staff happier and more satisfied and ensuring that the library staff are also providing patrons with the best possible service.

By connecting RUSA's guidelines to a mindful approach to reference, librarians hope to create a complete experience for the patron who interacts with the reference librarian. According to Stephen Bell, "Designing a reference experience is about creating a practice predicated on getting to know the users and making sure they know who we are and what we do. By designing a reference experience that is unique, memorable, and focused on building loyal relationships, our profession can create its preferred future."[32] Reference librarians who engage in at least some

[30] Landry, M.B., 2000. The effects of life satisfaction and job satisfaction on reference librarians and their work. Ref. User Serv. Q. 40 (2), 173.

[31] Ibid., 173.

[32] Bell, S., 2011. They need to know us and we need to know them: preparing today's students for tomorrow's reference. Ref. Libr. 52 (4), 327–328.

mindfulness-based practices on a limited basis will be more effective in creating this kind of user experience than those who do not. According to Mastel and Innes, "Mindful librarianship—practiced with awareness, intention, an open mind, and a spirit of compassion—could make the difference in the success of our students, our profession, and ourselves."[33]

RECOMMENDED RESOURCES

Bell, S., 2011. They need to know us and we need to know them: preparing today's students for tomorrow's reference. Ref. Libr. 52 (4), 320–328.

Harmeyer, D., 2014. The Reference Interview Today: Negotiating and Answering Questions Face to Face, on the Phone, and Virtually. Rowman and Littlefield, Lanham, MD.

International Federation of Library Affiliations. IFLA digital reference guidelines. Available from: <http://archive.ifla.org/VII/s36/pubs/drg03.htm> (accessed 13.12.14.).

Mastel, K.M., Innes, G., 2013. Insights and practical tips on practicing mindful librarianship to manage stress. LIBRES: Libr. Inf. Sci. Res. Electron. J. 23 (1), 1–8.

Onwuegbuzie, A.J., Jiao, Q.G., Bostick, S.L., 2004. Library Anxiety: Theory, Research, and Applications. Scarecrow Press, Lanham, MA.

Reference and User Services Association. Guidelines for behavioral performance of reference and information service providers. Available from: <http://www.ala.org/rus/resources/guidelines/guidelinesbehavioral> (accessed 13.12.14.).

BIBLIOGRAPHY

A few good men. Directed by Rob Reiner. Sony Home Pictures, 2002. DVD.

Bell, S., 2011. They need to know us and we need to know them: preparing today's students for tomorrow's reference. Ref. Libr. 52 (4), 320–328.

Brown, L., 2011. Trending now-reference librarians: how reference librarians work to prevent library anxiety. J. Libr. Admin. 51 (3), 309–317.

Delgado, A.L., 2013. One percent: a new definition: practicing mindfulness in the law library. AALL Spectr. 18, 27–29.

Deng, L., 2014. The evolution of library reference services: from general to special, 1876–1920s. Libri 64 (3), 254–262.

Freud, A., 1937. The Ego and the Mechanisms of Defense. Hogarth Press, London.

Hanson, R., Mendius, R., 2009. Buddha's Brain: The Practical Neuroscience of Happiness, Love & Wisdom. New Harbinger Publications, Oakland, CA.

International Federation of Library Associations. IFLA digital reference guidelines. Available from: <http://www.ifla.org/files/assets/reference-and-information-services/publications/ifla-digital-reference-guidelines-en.pdf> (accessed 01.12.14.).

Kown, N., Onwuegbuzie, A.J., Alexander, L., 2007. Critical thinking disposition and library anxiety: affective domains on the space of information seeking and use in academic libraries. Coll. Res. Libr. 68 (3), 268–278.

Landry, M.B., 2000. The effects of life satisfaction and job satisfaction on reference librarians and their work. Ref. User Serv. Q. 40 (2), 166–177.

---

[33] Mastel, K., Innes, G., Insights and practical tips on practicing mindful librarianship to manage stress, 6.

Mastel, K., Innes, G., 2013. Insights and practical tips on practicing mindful librarianship to manage stress. LIBRES: Libr. Inf. Sci. Res. Electron. J. 23 (1), 1–9.

McCown, D., Reibel, D., Micozzi, M.S., 2011. Teaching Mindfulness: A Practical Guide for Clinicians and Educators. Springer, New York, NY.

Olszewski, L., Rumbaugh, P., 2010. An international comparison of virtual reference services. Ref. User Serv. Q. 49 (4), 360–368.

Platt, J., Platt, T., 2013. Library anxiety among undergraduates enrolled in a research methods in psychology course. Behav. Soc. Sci. Libr. 32 (4), 240–251.

Reference and User Services Association. Bylaws. Available from: <http://www.ala.org/rusa/about/bylaws> (accessed 01.12.14.).

Reference and User Services Association. Guidelines for behavioral performance of reference and information service providers. Available from: <http://www.ala.org/rusa/resources/guidelines/guidelinesbehavioral> (accessed 01.12.14.).

Robinson, C.M., Reid, P., 2007. Do academic enquiry services scare students? Ref. Serv. Rev. 35 (3), 405–424.

Rothstein, S., 1953. The development of the concept of reference service in American libraries, 1850–1900. Libr. Q. 23 (1), 1–15.

Saunders, L., Kurbanoglu, S., Jordan, M.W., Boustany, J., Chawner, B., Filas, M., et al., 2013. Culture and competencies: a multi-country examination of reference service competencies. Libri: Int. J. Libr. Inf. Serv. 63 (1), 33–46.

Shachaf, P., Horowitz, S., 2008. Virtual reference service evaluation: adherence to RUSA behavioral guidelines and IFLA digital reference guidelines. Libr. Inf. Sci. Res. 30 (2), 122–137.

Smalley, S., Winston, D., 2010. Fully Present: The Science, Art, and Practice of Mindfulness. Da Capo Lifelong, Cambridge, MA.

Toot, L., 2002. Zen and the art of dealing with the difficult patron. Ref. Libr. 36 (75–76), 217–233.

CHAPTER 6

Building Mindful Relationships with Faculty

Jo Henry and Howard Slutzky

INTRODUCTION

The importance of academic librarians building relationships with faculty in order to support, assist, and collaborate in the academic realm is now an accepted concept. The execution, however, is hardly simple. Lars Christiansen, Mindy Stombler, and Lyn Thaxton cite numerous studies of library–faculty relations dating back to the late 1980s before laying out their own findings at a 2004 conference, which confirmed "an asymmetrical disconnection … exists between librarians and faculty."[1] In 2009, Kristin Anthony discussed at length librarians' challenge of overcoming their perceived service status by faculty and becoming a part of the teaching community.[2] More recently, Kara J. Malenfant described librarians' perceptions of inferiority to faculty in terms of their credentials and academic titles and lent additional support to the division between the two parties due to status or rank.[3] Finally, Lan Shen explored the impact of the librarian–faculty disconnect as it affects collection development collaboration in her 2012 article and suggested that librarians must "master the art of interdependence" with faculty.[4] With these types of long, entrenched barriers, how can a librarian establish a mindful, working relationship with faculty members?

The 2014 publication *Fundamentals for the Academic Liaison* lays out numerous methods for establishing and supporting a librarian–faculty

---

[1] Christiansen, C., Stombler, S., Thaxton, L., 2004. A report on librarian–faculty relations from a sociological perspective. J. Acad. Libr. 30 (2), 117.

[2] Kristin, A., 2010. Reconnecting the disconnects: library outreach to faculty as addressed in the literature. Coll. Undergrad. Libr. 17 (1), 79–92.

[3] Malefant, K.J., 2010. Leading change in the system of scholarly communication: a case study of engaging liaison librarians for outreach to faculty. Coll. Res. Libr. 71 (1), 74.

[4] Shen, L., 2012. Improving the effectiveness of librarian–faculty collaboration on library collection development. Collab. Libr. 4 (1), 21.

The Mindful Librarian.
© 2016 by R. Moniz, J. Eshleman, J. Henry, H. Slutzky and L. Moniz. Published by Elsevier Ltd. All rights reserved.

relationship, which involve a variety of opportunities for personal inter-activity. These include social interactions such as attending faculty meet-ings, orientation meetings, or having a cup of coffee together, as well as work-related exchanges that include information literacy facilitation, research assistance, and library resource support activities, among other mechanisms.[5] The importance of relationships and communication with faculty is woven throughout the book, suggesting that library liaisons find a variety of ways to interact with faculty in their role as "a master of communication."[6] In addition to all of these practical tips, mindful-ness can enhance this challenging task. From a mindful perspective, the development of a relationship with a faculty member comes down to fully understanding communication. First, a mindful librarian must com-prehend the relationship of social interaction and the state of mind of both parties. Second, mindful listening must be employed by the librar-ian when interacting with faculty in order to have meaningful exchanges. Finally, this chapter will explore the impact of mindfulness and interper-sonal synchrony when working toward the collaborative efforts of librar-ians and faculty members. Through a better understanding of these three areas of mindfulness, the librarian is better equipped to interact and build a positive faculty relationship at their institution.

SOCIAL INTERACTION AND STATE OF MIND

Social interaction and state of mind are intertwined. They are insepa-rable as an interactive social experience cannot take place without feel-ings, expressions, thoughts, words, and ideas. In a social exchange, the relationships between all parties are affected by what each participant is mentally processing as the verbal and nonverbal interaction takes place. This exchange can occur between any two or more individuals, but this chapter's examples will focus on librarian–faculty interactions. A librar-ian cannot develop a relationship in a mindful way without understanding the interrelatedness of these two concepts. For a better understanding of social interaction and state of mind, this section reviews the essential steps of social communication, the purpose of these communication exchanges, and the impact that mindfulness has on such interactions.

---

[5] Moniz, R., Henry, J., Eshleman, J., 2014. Fundamentals for the Academic Liaison. Neal-Schuman, Chicago, IL.
[6] Idid., p. 35.

The essential steps of social interaction and state of mind are rooted in communication, and when mindfulness is applied, this exchange becomes more meaningful. Mindful researchers Ellen Langer and Mihnea Moldoveanu define mindfulness as a "process of drawing novel distinctions" and "drawing on these distinctions."[7] When an individual experiences something in a new way, it triggers a more thoughtful and engaged response or a more mindful response. Interpersonal exchanges can also become a more mindful experience if the participants truly focus on the messages conveyed and on nonverbal clues from the speaker. The actual process of this mindful exchange taking place is best described by Judee K. Burgoon, Charles R. Berger, and Vincent R. Waldron in three steps—communication signals, information exchange, and the mindful or mindless brain response.[8]

First, both verbal and nonverbal communication signals and their level of mindfulness influence the interaction.[8] This verbal and nonverbal component involves how something is presented, such as choice of words, tone of voice, body language, and facial expressions, among other attributes. The degree of mindfulness that each party uses to collect the verbal and nonverbal clues during the exchange is the second influencing factor that affects their processing. For example, a faculty member may ask for help from the librarian on creating a writing assignment for a course. However, the faculty member may have simply dropped in unannounced at the library on the way to class, when the librarian was actually focused on another matter entirely. In this instance, both parties may have been distracted during the exchange and failed to be mindful. The faculty member may not have listened closely to the librarian's response because he was worried about getting to class on time. Conversely, the librarian may be frustrated with the interruption and more concerned with answering the question quickly than with mindfully explaining the solution. Such an exchange may have unfolded with the librarian suggesting to the faculty member that the use of reliable resources should be a part of the instructions for a student's writing assignment. Believing that was sufficient explanation, the faculty member agreed to incorporate it into the assignment and left. Later, when the assignment was released to

[7] Langer, E.J., Moldoveanu, M., 2000. The construct of mindfulness. J. Soc. Issues 56 (1), 1–2.
[8] Burgoon, J.K., Berger, C.R., Waldron, V.R., Mindfulness and interpersonal communication. J. Soc. Issues 56 (1), 107.

the students, the instructor required that only books and the academic electronic database called JSTOR (short for "Journal Storage") should be used to find credible information. Because the librarian failed to mindfully explain the specifics of the statement and that many other electronic databases were available to students as well, the instructor simply wrote about two possible sources. Equally mindlessly, the professor acted on the librarian's suggestion by offering just the two resources with which he was most familiar, believing that he was doing exactly the right thing. Both parties failed in mindfully reading basic verbal and nonverbal clues during the exchange, and a disconnect in understanding resulted.

Related to communication signals, the second part of the process is the mindful exchange of information, which involves actual message encoding and decoding in the brain from both parties.[8] This is how the brain gathers and delivers a message (encoding) and, conversely, the brain's processing of the information received (decoding). In the example of the writing assignment mentioned previously, the librarian received the message from the instructor of needing assistance (decoding) and then responded with a new message about using reliable resources (encoding). The faculty member decoded the message and ultimately responded by requiring that the resources be books and the JSTOR database. The professor's use of only books and the JSTOR electronic resource most likely was out of habit. In fact, such habits have been shown to be an automatic behavioral response and a way to connect goals and actions.[9] However, the encoding and decoding of this example exchange were not particularly mindful by either party. Librarians must be aware that messages delivered and received can easily be misinterpreted or misunderstood as each individual processes information differently.

The last step in the mindful communication process is the exchange between the parties, which may provoke a more mindful or mindless state.[10] This means that one's mindful or mindless state can be altered depending on how an exchange unfolds. Continuing with the previous example, the librarian's suggestion of reliable resources, with no further explanation, was somewhat mindless. This may have been due to both the work interruption and the urgency of the faculty member's need to get

---

[9] Aarts, H., Dijksterhuis, A., 2000. Habits as knowledge structures: automaticity in goal-directed behavior. J. Pers. Soc. Psychol. 78 (1), 55.

[10] Burgoon, J.K., Berger, C.R., Waldron, V.R., 2000. Mindfulness and interpersonal communication. J. Soc. Issues 56 (1), 107.

to class quickly. However, if the librarian had actually heard the instructor's response of using books and JSTOR (rather than seeing it later in the written assignment), his or her state of mind may have shifted to a more mindful place and the miscommunication corrected immediately. The mindful librarian response would have been to explain other electronic database options and resources available to students and suggest that a broader resource selection be allowed for the paper. While this is a simple example, it does illustrate the process of mindful communication in an academic setting. These communication patterns, coding and encoding of information, and the changing of mindful states lie at the core of mindful communication exchanges.

In addition to the essential steps of mindful communication, the second component of understanding social interaction and state of mind is an understanding of purposeful communication. What is meant by purposeful communication? In some way, every communication is purposeful and "goal-directed."[11] That simple statement brings about a mindful pause to reflect on exactly what that means. Is it not true that everything we say or write has a purpose behind it? Purposeful communication is rooted in controlled areas of "awareness, intentionality, controllability, and cognitive effort."[12] There can be a variety of motives behind these communications, from simply communicating for pleasure to communicating for the purpose of accomplishing a task. For example, a librarian may contact a faculty member for the purpose of discussing collection development or an information literacy-related classroom visit. Even a social exchange, such as having lunch with a faculty member, may have behind it the purpose of furthering a relationship and getting to know the person better to establish trust for future avenues of library/faculty interaction. Regardless, every exchange between librarian and faculty member not only has meaning, it also has purpose. Fundamentally, at the core of all social interactions lies a purpose.

On a deeper level, purposeful exchanges during social interactions have both primary goals and secondary goals, which often occur simultaneously.[11] Librarians should be aware of the existence of these two goal levels during conversations. The primary goal is often a more obvious

---

[11] Idid., 108.

[12] Lakin, J.L., 2006. Automotive cognitive processes and nonverbal communication. In: Manusov, V., Patters, M.L. (Eds.), The Sage Handbook of Nonverbal Communication. Sage Publications, Inc., Thousand Oaks, CA, p. 60.

reason for an exchange or the primary purpose behind the interaction. The secondary goals are more subtle, often occurring in the subconscious, but they also influence the interaction. To illustrate this in another example, if a librarian is talking with an instructor about setting up an embedded librarian component with an online class (the primary goal), he or she may be processing verbal and nonverbal responses which may indicate if the professor is receptive to the embedment (secondary goal) or may have an entirely different agenda for the librarian's participation. The processing of the interaction on primary and secondary goal levels in the brain provides feedback to the librarian, who determines if the exchange is accomplishing the primary purpose or if a different tack must be used.

While the influence of mindfulness on social interaction is apparent, mindless interaction is also possible. It is easy to have a mindless exchange in situations where responses are habitual and routine. Sometimes a mindless response may be appropriate to avoid overanalysis, and it may not be detrimental to the communication at all.[13] Not every situation has to be handled in a focused and mindful way. However, mindfulness can assist with clear communication, proper responding, and the achievement of purposeful goals. What would make a person shift from mindless exchanges to a more mindful state? A number of researchers have identified nine areas which make someone more thoughtful or mindful during communications:

1. Novel behavior
2. Novel communication formats
3. Uninvolving situations
4. Interruptions by external factors … with completion of a script
5. Conflict, competition, or confusion arising among two or more message goals
6. Anticipating negative consequences of a message
7. Nonroutine time delay or processing difficulty
8. Suspicion-arousing features of the modality, message, source, or situation
9. Experiencing a positive or negative consequence … discrepant from previous consequences.[14]

Does it get one's attention if a professor interrupts a librarian's information literacy class presentation? What if a faculty member asks for advice on a situation unrelated to oneself? If the faculty member announced that she was changing the semester's assignments, would the librarian be more

[13] Idid., 109.
[14] Idid., 110; Langer, E.J., Moldoveanu, M., 2000. The construct of mindfulness. J. Soc. Issues 56 (1), 2.

attentive? Would a librarian be more focused on an email that responds to a negative situation, such as cancellation of a class, than on an email with routine, mundane news? It is when the communicator experiences any of these unique situations that the state of mind is heightened or altered in the area of mindfulness. In addition, mindful communication is triggered if the message is "important to you," or it is being delivered by someone "you care about [who] is speaking about a matter that is important to him or her."[15] All of these factors are situations which lie outside the norm or the expected. They illustrate how easily (and quickly) a mindless conversation or experience shifts to something more mindful.

Through these social interactions, verbal and nonverbal messages are continuously interpreted and sent. Each message influences the state of mind of the receiver and can alter the level of mindfulness. Through such purposeful exchanges, both primary and secondary goals bring into play the constant coding and encoding tools in the mind. Any unique or unconventional attributes of social interactions can trigger a more mindful state. Finally, the interconnectedness of back-and-forth communications brings on constant analysis and processing, as well as shifts from mindless to mindful states, depending on the circumstances. These social interactions and the state of mind are indeed inseparable, and librarians should be aware of the dynamics in play as they move toward more mindful communications.

MINDFUL LISTENING

A large component of mindful communication is mindful listening. In a world filled with electronic distractions and brief exchanges, paying close attention to what someone says or listening in a mindful, deliberate way is challenging for anyone. For librarians, the art of listening is critical in order to assist faculty and other patrons. It lies at the heart of the reference interview and almost all exchanges where there is a need to solve a problem. As with the state of mind during social interactions, listening can also be mindful and mindless. Similarly, both verbal and nonverbal components are involved, and mindful listeners are active listeners with listening goals in mind. In addition, there are a number of listening styles that play a role in this aspect of communication. Mindful listening can be challenging, but it is possible with practice and an understanding of what mindful listening involves.

---

[15] Cline, B.J., 2013. The science and sanity of listening. ETC.: Rev. Gen. Semant. July, 250.

Mindful listening is not singularly focused; rather, it is an open and receptive state to process what is being said. Remember that mindfulness involves an openness to take in what is happening in the moment in a nonjudgmental way. Mindful listening involves giving "thoughtful attention and responses to the messages we receive," rather than an automatic response without "mental investment."[16] Rebecca Shafir, a speech and language pathologist and neurotherapist, has identified four common qualities of an engaged listener who retains the conversation at a later date:

1. [The listener can] sustain their attention over time
2. Hear and see the whole message
3. Make the speaker feel valued and respected
4. Listen to themselves.[17]

Good listening has also been described as active listening. This process involves attending, following, and reflecting skills in the communication.[18] More specifically, this means focusing attention during the exchange, following the pattern of thought by the speaker, and reflecting on or processing what is said. The mindful listener must be actively engaged, focused, and openly receptive to have a substantive exchange.

Listening Tips
- Write down the main points of the conversation.
- Be focused and do not let your attention wander.
- Listen to the verbal and nonverbal aspects of the conversation.
- Push aside the urge to be distracted by the environment.
- Control your emotions in response to what is being said.[19]

Listening Stoppers
- Interrupting the person talking
- Giving advice to the speaker
- Stating disbelief in the speaker's words or situation[20]

---

[16] Adler, R., Proctor, R. II, 2014. Looking Out, Looking In, 14th ed. Wadsworth, Boston, MA, pp. 219–220.

[17] Shafir, R., 2010. Mindful listening for better outcomes. In: Hick, S.F., Bien, T. (Eds.), Mindfulness and the Therapeutic Relationship. Guildford Press, New York, NY, p. 219.

[18] Hartley, P., 1999. Interpersonal Communication. Routledge, New York, NY, p. 59. PDF eBook.

[19] Romero, D.B., 2009. The Business of Listening: Become a More Effective Listener. Axzo Press, Rochester, NY, p. 90.

[20] Shafir, R., 2010. Mindful listening for better outcomes. In: Hick, S.F., Bien, T. (Eds.), Mindfulness and the Therapeutic Relationship. Guildford Press, New York, NY, pp. 227–229.

When in listening mode, nonverbal information can also be obtained from the speaker, and these signals often differ depending on the culture. For example, in Japan, the nonverbal clues are critically linked to the emotion of the speaker, while in Argentina, facial expressions are used more with family or friends than strangers.[21] The first of these varied components is the voice. Characteristics such as tone, speaking rate, use of pauses, and intensity can frame the actual words and add meaning to what is being said. As would be expected, studies have shown that emotion can change the acoustics of speech.[22] Next, gestures also can provide some feedback to the listener. While the use of gestures were first documented in the seventeenth century, today it is believed they are used to better communicate with the listener and to facilitate understanding of what is being said.[23] Use of gestures also can change depending on culture. In Great Britain, gestures are kept to a minimum, and the Irish nod rather than point at an object during conversations.[24]

Much research has been done in the area of eye contact and movement and goes beyond the scope of this discussion. However, the degree of eye contact does vary depending on culture or subculture.[25] For example, in Australia avoiding eye contact is considered rude, and in Germany it is a sign of respect, but in Indonesia indirect eye contact is preferred.[26] In the United States, eye contact is related to a positive patron response in

[21] Japan—language, culture, customs and etiquette. Kwintessential. Available from: <http://www.kwintessential.co.uk/resources/global-etiquette/japan-country-profiles.html> (accessed 14.12.14.). Cultural information-Argentina. Centre for Intercultural Learning, last modified October 15, 2009. Available from: <http://www.intercultures.ca/cil-cai/ci-ic-eng.asp?iso=ar#cn-2>.

[22] Knapp, M.L., Hall, J.A., 2013. Nonverbal Communication. De Gruyter Mouton, Boston, MA, p. 184. PDF eBook.

[23] Idid., p. 206.

[24] Cultural information-United Kingdom. Centre for Intercultural Learning, last modified October 15, 2009. Available from: <http://www.intercultures.ca/cil-cai/ci-ic-eng.asp?iso=gb#cn-2>.

[25] Idid., pp. 676–677.

[26] Culture crossing guide: Australia. Culture Crossing. Available from: <http://guide.culturecrossing.net/basics_business_student_details.php?Id=10&CID=13> (accessed 14.12.14.). Culture crossing guide: Germany. Culture Crossing. Available from: <http://guide.culturecrossing.net/basics_business_student_details.php?Id=10&CID=79> (accessed from 14.12.14.). Culture crossing guide: Indonesia. Culture Crossing. Available from: <http://guide.culturecrossing.net/basics_business_student_details.php?Id=10&CID=97> (accessed from 14.12.14.).

a customer service setting.[27] Similarly, in the United States and Australia, a direct rather than averted gaze is associated with approachability as noted in an earlier chapter of this book.[28] A mindful listener must have an awareness of these cultural norms and pay attention to voice, gestures, and eye contact in order to truly process what is being expressed by the speaker.

One final area of nonverbal communication is overall facial expression. A leading researcher in the area of facial expression in communication is Paul Ekman. Ekman began his research of facial expression in 1954 and spent his working life studying the field of facial and body movements. His work has identified seven emotions through facial expressions (fear, anger, sadness, disgust, surprise, happiness, and contempt) and led him to create several tools, including the Facial Action Coding System (measuring all facial expressions or macroexpressions) and the Subtle Expression Training Tool (measuring microexpressions).[29] The face can express 43 total macromovements, with changes of the upper part of the face almost involuntary and lower parts more under one's control.[30] When someone is trying to repress an emotion, facial movements are called "microfacial expressions" (lasting only 1/15th to 1/25th of a second), and they may include "inflection in the voice, the duration of a pause, a swallowing in the throat, or … body movement" that affect the actual words being spoken.[31] A mindful listener must not only hear the words, but also watch the speaker's facial clues in message delivery.

[27] Patterson, M.L., Manusov, V.L. (Eds.), 2006. The SAGE Handbook of Nonverbal Communication. SAGE Publications, Thousand Oaks, CA, p. 513. PDF eBook.

[28] Knapp, M.L., Hall, J.A., 2013. Nonverbal Communication. De Gruyter Mouton, Boston, MA, p. 242. PDF eBook. Willis, M.L., Palermo, R., Burke, D., 2011. Judging approachability on the face of it: the influence of face and body expressions on the perception of approachability. Emotion 11 (3), 521.

[29] Honan, D., 2012. Lie to me: the biological basis of emotion. bigthink, last modified 2012. Available from: <http://bigthink.com/think-tank/lie-to-me>. Research resources: about Dr. Ekman's research. Paul Ekman Group. Available from: <http://www.paulekman.com/research/> (accessed 14.12.14.).

[30] Shafir, R., 2010. Mindful listening for better outcomes. In: Hick, S.F., Bien, T. (Eds.), Mindfulness and the Therapeutic Relationship. Guildford Press, New York, NY, p. 223.

[31] Shafir, R., 2010. Mindful listening for better outcomes. In: Hick, S.F., Bien, T. (Eds.), Mindfulness and the Therapeutic Relationship Guildford Press, New York, NY, p. 218. Micro expressions. Paul Ekman Group. Available from: <http://www.paulekman.com/micro-expressions/> (accessed 14.12.14.).

In addition to picking up on nonverbal clues, a mindful listener must have knowledge of listening styles. As a part of becoming a good listener, one should also build an aware of four types of listening styles. Everyone has a preferred listening style, but some people change the style depending on the situation. First, action-oriented listeners want the speaker to be brief and get to the point quickly.[32] They become frustrated with a long-winded conversation because of their urge to move on and get something else done. Second, time-oriented listeners assign a designated amount of time to the speaker depending on what is available.[32] Everything, including the interaction, is scheduled. Third, people-orientated listeners enjoy conversations because they enjoy connecting.[32] For example, a faculty member who wanders into the office to have a chat about general happenings without an agenda simply wants to engage and socialize. Finally, content-oriented listeners expect to be stimulated by what someone says.[32] An exchange between a librarian and faculty member about a recent study in a specific field would relate to a content-oriented listening situation. These four listening types affect both parties in the interaction. Frustration may arise when the styles conflict, so librarians must recognize not only which style they prefer, but also the preference of the faculty members they converse with. Armed with this information, librarians can better adapt to and cope with each situation as mindful listeners.

Finally, just as there are goals (or purpose) for communication, there are goals for mindful listening. Mindful listening is about getting to the true meaning of the conversation or critical listening.[33] Why is the exchange taking place? What is the purpose of the discussion? If the librarian is sitting on a departmental meeting discussing an upcoming accreditation meeting, what aspect of the accreditation process is really being talked about? Who is involved? Will the library need to play a role? Second, mindful listening is about gathering facts or informational listening.[33] Without facts, one cannot react appropriately to the situation. For example, if an instructor is trying to find help for a student's difficulty with obtaining good research articles, the librarian must listen carefully to what is being communicated in order to offer an appropriate solution. Third, mindful listening is about understanding emotion or empathic listening.[33] What is the meaning behind the conversation? How does the

---

[32] Cline, B.J., 2013. The science and sanity of listening. ETC: Rev. Gen. Semant. 70 (3), 252.
[33] Ibid., 251.

speaker feel? How does the listener feel in response? Finally, listening can be simply for the appreciation for "sensory pleasure" void of analysis.[33] Imagine listening to a concert, or perhaps a poetry reading, and simply enjoying the moment. This is listening for pleasure. Mindful listeners must understand the four categories of purposeful listening—conceptual, factual, empathic, and pleasurable. To assist a faculty member or respond appropriately, one must listen for the true meaning and emotions behind what is being said.

Mindful listening is active listening. It is being engaged in the conversation, following along, and processing what is spoken. Part of this includes awareness of nonverbal clues, such as tone of voice, gestures, eye movement, or macrofacial and microfacial movements, which influence the meaning behind the actual words. Librarians must take time to not only hear the words spoken, but to obtain nonverbal clues from the speakers. They also must be aware that mindful listening is influenced by the overall listening goal (conceptual, factual, empathetic, or pleasurable), as well as the listening style (action-, time-, people-, or content-oriented). Through mindful listening, proper, mindful responses result.

Dr Howard Slutzky's Tips for Successful Communication

A primary component of this chapter is the development of collaborative communication between librarians and faculty. A mindful approach to doing so will help both parties prevent or minimize potential barriers that could otherwise undermine their efforts to form a working alliance.

One such barrier is a *busy schedule*. Both librarians and faculty alike are prone to feeling overworked and overwhelmed, with little time to spare for additional projects. With the popularity and convenience of indirect communication (e.g., email, voicemail, texting) and untimely follow-through by one or both parties, initial efforts to forge this alliance may be quite fragile and short-lived. Before embarking on such collaborative relationships, it is important to be mindful of this barrier so that proactive steps can be taken to minimize its impact. I recommend scheduling a face-to-face meeting as soon as possible. Lengthy or frequent emails have a tendency to feel overwhelming and can easily fade into the background.

Another barrier is *lack of planning*. Taking a reactive approach to this collaboration is often less constructive than a proactive one. Coming up with talking points prior to the meeting will help make it much more productive. We may often overestimate our ability to remember all of the key points that we wanted to present or important questions that we wanted to ask. Constructing these talking points and questions proactively will help prevent important things from slipping through the cracks, and it will maximize the efficiency of the collaborative meeting.

The next barrier involves ***interrupting others*** while they are speaking. This is not only disrespectful, but it also breaks down the communication and undermines the collaborative relationship. Being mindful of our tendency to interrupt, as well as the reasons we may be doing so, is extremely important for effective communication. So why do people interrupt? One reason is that they disagree with the other person and feel they have something better to offer. Even in cases where this may actually be true, addressing it through interruptions is counterproductive. But often our initial interpretations are not entirely accurate. I always recommend the approach of gathering more information, but with an open mind. Asking the other person to elaborate or clarify may shift your initial opinion. Be mindful of any tendency to ask questions for the sole purpose of gathering evidence against the other person's ideas. Another reason for interruption is a fear of forgetting what we want to say and a belief that it is best to interrupt before this happens. I can relate to this one personally; to combat this tendency, I recommend writing down a quick word or two to serve as a prompt for your memory when it is your turn to speak. Anything lengthier will be as disruptive to the present communication as the interruption itself.

Another barrier is ***advice giving***. Often we are very happy to help others, and our interest in doing so may be guided by the best intentions. When someone is coming to us for assistance, we may have a tendency to go directly and prematurely into offering our recommendations. Even when our advice appears to be well received, it may still undermine the collaborative process. This may be compounded by one or more of the previous barriers, such as rushing the communication due to a busy schedule. In my clinical work as a psychologist, I have come to recognize the importance of simply gathering more information. I've sat in on team meetings where therapists discuss cases with their colleagues for the purpose of gaining assistance in formulating a diagnosis, as well as treatment recommendations. It has always surprised me how quickly their colleagues immediately offer possible diagnoses for consideration. When asked my clinical opinion, I almost always acknowledge that there is insufficient information to formulate a diagnosis at this time; and I subsequently recommend additional questions that they should ask. In any collaborative relationship, the importance of gathering more information cannot be overemphasized. I recommend that before offering advice, recommendations, or solutions, additional information be gathered so that the needs of the person asking for assistance can be appropriately and accurately assessed, and accurate assistance can be offered. As simple as it may sound, I suggest starting off with the question, "What would be helpful?" I also suggest asking clarifying questions at several points throughout the meeting. And as the meeting is coming to a close, I suggest asking the questions, "Was this helpful?" and "Is there anything else you needed today that I haven't addressed?" Of course, use your own variations of these questions.

MINDFULNESS AND INTERPERSONAL SYNCHRONICITY

The term *interpersonal synchronicity* refers to an interpersonal interaction that takes place at the same time between individuals. For example, this could be dyads tapping at the same time or having a similar heart rate when working together. To understand how the concept of synchronicity has developed and how it plays a role in mindfulness, it is good to take a very brief examination of its history.

The concept of synchronicity began with Carl Jung in the first part of the twentieth century. He theorized that certain unique or synchronistic events had meaningful connections based in perception and apprehension.[34] Jung wrote, "I found where 'coincidences' which were connected so meaningfully that their 'chance' concurrence would represent a degree of improbability that would have to be expressed by an astronomical figure."[35] While Jung started the research into the idea of synchronicity for the first time, it was not until the 1970s that studies surfaced about the interpersonal synchronicity with the interaction of mothers and their infants.[36] Since that time, synchronicity has been analyzed in other types of relationships as well. These studies have revealed that interpersonal synchronicity is an optimal experience. Studies have also shown that synchronicity and social interaction alter the neural system of the brain. In addition, research has indicated that mindfulness influences synchronicity and actually improves the relationship between two people.

[34] Hogenson, G.B., 2009. Synchronicity and moments of meeting. Soc. Anal. Psychol. 184, 186.

[35] Main, R., 2004. Rupture of Time: Synchronicity and Jung's Critique of Modern Western Culture. Brunner-Routledge, New York, NY, p. 80.

[36] Hogenson, G.B., 2009. Synchronicity and moments of meeting. Soc. Anal. Psychol. 184, 188–191.

The optimal feeling that interpersonal synchronicity creates has been explained as being in sync with another person or working together in the zone. It is a feeling often described by jazz musicians who are improvising music together and feel like it "jams" (or simply gels perfectly). When this happens, the music becomes more than just notes being played and takes on its own meaning. Professor Mihaly Csikszentmihalyi, director of the Quality of Life Research Center at Claremont University, has spent his life studying this state of mind, which he terms "flow," or the feeling someone has during an optimal experience.[37] His research interviewing people from across the world doing different things indicated that they experience eight commonalities when experiencing this flow, and after the experience, there is always a positive feeling. These characteristics of flow are as follows:

1. The task can be completed.
2. Concentration to complete the task is possible.
3. Clear goals are outlined.
4. There is immediate feedback delivered.
5. Immersion in the work brings an escape from the real world.
6. Actions are able to be controlled.
7. Who we are is lost during task completion.
8. Sense of time is altered.[37]

This sensation is also defined by Timothy D. Richie and Fred B. Bryant, who concluded in their 2012 study that a positive experience involves three aspects that must be present—"focused attention, appreciation of novel stimuli, and open-ended expectations."[38] All of these characteristics define the feeling experienced during interpersonal synchronicity.

When synchronicity and social interaction are combined, it alters the neural system in the brain. This change is supported by biophysical evidence. In 2011, Alan Haas studied the brain changes between two individuals who had an interpersonal exchange, and he showed that the brain's neural activity becomes positive or negative, depending on which regions were activated.[39] For example, an active listener would have negative areas

[37] Csikszentmihalyi, M., 1990. FLOW: The Psychology of Optimal Experience. Harper & Row, New York, NY, p. 49.
[38] Ritchie, T.D., Bryant, F.B., 2012. Positive state mindfulness: a multidimensional model of mindfulness in relation to positive experience. Int. J. Wellbeing 2 (3), 173.
[39] Haas, A.S., 2012. A brain charge mechanism modeled in synchronistic dyadic interpersonal interaction. NeuroQuantology 10 (3), 482–488.

of the brain for speaking, but positive areas for attention and memory.[40] Conversely, the active speaker would have positive electromagnetic charges in the speaking areas of the brain and negative charges in the attention and memory areas.[40] When the brains are charged in opposite ways like this, these two individuals would be interacting in sync with each other. The brains would complement each other in the negative and positive areas during their interaction. When dyads and groups reach this state, this complimentary brain activity is typically beneath the conscious level and often continues even when external interacting clues cease.[41]

Relationships are affected by synchrony between dyads. Positive feelings experienced by the participants of a synchronous collaboration have been documented. In 2009, Michael J. Hove and Jane L. Risen were the first to theorize in a simple foot-tapping study that tapping in sync with a person rather than a metronome was associated with a positive likability between the parties.[42] Since then, other researchers have also proven that when people become aligned in their actions, their coordination increases their positive feeling about the overall experience.[43] Additionally, studies show synchrony enhances perception, altruistic behavior, and sociability.[43] Synchronicity's association with prosocial behavior was studied by Lumsden et al. (2012). Their study of 70 female undergraduates showed that those who were prosocial showed more spontaneous synchrony with a partner than those who were less social.[44] Thus, higher sociability is directly related to the ability to work with another person harmoniously or in sync. Overall, positive feelings of collaboration result from a more social librarian, faculty member, or both, as well as a shared synchronous experience.

Mindfulness also has a positive influence on the level of synchrony between people. Alan S. Haas and Ellen J. Langer published a study in 2014 that supported this concept. A group of 92 Harvard participants were measured for their degree of mindfulness and then divided into groups

[40] Ibid., 485.
[41] Ibid., 487.
[42] Knapp, M.L., Hall, J.A., 2013. Nonverbal Communication. De Gruyter Mouton, Boston, MA, p. 557. PD eBook.
[43] Lumsden, J., Miles, L.K., Richardson, M.J., Smith, C.A., Neil Macrae, C., 2012. Who syncs? Social motives and interpersonal coordination. J. Exp. Soc. Psychol. 48 (6), 746.
[44] Ibid., 749.

in order to complete tasks.[45] The more mindful group had a more plea-surable experience, a quicker return time to perform an additional task, a higher comfort level with their group, and similar heart rates to group members.[45] Haas and Langer concluded that "mindfulness ... enhance[d] relationships when it [was] desirable to be socially tuned with others."[46] Simply put, mindfulness increased synchronicity. For a librarian, mindful-ness opens the door to better, harmonious relationships and interactions with faculty members. A mindful librarian is more likely to have a positive, cooperative experience, and because of that, the faculty member is more likely to want to repeat the collaboration in the future.

In order to encourage more mindful interpersonal relationships, aca-demic centers, including libraries, are becoming involved in facilitating meditation. As illustrated throughout this book, meditation is an impor-tant component to increasing mindfulness (and in turn synchronicity) in working relationships. For example, the University of Redlands has a des-ignated Meditation Room that is used not only for mindfulness classes, but as a place for faculty to go to meditate.[47] The Pollak Library at California State University, Fullerton, offers "Meditation in the Library on Mindful Mondays," and the Humbolt State University Library offers a meditation room to students and staff.[48] In another example, a group of six Fairfield University faculty members met 2 hours a week to explore the mindful integration of spirituality into their professional lives.[49] After the experi-ence, one professor stated that these interactions created a sense of connec-tion to and caring for each other and the university. Similarly, in fall 2014, Charlotte Library at Johnson & Wales University implemented a practice of offering meditation time to faculty members at the end of the semester in

---

[45] Haas, A.S., Langer, E.J., 2014. Mindful attraction and synchronization: mindfulness and regulation of interpersonal synchronicity. NeuroQuantology 12 (1), pp. 24–32.

[46] Haas, A.S., Langer, E.J., Mindful attraction and synchronization: mindfulness and regula-tion of interpersonal synchronicity. NeuroQuantology 12 (1), 32.

[47] Academics: meditation room. The University of Redlands. Available from: <http://www.redlands.edu/academics/meditation-room.aspx#.VIRmxzHF_xo> (accessed 14.12.14.).

[48] Breitbach, W., Meditate in the Library on Mindful Mondays. California State University, Fullerton, CA, last modified February 21, 2013. Available from: <http://libraryblogs.ful-lerton.edu/2013/02/21/meditate-in-the-library-on-mindful-mondays/>.

[49] O'Shea, E.R., Torosyan, R., Robert, T., Haug, I., Wills, M., Bowen, B.A., 2011. Spirituality and professional collegiality: *Esprit de "Core"*. In: Heewon, C., Boyd, D., Spirituality in Higher Education Autoethnographies. Left Coast Press, Walnut Creek, CA, pp. 87, 97.

order to create a more positive, harmonious working environment. As this mindful movement continues, librarians are taking the lead to provide quiet meditation spaces and encouraging mindfulness, which in turn enhances interpersonal synchronicity and benefits the entire academic community.

Interpersonal synchronicity and the positive benefits of working harmoniously with one another have been scientifically proven. Working in sync with others has its own optimal experience characteristics (such as the feeling of escape or no sense of real time), but it also involves complimentary positive and negative neural activity in the brain between dyads. When mindfulness is added to the relationship mix, synchronicity is enhanced and participants have a more positive feeling about each other and the experience that they are sharing together. In fact, interpersonal synchronicity and mindfulness play a role in the development of a positive, social relationship between librarians and faculty members. For librarians, all this comes together with increasing mindfulness through meditation while encouraging faculty to join in the spiritual journey, which will enhance everyone's shared experiences.

CONCLUSION

For the academic librarian, building relationships with faculty to support, assist, and collaborate is necessary but challenging. Mindfulness can assist with this relationship-building process and have a positive impact. This social interaction between librarian and faculty member involves an awareness of communication methods, including nonverbal clues and differences in encoding and decoding of messages. Not only are exchanges purposeful, but they can shift from a mindful to a more mindless state, depending on the level of focus. Part of these interactions includes mindful listening. Librarians must pick up on nonverbal clues and listening styles while practicing active listening. Being truly engaged in the conversation is an important aspect of being a mindful librarian. Finally, both mindfulness and the role of interpersonal synchronicity have a significant impact on the establishment and growth of library–faculty relationships. The interaction of these two individuals will be more positive and productive if they are in tune with one another. In addition, with mindful, interpersonal synchronicity, each party will come away with an increased feeling of satisfaction and be eager to collaborate again in the future. With an increased awareness of the dynamics surrounding communication, the librarian is better equipped to interact and build a positive faculty relationship at their institution.

RECOMMENDED RESOURCES

Burgoon, J.K., Berger, C.R., Waldron, V.R., 2000. Mindfulness and interpersonal communication. J. Soc. Issues 56 (1).

Csikszentmihalyi, M., 1990. FLOW: The Psychology of Optimal Experience. Harper & Row, New York, NY.

Haas, A.S., Langer, E.J., 2014. Mindful attraction and synchronization: mindfulness and regulation of interpersonal synchronicity. NeuroQuantology 12 (1), 24–32.

Langer, E.J., Moldoveanu, M., 2000. The construct of mindfulness. J. Soc. Issues 56 (1).

BIBLIOGRAPHY

Aarts, H., Dijksterhuis, A., 2000. Habits as knowledge structures: automaticity in goal-directed behavior. J. Pers. Soc. Psychol. 78 (1), 53–63. Available from: <http://dx.doi.org/10.1037/0022-3514.78.1.53> (accessed 07.12.14.)

Academics: meditation room. The University of Redlands. Available from: <http://www.redlands.edu/academics/meditation-room.aspx#.VIRmxzHF_xo> (accessed 14.12.14.).

Adler, R., Proctor II, R., 2014. Looking Out, Looking In, 14th ed.. Wadsworth, Boston, MA.

Anthony, K., 2010. Reconnecting the disconnects: library outreach to faculty as addressed in the literature. Coll. Undergrad. Libr. 17 (1), 79–92. Available from: <http://dx.doi.org/10.1080/10691310903584817> (accessed 02.12.14.)

Breitbach, W., 2013. Meditate in the Library on Mindful Mondays. California State University, Fullerton, CA, Last modified February 21, 2013. Available from: <http://libraryblogs.fullerton.edu/2013/02/21/meditate-in-the-library-on-mindful-mondays/>.

Burgoon, J.K., Berger, C.R., Waldron, V.R., 2000. Mindfulness and interpersonal communication. J. Soc. Issues 56 (1), 105–127. Available from: <http://dx.doi.org/10.1111/0022-4537.00154> (accessed 05.12.14.)

Christiansen, L., Stombler, M., Thaxton, L., 2004. A report on librarian–faculty relations from a sociological perspective. J. Acad. Libr. 30 (2), 116–121. Available from: <http://dx.doi.org/10.1016/j.acalib.2004.01.003> (accessed 02.12.14.)

Cline, B.J., 2013. The science and sanity of listening. ETC: Rev. Gen. Semant. 70 (3), 247–259. Available from: <http://connection.ebscohost.com/c/articles/93297892/science-sanity-listening> (accessed 20.11.14.)

Csikszentmihalyi, M., 1990. FLOW: The Psychology of Optimal Experience. Harper & Row, New York, NY.

Cultural information-Argentina. Centre for Intercultural Learning. Last modified October 15, 2009. Available from: <http://www.intercultures.ca/cil-cai/ci-ic-eng.asp?iso=ar#cn-2>.

Cultural information-Ireland. Centre for Intercultural Learning. Last modified October 15, 2009. Available from: <http://www.intercultures.ca/cil-cai/ci-ic-eng.asp?iso=ie#cn-2>.

Cultural information-United Kingdom. Centre for Intercultural Learning. Last modified October 15, 2009. Available from: <http://www.intercultures.ca/cil-cai/ci-ic-eng.asp?iso=gb#cn-2>.

Culture crossing guide: Australia. Culture Crossing. Available from: <http://guide.culturecrossing.net/basics_business_student_details.php?Id=10&CID=13> (accessed 14.12.14).

Culture crossing guide: Germany. Culture Crossing. Available from: <http://guide.culturecrossing.net/basics_business_student_details.php?Id=10&CID=79> (accessed 14.12.14.).

Culture crossing guide: Indonesia. Culture Crossing. Available from: <http://guide.culturecrossing.net/basics_business_student_details.php?Id=10&CID=97> (accessed 14.12.14.).

Haas, A.S., 2012. A brain charge mechanism modeled in synchronistic dyadic interpersonal interaction. NeuroQuantology 10 (3), 482–488. Available from: <http://dx.doi.org/10.14704/nq.2012.10.3.562> (accessed 05.12.14.)

Haas, A.S., Langer, E.J., 2014. Mindful attraction and synchronization: mindfulness and regulation of interpersonal synchronicity. NeuroQuantology 12 (1), 21–34. Available from: <http://dx.doi.org/10.14704/nq.2014.12.1.728> (accessed 15.11.14.)

Hogenson, G.B., 2009. Synchronicity and moments of meeting. J. Anal. Psychol. 54 (2), 183–197. Available from: <http://dx.doi.org/10.1111/j.1468-5922.2009.01769.x> (accessed 15.11.14.)

Honan, D.H., 2012. Lie to me: the biological basis of emotion. Bigthink. Last modified Sept. 29, 2012. Available from: <http://bigthink.com/think-tank/lie-to-me>

Japan—language, culture, customs and etiquette. Kwintessential. Available from: <http://www.kwintessential.co.uk/resources/global-etiquette/japan-country-profiles.html> (accessed 14.12.14.).

Knapp, M.L., Hall, J.A., 2013. Nonverbal Communication. De Gruyter Mouton, Boston, MA, PDF eBook.

Lakin, J.L., 2006. Automatic cognitive processes and nonverbal communication. In: Manusov, V., Patters, M.L. (Eds.) The Sage Handbook of Nonverbal Communication, Sage Publications, Inc., Thousand Oaks, CA, pp. 59–77.

Langer, E.J., Moldoveanu, M., 2000. The construct of mindfulness. J. Soc. Issues 56 (1), 1–9. Available from: <http://www.communicationcache.com/uploads/1/0/8/8/10887248/the_construct_of_mindfulness.pdf> (accessed 25.11.14.)

Lumsden, J., Miles, L.K., Richardson, M.J., Smith, C.A., Neil Macrae, C., 2012. Who syncs? Social motives and interpersonal coordination. J. Exp. Soc. Psychol. 48 (6), 746–751. Available from: <http://dx.doi.org/10.1016/j.jesp.2011.12.007> (accessed 07.12.14.)

Main, R., 2004. Rupture of Time: Synchronicity and Jung's Critique of Modern Western Culture. Brunner-Routledge, New York, NY.

Malefant, K.J., 2010. Leading change in the system of scholarly communication: a case study of engaging liaison librarians for outreach to faculty. Coll. Res. Libr. 71 (1), 63–76. Available from: <http://crl.acrl.org/content/71/1/63.full.pdf> (accessed 25.11.14.)

Moniz, R., Henry, J., Eshleman, J., 2014. Fundamentals for the Academic Liaison. Neal-Schuman, Chicago, IL.

O'Shea, E.R., Torosyan, R., Robert, T., Haug, I., Wills, M., Bowen, B.A., 2011. Spirituality and professional collegiality: Esprit de 'Core'. In: Heewon, C., Boyd, D. (Eds.) Spirituality in Higher Education Autoethnographies, Left Coast Press, Walnut Creek, CA, pp. 87–108.

Patterson, M.L., Manusov, V.L. (Eds.), 2006. The Sage Handbook of Nonverbal Communication, SAGE Publications, Thousand Oaks, CA, PDF eBook.

Research Resources: About Dr. Ekman's Research. Paul Ekman Group. Available from: <http://www.paulekman.com/research/> (accessed 14.12.14.).

Ritchie, T.D., Bryant, F.B., 2012. Positive state mindfulness: a multidimensional model of mindfulness in relation to positive experience. Int. J. Wellbeing 2 (3), 150–181. Available from: <http://dx.doi.org/10.5502/ijw.v2.i3.1> (accessed 07.12.14.)

Shafir, R.Z., 2010. Mindful listening for better outcomes. In: Hick, S.F., Bien, T. (Eds.) Mindfulness and the Therapeutic Relationship, Guildford Press, New York, NY, pp. 176–194.

Shen, L., 2012. Improving the effectiveness of librarian–faculty collaboration on library collection development. Collab. Libr. 4 (1), 14–22. Available from: <http://collaborativelibrarianship.org/index.php/jocl/article/view/168/126> (accessed 05.12.14.)

CHAPTER 7

Mindful Library Leadership

Jo Henry and Howard Slutzky

INTRODUCTION TO MINDFUL LEADERSHIP

The concept of leadership encompasses a variety of logistical and humanistic attributes, which have been studied and grouped into numerous theories. Within many of the modern leadership theories, mindfulness is a component. However, mindfulness more recently has developed into a separate area of study. It is the subject of conferences, retreats, and training for many organizational leaders, including library leaders. In fact, the First International Mindfulness Conference was held in Madrid, Spain, in 2013, bringing together people from all areas of work, including academics, teachers, and other community workers.[1] Mindfulness plays a role not only in an individual leader's growth, but it can affect the employees and the organization itself. While mindfulness could be a concept that is applied in a singular instance, when used consistently and across an entire organization, it has positive, wide-ranging effects on operations. Because of the continual search for the best method of library leadership, an exploration of mindfulness has led to this chapter.

In their 2007 book, Nancy Rossiter and Peter Hernon state simply, "management and leadership are not synonymous terms."[2] Management deals with the logistic side of a library operation. This includes tasks such as staffing, budgeting, equipment acquisition and maintenance, operating procedures, and collection development, among other duties. Leadership "is communicating a vision, building trust, and knowing yourself" in furthering the goals of the library operation.[3] Communicating this "shared

---

[1] American Health and Wellness Institute. First International Conference on Mindfulness. Last updated 2014. Available from: <https://www.ahwinstitute.com/first-international-conference-on-mindfulness>.

[2] Rossiter, N., Hernon, P., 2007. Making a Difference: Leadership and Academic Libraries. Libraries Unlimited, Westport, CT, PDF e-Book, p. 3.

[3] Rossiter, N., Hernon, P., 2007. Making a Difference: Leadership and Academic Libraries. Libraries Unlimited, Westport, CT, PDF e-Book, p. 4.

vision" is the job of the library leader.[4] Successfully achieving overall library goals will include establishing trusting relationships with employees and applying mindful leadership principles.

What exactly is mindful leadership? Ellen J. Langer and Mihnea Moldoveanu define mindfulness as "the process of drawing novel distinctions" in a state of heightened awareness of the present.[5] This leads to a "greater sensitivity to the environment, more openness to new information, the creation of new categories for structuring perception, and enhanced awareness of multiple perspectives in problem solving."[6] A good leader is constantly aware of operations and always looking for new ideas or methods. Mindful practices make this possible for organizational leaders. On an individual level, mindful attributes of a leader are necessary for the concept to be carried down through the organization and positively affect his or her followers. Mindfulness of the individual includes an "awareness of one's behavior, experience, and various stimuli" of the surrounding environment.[7] The Institute for Mindful Leadership, based in Oakland, New Jersey, defines mindful leadership as follows: "A mindful leader embodies leadership presence by cultivating focus, clarity, creativity, and compassion in the service of others."[8] As both definitions indicate, mindfulness is all of these elements, which can be applied to the overall operation of the organization and the interaction of the working group with a mindful leader. While the concept of mindfulness can mean focused attention in the moment, mindful leadership carries this concept much further, affecting both the actions and the relationships of the organization.

The idea of mindful leadership is the culmination of a long evolution of leadership theories traced back to the mid-1800s. At that time, leadership theories began with the emergence of trait theories. The "Great Man" theory was one of the first trait theories to state that leadership characteristics could be defined and were linked to heredity.[9] Subsequent leadership

---

[4] Rossiter, N., Hernon, P., 2007. Making a Difference: Leadership and Academic Libraries. Libraries Unlimited, Westport, CT, PDF e-Book, p. 8.

[5] Langer, E.J., Moldoveanu, M., 2000. The construct of mindfulness. J. Soc. Issues 56 (1), 1.

[6] Langer, E.J., Moldoveanu, M., 2000. The construct of mindfulness. J. Soc. Issues 56 (1), 1.

[7] Brown, K.W., Ryan, R.M., 2003. The benefits of being present: mindfulness and its role in psychological well-being. J. Pers. Soc. Psychol. 84 (4), 843.

[8] Institute for Mindful Leadership. Definitions. Last updated 2014. Available from: <http://instituteformindfulleadership.org/definitions/>.

[9] Smith, E., Tapscott, L., 2010. Historic ideas into contemporary leadership theories: have formalized theories improved the field of leadership? Mid-Atl. Leader. Rev. 3 (1), 37.

theories at this time centered on lists of traits that, while not attributed to heredity, defined a good leader. Each theory spouted a variety of characteristics of a good leader. No consideration was given to the environment or interpersonal communication in these early theories. However, these trait theories had a long-lasting effect. Even today, attributes of the early trait theories have resurged as a component of modern leadership theories.

The next significant change in leadership thinking came in the middle of the twentieth century. A number of studies conducted from 1946 to 1956 by Rensis Likert (at the University of Michigan) and Ralph Stogdill and Carroll Shartle (at Ohio State) added a critical component to leadership theory. These theorists introduced the concept that leadership had two dimensions—task and interpersonal.[10] The introduction of the interpersonal component altered the common (trait-centered) view of leadership. These studies indicated that individuals who could develop their own methods to achieve a goal, rather than being given a method of execution, were more engaged in the activity and open to new concepts.[11] This simply meant that giving individual workers some freedom in their work decisions had a positive impact. More important, if trust and respect were a part of interpersonal relationships at work, "good rapport and two-way communication" in the workplace were achieved.[12] This study was significant because it shifted the concentration of leadership theories away from attributes and toward more humanistic elements.

With the acceptance that humanism was part of leadership, focus on behavior became the next wave of leadership theory. These behavioral theories began by analyzing the "best way to lead."[13] This way of thinking finally evolved into situational contingency theories of the 1960s and 1970s and added yet another layer of complexity. For the first time in the study of leadership, the situational contingency theories took into consideration the environment in which a leader was placed.[14] They were incorporating both

---

[10] Johns, H.E., Ronald Mosner, H., Fall 1989. From trait to transformation: the evolution of leadership theories. Education 110 (1), 116.

[11] Johns, H.E., Ronald Mosner, H., Fall 1989. From trait to transformation: the evolution of leadership theories. Education 110 (1), 117.

[12] Johns, H.E., Ronald Mosner, H., Fall 1989. From trait to transformation: the evolution of leadership theories. Education 110 (1), 117.

[13] Smith, E., Tapscott, L., 2010. Historic ideas into contemporary leadership theories: have formalized theories improved the field of leadership? Mid-Atl. Leader. Rev. 3 (1), 38.

[14] Dickmann, M.H., Stanford-Blair, N., 2009. Mindful Leadership: A Brain-Based Framework. Orwin Press, Thousand Oaks, CA, PDF e-Book, pp. 44–45.

the influence of the surroundings and the idea that leadership styles could be changed depending on the situation. By the 1970s, these types of leadership theories were evolving from well-known contributors such as Likert, Kenneth Blanchard, Paul Hersey, and James MacGregor.[15] The influence of the environment was layered onto the humanistic approach, adding another stage in the evolution of leadership theory.

Other modern approaches to leadership moving more toward mindful leadership were also drawing attention. Robert Greenleaf led the servant leadership approach (serving rather than leading employees) with his publications on the theory. While his ideas on servant leadership were more widely understood in the 1970s (along with the publication of his first book in 1977), he had already founded the Robert K. Greenleaf Center for Servant Leadership (originally "The Center for Applied Ethics") in 1964.[16] Another theory was introduced by James M. Burns, called *transformational leadership*. The elements of this theory included "transformational (focused on change) and transactional (focused on process and people)" aspects of leadership.[17]

The concept of transformational leadership was expanded in 1985 by Bernard Bass (among others) and identified leadership components that were "charismatic, inspirational, intellectually stimulating, and individually considerate."[18] Libraries, too, began to recognize the importance of humanistic leadership. During the 1980s and 1990s, libraries began to develop leadership programs that explored leadership skills and the path of "self-discovery."[19] Many of the elements of these theories and leadership styles lie at the root of mindful leadership.

Adding further to the mix of theories was a number of other collaborative leadership models that evolved in the mid-1990s. Examples include the Social Change Model, a collaborate values-based theory developed by Alexander and Helen Astin; authentic leadership (authentic self and behavior), developed by Avolio and William L. Gardner; and resonant

[15] Johns, H.E., Ronald Mosner, H., Fall 1989. From trait to transformation: the evolution of leadership theories. Education 110 (1), 117.

[16] Robert K Greenleaf Center for Servant Leadership. About the Robert K. Greenleaf Center. Last updated 2014. Available from: <https://greenleaf.org/about-us/>.

[17] Mason, F.M., Wetherbee, L.V., 2004. Learning to lead: an analysis of current training. Libr. Trends 53 (1), 190.

[18] Bass, B.M., Avolio, B.J., Atwater, L., 1996. The transformational and transactional leadership of men and women. Appl. Psychol. Int. Rev. 45 (1), 9.

[19] Mason, F.M., Wetherbee, L.V., 2004. Learning to lead: an analysis of current training. Libr. Trends 53 (1), 187.

leadership (mindful balance of sacrifice and renewal), by Annie McKee, Richard Boyatzis, and Francis Johnston.[20] Mindfulness is a component of all these theories. As many of these theories speak directly of mindful behavior, they will be explored in this chapter.

As theories of leadership have evolved from the 1800s to today, it is now understood that leadership involves more than a list of human traits. Leadership is a complex, interactive role than must consider the self, environment, and relationships. Its complexity and impact on the brain has been studied in recent decades through use of magnetic resonance imaging (MRI) scans proving the connection between body, mind, emotions, and the environment. When viewed as a whole, all of the modern theories point to similar, overall themes. These leadership theories speak to self-awareness, ethics and morals, social responsiveness, and shared leadership power.[21] It is through a *mindful approach* that these characteristics and actions are enhanced, improved, and utilized by a strong leader. Mindful leadership is taking its place in the developing leadership theory chain. It is happening now, and it is time for library leaders to pause for a moment of mindful learning.

Mindful Leadership Centers
- Institute for Mindful Leadership (est. 2011),
- 1440 Foundation (est. 2011),
- The Mindful Leadership Foundation (est. 2010),
- Garrison Institute (est. 2003),
- The Mindfulness Centre (est. 2006),
- Center for Courage and Renewal Australasia (est. 1997).

MINDFUL LEADERS

Mindful leadership will have an impact on the operation of, as well as relationships within, the organizational unit. With the emphasis on a more humanistic and mindful approach to leadership, this influence is inevitable.

[20] McKee, A., Boyatzis, R.E., 2008. Becoming a Resonant Leader: Develop Your Emotional Intelligence, Renew Your Relationships, Sustain Your Effectiveness. Harvard Business School Publishing, Boston, MA, p. x. Komives, S.P., Dugan, J.P., 2010. Contemporary leadership theories. In: Couto, R.A. (Ed.), Political and Civic Leadership. SAGE Publications, Washington, DC, pp. 115–116.

[21] Mason, F.M., Wetherbee, L.V., 2004. Learning to lead: an analysis of current training. Libr. Trends 53 (1), 117–118.

However, mindful leadership cannot take place without focusing first on the self. This is so critical that Richard J. Moniz, Jr, in *Practical and Effective Management of Libraries: Integrating Case Studies, General Management Theory, and Self-Understanding*, dedicated an entire chapter to the importance of library leaders understanding themselves.[22] Additionally, a Mindful Attention Awareness Scale (MAAS) study of 1253 participants indicated that mindfulness is "associated with heightened self-knowledge."[23] To accomplish this self-understanding, the leader must first implement mindful actions into the areas of self-awareness, self-management, ethics and morals, actions and effort, and reflection or meditation.

Any time that change is implemented, there must be a clear understanding of the present situation before an action can be applied. With self-awareness, a leader must have a clear understanding of the self before a mindful action can be taken. Leading resonant leadership theorists describe this as the gap between the "real self" and the "ideal self."[24] In trying to close that gap, Daniel Goleman, Boyatzis, and McKee suggests these defining steps to self-awareness in their book *Primal Leadership: Realizing the Power of Emotional Intelligence*.

1. "Who do I want to be?"
2. "Who am I?"
3. "How can I build on my strengths while reducing my gaps?"
4. "Experimenting and practicing new behaviors...."
5. "Developing supportive and trusting relationships that make change possible."[25]

The concept of understanding the self, evaluating strength gaps, and applying new behaviors put the leader on the path to mindfulness. Knowing oneself is also a component of many authentic leadership concepts. It is from these studies that the following questions can be addressed to begin thinking of important areas to identify in a self-analysis:

• What are your core values and beliefs?
• What attitudes and behaviors are consistent over time?

---

[22] Moniz, R.J., Jr, 2010. Practical and Effective Management of Libraries: Integrating Case Studies, General Management Theory, and Self-Understanding. Chandos Publishing, Oxford, pp. 19–40.

[23] Brown, K.W., Ryan, R.M., 2003. The benefits of being present: mindfulness and its role in psychological well-being. J. Pers. Soc. Psychol. 84 (4), 843.

[24] McKee, A., Boyatzis, R.E., 2008. Becoming a Resonant Leader: Develop Your Emotional Intelligence, Renew Your Relationships, Sustain Your Effectiveness. Harvard Business School Publishing, Boston, MA, p. 9.

[25] Goleman, D., Boyatzis, R., McKee, A., 2002. Primal Leadership: Realizing the Power of Emotional Intelligence. Harvard Business School Press, Boston, MA, pp. 111–112.

- How are your emotions expressed?
- What motivates you? What are your personal goals?
- How would you describe your personality?

Before reading further, take a moment to think about all these questions and begin to define the real self. For those who are already in a leadership role, an awareness of current leadership style is also important. For that insight in this area, the emotional intelligence theory of Goleman, Boyatzis, and McKee defined leadership styles as follows:

- Visionary
- Coaching
- Affiliative
- Democratic
- Pace-setting
- Commanding[26]

What kind of leader are you? What is your true self? The road to mindful leadership begins with a clear definition of the present.

Another aspect of understanding oneself involves ethics and morals. Leaders have an enormous responsibility to their followers and the organization and must make ethical choices. When applied to the concept of mindfulness, this sort of "right understanding" is derived from Buddhist philosophy and part of the Noble Eightfold Path.[27]

The Buddhist Noble Eightfold Path toward enlightenment is achieved through mindful practices that include right view, right intention, right speech, right action, right livelihood, right effort, right mindfulness, and right concentration.[28]

The Noble Eightfold Path is divided into three areas termed wisdom, ethics, and concentration, with the ethical components broken down into right speech, right action, and right livelihood.[29] When a leader is mindful

[26] Goleman, D., Boyatzis, R., McKee, A., 2002. Primal Leadership: Realizing the Power of Emotional Intelligence. Harvard Business School Press, Boston, MA, p. 55.

[27] Atkinson, L., Duncan, J.L., Fall and Winter 2013. Eight Buddhist methods for leaders. J. Org. Learn. Leader. 11 (2), 9.

[28] Allen, J., Buddhanet basic Buddhism guide: the Eightfold Path. Buddhanet.net. Last updated 2014. Available from: <http://www.buddhanet.net/e-learning/8foldpath.htm>.

[29] Bodhi, B., The Noble Eightfold Path: the way to the end of suffering. Access to Insight (Legacy Edition). Last updated November 30, 2013. Available from: <http://www.accesstoinsight.org/lib/authors/bodhi/waytoend.html>.

of these areas, he or she is truthful, makes morally correct decisions, and is honest and ethical in business decisions.[30] A leader understands the power of speech and refrains from using words or tone of voice in a negative way.[31] Put simply, mindful leaders do and say the right thing for the organization and its followers.

Once the self is defined and a path toward ethical behavior set, mindful management along with right actions, and effort can be applied. What exactly are the right actions of a library leader? A study of 66 library directors listed the top 5 self-regulation traits as follows:

1. Stable temperament and ability to maintain an emotional balance under constant tensions
2. Integrity
3. (tie) Comfortable in making judgment calls
4. (tie) Comfortable with ambiguity
5. Flexible in adapting to change or overcoming obstacles
6. Skill at diagnostic, strategic, and tactical reasoning[32]

In 2009, another study of library staff noted the top two self-management traits for library directors and management team members as giving the library direction and having integrity.[33] Honesty ranked third for directors, and comfort in judgment calls ranked third for senior management.[34] These studies both point to attributes of honesty, integrity, good judgment, emotional stability, and perseverance. All of these concepts are in line with mindful actions. Through these kinds of right action, library leaders make a positive impact on their organization.

Emotion also plays a critical role in library leadership success. Effectively using emotion requires emotional intelligence. Emotional Intelligence theories have at their foundation the understanding of one's state of

---

[30] Buddha Dharma Education Association, Inc., Buddhanet basic Buddhism guide: the eight fold path. Last updated 2014. Available from: <http://www.buddhanet.net/e-learning/8foldpath.htm>.

[31] Atkinson, L., Duncan, J.L., Fall and Winter 2013. Eight Buddhist methods for leaders. J. Org. Learn. Leader. 11 (2), 11.

[32] Hernon, P., Rossiter, N., 2006. Emotional intelligence: which traits are most prized? Coll. Res. Libr. 67 (3), 264.

[33] Kreitz, P.A., 2009. Leadership and emotional intelligence: a study of university library directors and their senior management teams. Coll. Res. Libr. 70 (6), 539.

[34] Kreitz, P.A., 2009. Leadership and emotional intelligence: a study of university library directors and their senior management teams. Coll. Res. Libr. 70 (6), 539.

mind and emotions.[35] In this way, these theories incorporate mindfulness. Leading researchers McKee, Boyatzis, and Johnston define this most clearly: "Emotional self-awareness is the ability to process one's own emotional information quickly and accurately, to recognize one's own emotions as they happen, and to immediately understand their effects on oneself and on others."[36] This level of emotional self-awareness is challenging and must be learned. It requires a good deal of self-control, an objective view of an emotional situation, and the ability to harness personal emotions to have a positive effect. While this type of response is challenging, it can be achieved. It is through mindful self-reflection and meditative practice that this level of recognition and control of emotions can be mastered. Leaders are encouraged to make space for quiet reflection every day.

One final leadership theory that touches on self-awareness and control is authentic leadership. This theory states that being an authentic leader can be achieved through self-regulation in four areas. First, the leader's behavior is based on what is important to the self (rather than others).[37] These types of actions by the leader are perceived as real by his or her followers. Second, leaders should objectively analyze strengths and weaknesses and work to improve both.[38] As in other theories, this theme of self-analysis in authentic leadership is a component of mindfulness. The final two characteristics of authentic leaders are that they act on their personal belief system and present a "true self" to others.[39] Studies show that leaders who focus on these areas of self-regulation are more hopeful,

---

[35] McKee, A., Boyatzis, R.E., 2008. Becoming a Resonant Leader: Develop Your Emotional Intelligence, Renew Your Relationships, Sustain Your Effectiveness. Harvard Business School Publishing, Boston, MA, p. 25.

[36] McKee, A., Boyatzis, R.E., 2008. Becoming a Resonant Leader: Develop Your Emotional Intelligence, Renew Your Relationships, Sustain Your Effectiveness. Harvard Business School Publishing, Boston, MA, p. 26.

[37] Kinsler, L., 2014. Born to be me… who am I again? The development of authentic leadership using evidence-based leadership coaching and mindfulness. Int. Coach. Psychol. Rev. 9 (1), 95.

[38] Kinsler, L., 2014. Born to be me… who am I again? The development of authentic leadership using evidence-based leadership coaching and mindfulness. Int. Coach. Psychol. Rev. 9 (1), 95.

[39] Kinsler, L., 2014. Born to be me… who am I again? The development of authentic leadership using evidence-based leadership coaching and mindfulness. Int. Coach. Psychol. Rev. 9 (1), 95.

have a higher self-esteem, and have a positive influence on followers.[40] Throughout the mindful journey of a leader, authenticity through a true understanding of oneself, others, and the organization is essential.

To facilitate the achievement of self-awareness, self-management, ethics, and actions, a mindful leader should take time to meditate and reflect. This is the antipathy of the multitasking, overloaded work environment that many experience on the job. It is easy to get caught up in the time demands of work and home and push quiet reflection aside. How many leaders may think, "Quiet reflection sounds like a good idea, but I simply do not have the time"? Unfortunately, with this approach, many leaders fall into a "sacrifice and renewal" cycle.[41] They will fill their schedules, multitask, work extra hours until they are spent, and then take a vacation in hopes of rejuvenation. Yet, when they return to the workplace, their approach is the same and the stress cycle starts again. The answer to "sustaining resonance and effectiveness over time … is tapping into mindfulness."[42]

A simple way to begin is to "STOP."[43] "STOP" is an acronym reminder to stop during the day, "take a … breath, observe your bodily sensations, and then proceed with what … you were doing."[44] At the next stage, leaders should try to meditate twice a week for 10–15 min, building toward the goal of meditating every day. Each meditation should have a specific goal or focus in mind. A 2007 study of meditation training indicated that groups given this training had a more positive mood, increased attention, and improved self-regulation.[45] Other studies have also shown that meditation has other positive results for leaders. These affects include reduced stress, improved concentration, and improved communication

---

[40] Kinsler, L., 2014. Born to be me… who am I again? The development of authentic leadership using evidence-based leadership coaching and mindfulness. Int. Coach. Psychol. Rev. 9 (1), 95–96.

[41] McKee, A., Boyatzis, R.E., 2008. Becoming a Resonant Leader: Develop Your Emotional Intelligence, Renew Your Relationships, Sustain Your Effectiveness. Harvard Business School Publishing, Boston, MA, p. x.

[42] McKee, A., Boyatzis, R.E., 2008. Becoming a Resonant Leader: Develop Your Emotional Intelligence, Renew Your Relationships, Sustain Your Effectiveness. Harvard Business School Publishing, Boston, MA, p. x.

[43] Hopper, L., Spring 2010. Mindful leadership. Georgia Libr. Q. 47 (2), 16.

[44] Hopper, L., Spring 2010. Mindful leadership. Georgia Libr. Q. 47 (2), 16.

[45] Tang, Y.-Y., Ma, Y., Wang, J., Fan, Y., Feng, S., Lu, Q., Yu, Q., Sui, D., Rothbart, M.K., Fan, M., Posner, M.I., 2007. Short-term meditation improves attention and self-regulation. Proc. Natl Acad. Sci. 104 (43), 17153.

with others.[46] Incorporating quiet moments in the workweek is necessary in becoming a mindful leader.

Dr Howard Slutzky on Intelligent Leadership

The predominating view of intelligence has been the existence of an underlying *general intelligence* that influences performance on all cognitive tasks. Within this school of thought, it is believed that intelligence can be measured and expressed by a single intelligence quotient (IQ) score. The existence of general intelligence was first described by Charles Spearman in 1904, and the standardized intelligence tests being used in clinical and educational settings largely reflect this traditional approach.[47] However, this is a highly restrictive view of intelligence, limiting its scope to only a small portion of the intellectual spectrum.

Rather than seeing intelligence as dominated by a single general ability, Howard Gardner proposed a model that conceptualized intelligence across multiple areas of ability including interpersonal and intrapersonal intelligence. In his 1983 book *Frames of Mind: The Theory of Multiple Intelligences*, Gardner originally articulated seven areas of intelligence, including interpersonal and intrapersonal intelligence. *Interpersonal intelligence* refers to our interaction with others. It represents the degree to which we are able to read others' emotions, navigate social interaction, communicate effectively, resolve conflicts, and collaborate with others toward a common goal. *Intrapersonal intelligence* refers to our interaction with ourselves. It represents our capacity for introspection and reflection regarding our thoughts, emotions, and motivations.[48]

In my experience as a student and as a professor, I have often encountered educators who are extremely knowledgeable in their field but who lack the skills to teach effectively. This brings to mind a psychology professor from my undergraduate education who spent the entire class strolling back and forth in the front of the classroom, lecturing with no notecards or overhead slides. Pretty impressive! However, he also had no eye contact with students and offered no opportunity for questions, discussion, or the development of rapport. While he was certainly an expert in his field, he appeared to be deficient in (or not mindful of) other factors equally important for maximizing the effectiveness of his class instruction.

---

[46] Atkinson, L., Duncan, J.L., Fall and Winter 2013. Eight Buddhist methods for leaders. J. Org. Learn. Leader. 11 (2), 15.

[47] Spearman, C., 1904. General intelligence, objectively determined and measured. Am. J. Psychol. 15, 201–293.

[48] Gardener, H., 1983. Frames of Mind: The Theory of Multiple Intelligences. Basic Books, New York, NY.

Another iconic figure from today's pop culture is the character of Dr Sheldon Cooper, a theoretical physicist on the television show *The Big Bang Theory*. Clearly, Sheldon demonstrates an expertise in a field that exceeds the intellectual capacity of most individuals. However, he is deficient in the areas of both interpersonal and intrapersonal intelligence. Specifically, he demonstrates exceptional difficulty navigating social interaction, he is inflexible with others regarding his schedule and routine, he has little to no capacity for reading others' emotions and nonverbal communication, and he is deficient in the areas of self-reflection and emotional insight. So while Sheldon may excel within his field, he clearly lacks the broader range of intelligence necessary to be an effective leader.[49]

Bill George, Harvard Business School professor and former CEO of Medtronic, has identified a similar (but perhaps less extreme) issue as the reason that many leaders within his industry have ultimately failed. In an online blog post he stated, "In examining these failures, I cannot identify a single leader who failed due to lack of intelligence (IQ). On the contrary, the unsuccessful leaders I have observed in person or through their words and deeds appear to have failed due to low levels of emotional intelligence (EQ)."[50]

The concept of emotional intelligence was articulated by Daniel Goleman in his 1995 book *Emotional Intelligence: The Groundbreaking Book That Redefines What It Means to Be Smart*. High EQ doesn't mean an absence of difficult emotions such as anger, sadness, fear, or jealousy. Instead, it reflects an insight into our emotional experience, a willingness to engage in self-reflection, and a concerted effort to interact with others in a responsible, constructive, and authentic manner. It also means taking responsibility for our mistakes as well as recognizing the defenses that often arise when we fall short of the standards set by ourselves or others.[51] Emotional intelligence entails both the intrapersonal and interpersonal components articulated by Gardner.

It has long been proposed that intelligence is a product of both nature and nurture. In other words, the development of our intellectual abilities is thought to be influenced by both environmental and genetic factors. This school of thought argues that while we have a genetically determined intellectual capacity, factors within our environment (i.e., nutrition, quality of education, parental influence, peers, culture) can affect the degree to which this capacity is achieved. I believe that the same holds true for

---

[49] *Big Bang Theory*. Produced by Chuck Lorre, Bill Prady, Steven Molaro. Warner Home Video, 2014, DVD.

[50] George, B., Bill George. Available from: <http://www.billgeorge.org/page/mindful-leadership-compassion-contemplation-and-meditation-develop-effective-leaders>.

[51] Goleman, D., 1995. Emotional Intelligence: The Groundbreaking Book that Redefines What It Means to be Smart. Bantam Books, New York, NY.

emotional intelligence. This leaves room for the development of skills that are lacking, the improvement of those that are weak, and the refinement of those that need adjustment. There are numerous online training programs, live conferences and workshops, and self-help books to assist leaders this process. Those who offer such resources argue (as I do) that emotional intelligence is a skill that can be developed.

It is a lifelong journey from the present self to a more ideal and mindful self. It starts with a clear understanding of one's current self. Personality, character, strengths, and weaknesses should be honestly reviewed. Then, a leader should define an ideal character and self before using self-management techniques to close the gap between the two. As a leader develops in a mindful way, using right actions marked by upstanding ethics and morals will add to leadership credibility. All of these steps should be supported with mindful reflection and meditation. Becoming a mindful leader is a slow, learned process, but it is an achievable goal.

MINDFUL RELATIONSHIPS

As a leader, building relationships with employees is a part of the position. When this is done in a mindful way, leaders empower the employees and the organization will flourish. For this to happen, inspirational and compassionate leadership is required. In addition, leaders must work toward developing others, distributing power, coaching for success, and correctly utilizing teams in their organization. Goleman, Boyatzis, and McKee, in *Primal Leadership: Realizing the Power of Emotional Intelligence,* term dealing with these relationships as "relational management."[52] While none of these concepts are new, what is different here is to approach them from a mindful perspective.

Leaders must be inspirational or visionary as well as compassionate. Inspirational leadership is mentioned in resonant leadership as bringing people together through relationships "around an optimistic vision of the future."[53] The importance of vision and compassion for libraries is noted in a number of studies. A study of 70 library directors indicates that in the area of social skills, leading "effective change" ranked second among 19

[52] Goleman, D., Boyatzis, R., McKee, A., 2002. Primal Leadership: Realizing the Power of Emotional Intelligence. Harvard Business School Press, Boston, MA, p. 51.

[53] McKee, A., Boyatzis, R.E., 2008. Becoming a Resonant Leader: Develop Your Emotional Intelligence, Renew Your Relationships, Sustain Your Effectiveness. Harvard Business School Publishing, Boston, MA, p. 21.

traits, and the ability to "develop and foster partnerships" ranked third.[54] In the United Kingdom and Australia, a study of library leaders indicated the importance of "wider organization structure and operation," which included skills "described as … 'relationship management'."[55] Another study of 13 Association of College and Research Libraries (ACRL) libraries ranked knowing where to take the organization number one in importance and listening and delegating second in traits for both library directors and senior managers.[56] Some of the most primary jobs of senior library leaders include developing and supporting the organization's vision, as well as relaying this information to employees through established relationships.

However, having a vision is not enough. A leader must get employees to embrace the vision and support it. Here is where mindfulness plays a role. Through relationships, the leader must really listen to employees, show compassion, and inspire trust.[57] Successful library leaders must have the ability "to understand [employees] in terms of their needs and concerns."[58] It is through these established relationships and the trust developed from them that leaders derive the power to drive a vision forward. Simply telling an employee is not enough. An employee must trust the source of information and because of that trust, be willing to go along with the concept. As execution of a vision progresses, leaders must also be empathetic and understanding of the variety of emotions that employees will display as challenges develop. However, this long-term, mindful, and compassionate approach will be sustaining and is reflective of resonant leaders.[59]

As the organization's employees work to support the leader's vision, the leader in turn must support the employees through training. Part of this training should include mindful approaches to work, task execution, and

---

[54] Hernon, P., Rossiter, N., 2006. Emotional intelligence: which traits are most prized? Coll. Res. Libr. 67 (3), 267.

[55] Goulding, A., Walton, G., Stephens, D., 2012. The importance of political and strategic skills for UK library leaders. Aust. Libr. J. 62 (2), 110.

[56] Kreitz, P.A., 2009. Leadership and emotional intelligence: a study of university library directors and their senior management teams. Coll. Res. Libr. 70 (6), 537.

[57] McKee, A., Boyatzis, R.E., 2008. Becoming a Resonant Leader: Develop Your Emotional Intelligence, Renew Your Relationships, Sustain Your Effectiveness. Harvard Business School Publishing, Boston, MA, p. 13.

[58] Moniz, R.J., Jr, 2010. Practical and Effective Management of Libraries: Integrating Case Studies, General Management Theory, and Self-Understanding. Chandos Publishing, Oxford, p. 24.

[59] Boyatzis, R., McKee, A., Summer 2006. Inspiring others through resonant leadership. Bus. Strat. Rev. 17 (2), p. 17.

handling stress. Mindful training may include simplifying the work environment and allowing employees to focus on one task at a time. Focused execution of the task to minimize mistakes and lost time is also encouraged. A 2012 study of 31 participants found that meditation resulted in slower body movements and improved motor control.[60] Another study shows that mindful meditation increases bodily awareness in execution of a physical task playing a role in accurate execution.[61] Mindful training can also be used to reduce stress in employees. For example, the US military uses a Mindfulness-based Mindful Fitness Training (MMFT) to assist enlisted soldiers with handling stress, attention, emotional intelligence, and situational awareness.[62] In fact, the 8-week, 20 hours MMFT course is one of three essential components used for "combat readiness."[63] In addition to military use, over 250 medical centers in the United States use mindful training for stress reduction.[64] The British army has also used meditation to reduce posttraumatic stress from military service.[65] Throughout the process of executing organizational goals, mindful training can play an important role in task execution and stress reduction.

In a less formal approach, the addition of mindfulness, meditation, and spirituality in the workplace has significant impact on stress. Complimentary alternative medicine in both Europe and Australia includes "mindful practices" such as meditation to reduce stress.[66] In a 2010 study

[60] Naranjo, J.R., Schmidt, S., 2012. Is it me or not me? Modulation of perceptual motor awareness and visuomotor performance by mindfulness meditation. BMC Neurosci. 13 (1), 16.

[61] Delevoye-Turrell, Y.N., Bobineau, C., 2012. Motor consciousness during intention-based and stimulus-based actions: modulating attention resources through mindfulness meditation. Front. Psychol. 3, 8, doi: 10.3389/fpsyg.2012.00290.

[62] Stanely, E.A., Schaldach, J.M., 2011. Mindfulness-based Mind Fitness Training (MMFT). Mind Fitness Training Institute, 6.

[63] Stanely, E.A., Schaldach, J.M., 2011. Mindfulness-based Mind Fitness Training (MMFT). Mind Fitness Training Institute, 7.

[64] Jha, A.P., Kiyonaga, A., Ling, W., Gelfand, L., 2010. Examining the protective effects of mindfulness training on working memory capacity and affective experience. Am. Psychol. Assoc. 10 (1), 54.

[65] Jha, G., British army to send 4,000 Buddhist troups to India for meditation to combat post-traumatic stress. Mail Online India. Last updated October 24, 2014. Available from: <http://www.dailymail.co.uk/indiahome/indianews/article-2246069/British-Army-send-4-000-Buddhist-troops-India-meditation-combat-post-traumatic-stress.html>.

[66] IVAA Office, Cam 2020 the contribution of complementary and alternative medicine to sustainable healthcare in Europe. Eurocam: 19. Last updated 2014. Available from: <http://ehtpa.eu/pdf/CAM2020-FINAL.pdf>. Australasian Integrative Medicine Association, 2014. Best practice for integrative medicine in Australian medical practice. Adv. Integr. Med. 1, 74. Available from: <http://dx.doi.org/10.1016/j.aimed.2013.12.001>.

of elementary teachers in the United Kingdom, work stress levels significantly decreased after the teachers took an 8-week meditation course.[67] From 2002 to 2008, Saul Neves de Jesusa conducted 12 studies of teachers in Portugal and in Brazil, and the results showed stress reduction from implementation of stress management courses, which included relaxation and breathing techniques.[68] Mindful training is also used by many top companies (such as Apple, Ford, GE, IBM, Microsoft, Reliance, and Google) "to reduce stress and increase well-being."[69] At Johnson and Wales University Charlotte in the United States, the library facilitates a meditation day inviting faculty, staff, and students to half-hour, stress-reducing meditation sessions. Mindfulness, spirituality, and relaxation methods can reduce stress from work environments and should be a consideration for all library leaders for their staff. Alongside mindful training techniques, mindful coaching or support of the individual has been shown to have significant positive effects as well. A number of other studies have shown that life coaching increases "goal striving, subjective well-being, psychological well-being, and hope."[70] Both professional and peer coaching studies have shown positive impacts on employees.[71] A 2013 study of Case Western Reserve University (Cleveland, Ohio, U.S.) undergraduate students compared MRI scans after positive life dreams talks verses their college studies.[72] Results show that parts of the brain involving imagination were still stimulated with dream talk and "stress, defensiveness, and guilt resulted in school talk."[73] The results indicate coaching to positive thoughts

[67] Gold, E., Smith, A., Hoper, I., Herne, D., Tansey, G., Hulland, C., 2010. Mindfulness-based stress reduction (MBSR) for primary school teachers. J. Child Family Stud. 19 (2), 186, doi: 10.1007/s10826-009-9344-0.

[68] de Jesusa, S.N., Miguel-Tobalb, J.J., Rusc, C.L., Viseua, J., Gamboaa, V., 2014. Evaluating the effectiveness of stress management training on teachers and physicians' stress related outcomes. Clínica y Salud 25, 112–114.

[69] Andrew Lee, R., 2012. Accelerating the development and mitigating derailment of high potentials through mindfulness training. Indus.-Organ. Psychol. 49 (3), 26.

[70] Kinsler, L., 2014. Born to be me... who am I again? The development of authentic leadership using evidence-based leadership coaching and mindfulness. Int. Coach. Psychol. Rev. 9 (1), 96.

[71] Kinsler, L., 2014. Born to be me... who am I again? The development of authentic leadership using evidence-based leadership coaching and mindfulness. Int. Coach. Psychol. Rev. 9 (1), 97.

[72] Boyatizis, R.E., Leadership and management development from neuroscience. Acad. Manage. Learn. Edu. 13 (2), 302.

[73] Boyatizis, R.E., Leadership and management development from neuroscience. Acad. Manage. Learn. Edu. 13 (2), 302.

has a greater impact than coaching to negative ones. With this in mind, how does coaching affect mindfulness? First, mindful leaders understand the importance of positive coaching in the relationship-building areas. Second, mindfulness should be integrated into coaching sessions and encouraged by mentors. Mindful attributes of compassion, self-awareness, and self-regulation should all be a part of the coaching relationship.[74]

The final aspect of relationship development is the distribution of power and use of teams. The mindful understanding of the self allows a leader to apply a style of leadership where followers can grow and contribute to the organization. Effective leaders distribute power to followers and use that influence to create change.[75] One way of distributing power is by using teams for execution and decision making. Since the 1990s, the concept of teams to increase productivity and allow self-direction has been used.[76] However, simply creating teams does not equate success. J. Richard Hackman, who has done extensive study in the area of teams, warns that teams must have six characteristics for success:

1. The task must be appropriate for team rather than individual work.
2. The team is a real unit, not just individuals in a group.
3. The team's direction or purpose is clearly defined.
4. The team works in tandem with other organizational structures.
5. The organization supports the team's needs.
6. Coaching and support is delivered at the beginning, middle, and end of teamwork.[77]

Additionally, Hackman states that for teams to succeed, the number of members in the group must be small (in single digits), stay together as a unit over time, and have a "deviant" in their group that challenges "homogeneity."[78] Mindful leaders must understand the dynamics of real team success and distribute power to both individuals and groups appropriately.

[74] Kinsler, L., 2014. Born to be me… who am I again? The development of authentic leadership using evidence-based leadership coaching and mindfulness. Int. Coach. Psychol. Rev. 9 (1), 100.

[75] Atkinson, L., Duncan, J.L., Fall and Winter 2013. Eight Buddhist methods for leaders. J. Org. Learn. Leader. 11 (2), 10.

[76] Richard Hackman, J., 1998. Why teams don't work. In: Scott Tindale, R. (Ed.), Theory and Research on Small Groups. Plenum Press, New York, NY, 245.

[77] Richard Hackman, J., 1998. Why teams don't work. In: Scott Tindale, R. (Ed.), Theory and Research on Small Groups. Plenum Press, New York, NY, 248–256.

[78] Coutu, D., 2009. Why teams don't work, an interview with J. Richard Hackman. Harvard Bus. Rev.

A mindful leader who has a full understanding of self and leadership style must develop relationships with employees of the organization as well. It is the ethical, authentic, and mindful practices of the leader that provide the foundation of its execution by followers. Followers must be supported with mindful coaching and training while given enough latitude and power to execute the necessary tasks. If teams are used in the distribution of power, a mindful leader must understand what necessary team components for effective results are. It is through these mindful relationships that the leader's vision can be conveyed and are supported by the followers.

MINDFUL ORGANIZATION

Organizational mindfulness has its roots in individual mindfulness. While mindfulness has been built by the work of many people, much of its foundation is attributed to the theories of Ellen Langer, who forged into the study of mindfulness in the late 1980s. She describes the concept of individual mindfulness as (1) creation of new categories; (2) openness to new information; and (3) awareness of more than one perspective.[79] Her concepts were based on more of a Western view of Buddhist thought than an Eastern view.[80] Building on these concepts of individual mindfulness, Karl E. Weick, Kathleen M. Sutcliffe, and David Obstfeld introduced their theory of organizational mindfulness based on high-reliability organizations in 1999, and have continued to build on the concept ever since. They quote Gene Rochlin, who wrote in 1993 the following. High-reliability organizations "seek an ideal of perfection but never expect to achieve it … demand safety but never expect it … dread surprise but always anticipate it … deliver reliability but never take it for granted."[81] Simply put, they define organizational mindfulness as a focus on threats and failure rather than reaching lofty goals in order to achieve success.

---

[79] Langer, E., 2014. Mindfulness 25th Anniversary Edition, Da Capo Press, Boston, MA, print, p. 64.
[80] Vogus, T.J., Sutcliffe, K.M., 2012. Organizational mindfulness and mindful organizing: a reconciliation and path forward. Acad. Manage. Learn. Edu. 11 (4), 721.
[81] Weick, K.E., Sutcliffe, K.M., Obstfeld, D., 1999. Organizing for high reliability: processes of collective mindfulness. In: Sutton, R.S., Staw, B.M. (Eds.), Research in Organizational Behavior. Jai Press, Stanford, CT, p. 53.

The organizational mindfulness theory of Weick, Sutcliffe, and Obstfeld was based on numerous high-reliability organization studies. These organizations were studied because they showed consistent outcomes with minimal "variance in performance."[82] In other words, these organizations did things right most of the time, even during stressful or highly detailed work. When put together collectively, these organizations showed a number of commonalities. These are the foundation of the organizational mindfulness theory and are as follows:

1. Preoccupation with failure
2. Reluctance to simplify interpretations
3. Sensitivity to operations
4. Commitment to resilience
5. Underspecification of structures.[83]

"Preoccupation with failure" refers to being aware of the possibilities of attention to detail, analyzing failures (of both this organization and other related organizations), and the reporting of problems.[84] The "reluctance to simplify" concept means being open to new and different ideas that may alter current methods rather than continuing with a historical norm.[85] "Sensitivity to operations" involves having real-time information and "maintaining situational awareness."[86] "Commitment to resilience" means that organizations not only anticipate problems, but that they also respond to them successfully when they occur.[87] Finally, this type of response often means that organizations turn to the person who is most skilled to solve the problem rather than using the set hierarchy of management; this is termed by Weike, Sutciffe, and Obstfeld as "underspecification

---

[82] Weick, K.E., Sutcliffe, K.M., Obstfeld, D., 1999. Organizing for high reliability: processes of collective mindfulness. In: Sutton, R.S., Staw, B.M. (Eds.), Research in Organizational Behavior. Jai Press, Stanford, CT, pp. 34–35.

[83] Weick, K.E., Sutcliffe, K.M., Obstfeld, D., 1999. Organizing for high reliability: processes of collective mindfulness. In: Sutton, R.S., Staw, B.M. (Eds.), Research in Organizational Behavior. Jai Press, Stanford, CT, p. 37.

[84] Ray, J.L., Baker, L.T., Plowman, D.A., 2011. Organizational mindfulness in business schools. Acad. Manage. Learn. Edu. 10 (2), 190.

[85] Ray, J.L., Baker, L.T., Plowman, D.A., 2011. Organizational mindfulness in business schools. Acad. Manage. Learn. Edu. 10 (2), 190.

[86] Ray, J.L., Baker, L.T., Plowman, D.A., 2011. Organizational mindfulness in business schools. Acad. Manage. Learn. Edu. 10 (2), 190.

[87] Weick, K.E., Sutcliffe, K.M., Obstfeld, D., 1999. Organizing for high reliability: processes of collective mindfulness. In: Sutton, R.S., Staw, B.M. (Eds.), Research in Organizational Behavior. Jai Press, Stanford, CT, p. 46.

of structures."[88] These five attributes of successful organizations are all components of organizational mindfulness.

The concepts of Weike, Sutcliffe, and Obstfeld were tested in the academic arena by Joshua Ray, Lakami Baker, and Donde Ashmos Plowman, who performed a study of colleges of business within universities. Their findings, published in 2011, supported the organizational mindfulness theory. Of the 154 business colleges responding, it was found that the five dimensions of organizational mindfulness as defined by Weike, Sutcliffe, and Obstfeld were all components of successful programs.[89] At the time of their study, there was only one other supportive empirical study of schools involving a relationship between mindfulness and trust.[90] However, all indications are that Weike, Sutcliffe, and Obstfeld's theory holds true in academic settings, as well as other types of organizations.

Organizational mindfulness does involve all levels of the organization, from senior management to middle management to front-line workers. Top administrators bring the concept of organizational mindfulness to the organization and promote its presence, and middle management carries this message from the top down to the front-line employees, who act as a "bridge."[91] Finally, the message is carried down to the lower-level employees, who are often involved in mindful organizing tasks.[92]

Top administrators set the tone for the organization. When incorporating organizational mindfulness into the operation, these leaders are hoping that others support their strategic outcomes and improve performance and services. These high-level leaders empower middle management to pass along mindful concepts. The Ray, Baker, and Plowman study of 154 business schools found that the higher the position held in the school, the more mindful the organization was perceived.[93] In this study, deans saw

[88] Weick, K.E., Sutcliffe, K.M., Obstfeld, D., 1999. Organizing for high reliability: processes of collective mindfulness. In: Sutton, R.S., Staw, B.M. (Eds.), Research in Organizational Behavior. Jai Press, Stanford, CT, p. 49.
[89] Ray, J.L., Baker, L.T., Plowman, D.A., 2011. Organizational mindfulness in business schools. Acad. Manage. Learn. Edu. 10 (2), 197.
[90] Ray, J.L., Baker, L.T., Plowman, D.A., 2011. Organizational mindfulness in business schools. Acad. Manage. Learn. Edu. 10 (2), 191.
[91] Vogus, T.J., Sutcliffe, K.M., 2012. Organizational mindfulness and mindful organizing: a reconciliation and path forward. Acad. Manage. Learn. Edu. 11 (4), 723.
[92] Vogus, T.J., Sutcliffe, K.M., 2012. Organizational mindfulness and mindful organizing: a reconciliation and path forward. Acad. Manage. Learn. Edu. 11 (4), 723.
[93] Ray, J.L., Baker, L.T., Plowman, D.A., 2011. Organizational mindfulness in business schools. Acad. Manage. Learn. Edu. 10 (2), 194.

the College of Business as being more mindful than do associate deans, assistant deans, or department heads (who perceived it the least).[94] Upper-level managers not only handle crises in mindful ways, but they also envision and pass along the bigger picture of the overall operation to others.

It is through middle managers that real-time data is pushed up to top administrators and mindful solutions or initiatives are pushed down. As part of being a mindful leader, real-time information is important for decision making and analysis. In reverse, middle management conveys information and expectations down from senior leaders to front-line workers. As expected, middle management plays an important in-between role within an organization, and without them, the flow or information and ideas would not be complete. These personnel allow flow of information from events at the lower levels up to decision makers of the larger organizational goals. They are the go-betweens for the two levels in terms of when developing guidelines for employees to accomplish the tasks that will merge together and support the organization's strategies. Timothy Vogus and Kathleen Sutcliffe have termed these actions as "pattern recognition" and "scenario formulation," and they lie at the heart of the middle management's role.[95]

Finally, front-line employees who work through their daily tasks in a mindful way all contribute to the mindfulness of the organization. It is at this level that mindful organizing or paying close attention to tasks and execution becomes more apparent. A large body of research has been done in support of mindfulness and reliability, which began with studies of power plants, naval aircraft carries, and air traffic control systems in the late 1980s into the 1990s, and has continued in the new millennium.[96] Discussion of this body of information far exceeds the scope of this chapter. It is at this front-line level of an organization that individuals evaluate methods and errors and communicate their findings and ideas to the middle-management level.

---

[94] Ray, J.L., Baker, L.T., Plowman, D.A., 2011. Organizational mindfulness in business schools. Acad. Manage. Learn. Edu. 10 (2), 197.

[95] Vogus, T.J., Sutcliffe, K.M., 2012. Organizational mindfulness and mindful organizing: a reconciliation and path forward. Acad. Manage. Learn. Edu. 11 (4), 726.

[96] Weick, K.E., Sutcliffe, K.M., Obstfeld, D., 1999. Organizing for high reliability: processes of collective mindfulness. In: Sutton, R.S., Staw, B.M. (Eds.), Research in Organizational Behavior. Jai Press, Stanford, CT, p. 32.

A mindful organization embodies the concept of mindfulness throughout all levels. An organization focused on task execution is more mindful. The analysis of failures or potential failures, the openness to new ideas on task execution, and awareness of how things are operating are all a part of organizational mindfulness. An organization's ability to react and rebound after failure, as well as its use of the employees with critical knowledge (rather than power) during these episodes, will mean long-term success. Finally, all of these attributes are not complete without the constant flow of information and ideas up and down a chain of command.

NEUROSCIENCE

Beyond the leadership and organizational studies of mindfulness, there is an ever-growing body of evidence in the area of neuroscience that supports the concept. While mindful neuroscience studies date back 50 years, it is over the last two decades that mindfulness-based meditation and neurobiology have produced a large number of studies that illustrate the effects of mediation on the brain.[97] The use of the MRI to study the brain and its changes has proven that changes in stress levels, problem-solving skills, negotiation skills, concentration, emotional intelligence, self-awareness, self-regulation, motivation, and empathy are all affected by mindfulness.[98] Many of these mindful attributes have been discussed in this chapter and have a huge impact on leaders, followers, and the organization they work in. Therefore, a short visit of supporting research of these areas is appropriate.

Brain Facts
* The brain has 100 billion neurons.
* A neuron has 5000 synapses.
* Synapses receive a message to fire 5–50 times per second.[99]

[97] Adkins Singh, A.N., Kristeller, J.L., Raffone, A., Giommi, F., 2013. Advances in mindfulness research. Neuropsychiatry 3 (5), 467.

[98] Canua, J., 2013. Mind over matter the art of mindful meditation. S. Afr. Leg. Inform. Inst. 48 (DEREBUS 153), 3.

[99] Hanson, R. with Mendius, R., 2009. Buddha's Brain: The Practical Neuroscience of Happiness, Love, and Wisdom. New Harbinger Publications, Inc., Oakland, CA, PDF e-Book, p. 6.

A number of studies involving leaders and brain activity have been conducted. One such study involves the brain activity of charismatic leaders. Conducted in 2011, the charismatic leader study at Arizona State University noted a difference in brain activity between charismatic leaders and noncharismatic leaders. Charismatic leaders were found to use both the right and left halves of the brain and had more interconnectivity between the halves.[100] In other words, they utilized both the logical and analytical sides of their brain and the creative and imaginative side. The use of both areas is required of a mindful leader. In 2012, a Case Western Reserve University and Cleveland Clinic study of executives analyzed positive (resonant) versus negative (dissonant) leadership actions and found that the use of threatening, demeaning, or negative behavior toward others resulted in the recipient's brains becoming stimulated toward avoidance.[101] The use of positive interaction and feedback with employees is a component of right-brain action. This same study indicated that positive leaders activated the recipient's default mode network (DMN), which allows them to be emotionally connected and open to new ideas.[102] Again, both emotional awareness and openness are mindful traits. All of these studies show that both mindful and supportive actions of a leader make an impact on brain activity.

Studies have also been conducted in the area of emotion and empathy—additional traits of a mindful leader. A 2008 study of brains compared 40 meditators with an average of 8.6 years and 2 hours of daily meditative practice against a nonmeditation control group.[103] The study showed that in the meditation group, there was greater amount of gray matter in the medial orbital frontal cortex.[104] This is the area that plays a role in controlling emotions, and the study indicates that those who meditate have developed this part of the brain to a greater extent.

[100] Boyatizis, R.E., Leadership and management development from neuroscience. Acad. Manage. Learn. Edu. 13 (2), 301.
[101] Boyatizis, R.E., Leadership and management development from neuroscience. Acad. Manage. Learn. Edu. 13 (2), 301.
[102] Boyatizis, R.E., Leadership and management development from neuroscience. Acad. Manage. Learn. Edu. 13 (2), 301.
[103] Holzel, B.K., Ott, U., Gard, T., Hempel, H., Weygandt, M., Morgen, K., Vaitl, D., 2007. Investigation of Mindfulness Meditation Practitioners with Voxel-Based Morphometry. Oxford University Press, Oxford, vol. 3, no. 1, p. 56.
[104] Holzel, B.K., Ott, U., Gard, T., Hempel, H., Weygandt, M., Morgen, K., Vaitl, D., 2007. Investigation of Mindfulness Meditation Practitioners with Voxel-Based Morphometry. Oxford University Press, Oxford, vol. 3, no. 1, p. 56.

In other words, members of the meditation group had greater control of their emotions. Antoine Lutz, Julie Brefczynski-Lewis, Tom Johnstone, and Richard J. Davidson studied expert meditators (who had done more than 10,000 hours of Buddhist meditation) and their brain's response to emotional sounds.[105] Results showed changes to the somatosensory cortex and insula cortex brain areas in members of in the meditation group. While both the meditation group and control group's brains indicated more empathy stimulation during meditation, the experienced meditation group showed significant increases in brain activation, especially when negative sounds were used.[106] Those who meditated were more in tune with emotional stimuli. Other studies have shown that the amygdala in the brain plays a role in emotion regulation as well.[107] Even empathy has been shown to activate different neural circuits, depending on if empathy is genuine or not.[108] There is a large body of evidence connecting the use of meditation with emotional control as well as empathy—both being essential to the mindful leader.

Finally, focused attention is a key aspect of mindfulness at all levels of an organization, and also at the center of numerous studies. In a 2005 study, Western meditation practitioners were compared to a nonmeditating group. It was found that the meditation group had thicker cortical regions.[109] This is the area of the brain that relates to somatosensory processing and attention. Interestingly, the study also showed an age-related cortical thickening in the meditation group, which suggests that it may "slow the rate of neural degeneration" associated with aging.[110] Therefore,

[105] Lutz, A., Brefczynski-Lewis, J., Johnstone, T., Davidson, R.J., 2008. Regulation of the neural circuitry of emotion by compassion meditation: effects of meditative expertise. PLoS ONE 3 (3), 1.

[106] Lutz, A., Brefczynski-Lewis, J., Johnstone, T., Davidson, R.J., 2008. Regulation of the neural circuitry of emotion by compassion meditation: effects of meditative expertise. PLoS ONE 3 (3), 7–8.

[107] Davidson, R.J., 2004. Well-being and affective style: neural substrates and biobehavioural correlates. Philos. Trans. R. Soc. 359 (1449), 1406.

[108] Boyatizis, R.E., Leadership and management development from neuroscience. Acad. Manage. Learn. Edu. 13 (2), 301.

[109] Lazar, S.W., Kerr, C.E., Wasserman, R.H., Gray, J.R., Greve, D.N., Treadway, M.T., McGarveye, M., Quinn, B.T., Dusek, J.A., Benson, H., Rauch, S.L., Moore, C.I., Fischl, B., 2005. Meditation experience is associated with increased cortical thickness. Neuroreport 16 (17), 1896.

[110] Jack, A.I., Dawson, A., Begany, K., Leckie, R.L., Barry, K., Ciccia, A., Snyder, A., 2012. fMRI reveals reciprocal inhibition between social and physical cognitive domains. Neuroimage 12. Available from: <http://dx.doi.org/10.1016/j.neuroimage.2012.10.061>.

meditation makes a positive difference in the ability to focus. In another area of attention, a 2012 study by Anthony Jack et al. focused on the task positive network (TPN) and DMN neural circuits.[111] The TPN deals with focused, task-related work, and the DMN is a more restful and open state. The study found that typically only one of these areas can be active and functioning at a time. When an individual is focused on a task, the TPN part of the brain is active and the DMN shuts off. The DMN is activated by observing others and their emotions and allowing new information to be processed.[112] Mindful leaders should be aware that when executing focused tasks, the worker's ability to be open and receptive is shut down. These attention studies are just a sample, but they illustrate the connection between meditation, mind, and focused attention.

The body of evidence studying the connection of the brain to mindful attributes continues to grow. These studies in neuroscience prove the connection between the brain and leadership style, attention, emotion, and empathy among other characteristics. While the studies noted here are just a few in the expansive collection of literature, they illustrate the neuroscience connection and leave no doubt that mindful actions and meditation make a neurological difference in the brain.

CONCLUSION

Mindfulness has made its way into leadership theories, and its attributes have proven to have a positive effect on leaders and their organizations. Mindfulness can affect leaders, employee relationships, and organizational operations. Leaders can increase self-awareness and self-management through mindful analysis and introspection. The concept can guide leaders to act in ethical, moral ways, and also can assist them in preventing burnout through a reflection, meditation, and renewal cycle. Mindful leadership concepts are passed down to middle management and then to front-line employees, affecting communication and output. Mindfulness is also applied to relationships with inspiring leadership, compassion, power distribution, training, coaching, and team concepts. In this way, mindfulness enhances

[111] Jack, A.I., Dawson, A., Begany, K., Leckie, R.L., Barry, K., Ciccia, A., Snyder, A., 2012. fMRI reveals reciprocal inhibition between social and physical cognitive domains. Neuroimage 12. Available from: <http://dx.doi.org/10.1016/j.neuroimage.2012.10.061>.

[112] Jack, A.I., Dawson, A., Begany, K., Leckie, R.L., Barry, K., Ciccia, A., Snyder, A., 2012. fMRI reveals reciprocal inhibition between social and physical cognitive domains. Neuroimage 12. Available from: <http://dx.doi.org/10.1016/j.neuroimage.2012.10.061>.

the actions and interactions of those within the entire organization. Mindful organizations as a whole focus on failure and operations, allow employees to openly communicate up the chain of command, and utilize talented employees in times of crisis, making them more successful. Finally, mindfulness has a rich history of neuroscience studies supporting its concepts. Scientific studies indicate a link between mindful practices and charismatic leaders, empathy and emotion, focused attention, and one's openness to new ideas, among other concepts. Through MRI studies, meditation has found to alter the brain and enhance positive qualities in leaders and employees in mindful ways. This rich body of scientific evidence now proves that mindful leadership is more than just a concept—it is a way leaders can change themselves, their organizations, and their employees for the better.

RECOMMENDED RESOURCES

Goleman, D., Boyatzis, R., McKee, A., 2002. Primal Leadership: Realizing the Power of Emotional Intelligence. Harvard Business School Press, Boston, MA.
Hernon, P., Rossiter, N., 2006. Emotional intelligence: which traits are most prized? Coll. Res. Libr. 67 (3), 260–275.
Moniz, R.J., 2010. Practical and Effective Management of Libraries: Integrating Case Studies, General Management Theory, and Self-Understanding. Chandos Publishing, Oxford.

BIBLIOGRAPHY

American Health and Wellness Institute. First international conference on mindfulness. Last updated 2014. Available from: <https://www.ahwinstitute.com/first-international-conference-on-mindfulness>.
Allen, J., 2014. Buddhanet basic buddhism guide: the eight fold path. Buddhanet.net. Available from: <http://www.buddhanet.net/e-learning/8foldpath.htm>.
Atkinson, L., Duncan, J.L., 2013. Eight buddhist methods for leaders. J. Organ. Learn. Leadersh. 11 (2), 8–18. Available from: <http://www.leadingtoday.org/weleadinlearning/Winter2013/Article_2_Atkinson_and_Duncan.pdf> (accessed 05.11.14.)
Australasian Integrative Medicine Association, 2014. Best practice for integrative medicine in Australian medical practice. Adv. Integr. Med. 1, 69–84. Available from: <http://dx.doi.org/10.1016/j.aimed.2013.12.001> (accessed 06.12.14.)
Bass, B.M., Avolio, B.J., Atwater, L., 1996. The transformational and transactional leadership of men and women. Appl. Psychol. Int. Rev. 45 (1), 5–34. Available from: <http://dx.doi.org/10.1111/j.1464-0597.1996.tb00847>.x (accessed 08.12.14.)
Big bang theory. Produced by Chuck Lorre, Bill Prady, Steven Molaro. Warner Home Video, 2014. DVD.
Bodhi, B., 2013. The noble eightfold path: the way to the end of suffering. Access to insight (legacy edition). Last updated November 30, 2013. Available from: <http://www.accesstoinsight.org/lib/authors/bodhi/waytoend.html>.
Boyatizis, R.E., 2014. Leadership and management development from neuroscience. Acad. Manage. Learn. Edu. 13 (2), 300–303. Available from: <http://dx.doi.org/10.5465/amle.2014.0084>. (accessed 20.10.14.)

Brown, K.W., Ryan, R.M., 2003. The benefits of being present: mindfulness and its role in psychological well-being. J. Pers. Soc. Psychol. 84 (4), 822–848. Available from: <http://dx.doi.org/10.1037/0022-3514.84.4.822> (accessed 15.11.14.)

Buddha Dharma Education Association, Inc., 2014. Buddhanet basic buddhism guide: the eight fold path. Last updated 2014. Available from: <http://www.buddhanet.net/e-learning/8foldpath.htm>.

Canua, J., 2013. Mind over matter the art of mindful meditation. S. Afr. Leg. Inform. Inst. 48 (DEREBUS 153), 3. Available from: <http://www.saflii.org/za/journals/DEREBUS/2013/153.html> (accessed 09.12.14.)

Coutu, D., Why teams don't work, an interview with J. Richard Hackman. Harvard Business Review. Last updated May 2009. Available from: <https://hbr.org/2009/05/why-teams-dont-work/ar/1>.

Daniel, G., 1995. Emotional Intelligence: The Groundbreaking Book that Redefines What it Means to be Smart. Bantam Books, New York, NY.

Davidson, R.J., 2004. Well-being and affective style: neural substrates and biobehavioural correlates. Philos. Trans. R. Soc. 359 (1449), 1395–1411. Available from: <http://www.psy.vanderbilt.edu/courses/hon182/Davidson_2004_Phil_Trans_Roy_Soc.pdf> (accessed 09.12.14.)

de Jesusa, S.N., Miguel-Tobalb, J.J., Rusc, C.L., Viseua, J., Gamboaa, V., 2014. Evaluating the effectiveness of stress management training on teachers and physicians' stress related outcomes. Clínica y Salud 25, 111–115. Available from: <http://dx.doi.org/10.1016/j.clysa.2014.06.004> (accessed 25.10.14.)

Delevoye-Turrell, Y.N., Bobineau, C., 2012. Motor consciousness during intention-based and stimulus-based actions: modulating attention resources through mindfulness meditation. Front. Psychol. 3, 8. http://dx.doi.org/10.3389/fpsyg.2012.00290

Dickmann, M.H., Stanford-Blair, N., 2009. Mindful Leadership: A Brain-Based Framework. Orwin Press, Thousand Oaks, CA, PDF e-Book.

Gardener, H., 1983. Frames of Mind: The Theory of Multiple Intelligences. Basic Books, New York, NY.

Gold, E., Smith, A., Hoper, I., Herne, D., Tansey, G., Hulland, C., 2010. Mindfulness-based stress reduction (MBSR) for primary school teachers. J. Child Fam. Stud. 19 (2), 184–189. Available from: <http://dx.doi.org/10.1007/s10826-009-9344-0> (accessed 09.12.15.)

Goleman, D., Boyatzis, R., McKee, A., 2002. Primal Leadership: Realizing the Power of Emotional Intelligence. Harvard Business School Press, Boston, MA.

Goulding, A., Walton, G., Stephens, D., 2012. The importance of political and strategic skills for UK library leaders. Aust. Libr. J. 62 (2), 105–118. Available from: <http://dx.doi.org/10.1080/00049670.2012.10722680> (accessed 24.10.14.)

Hackman, J.R., 1998. Why teams don't work. In: Tindale, R.S. (Ed.), Theory and Research on Small Groups, Plenum Press, New York, NY, pp. 245–267.

Hanson, R., Mendius, R., 2009. Buddha's Brain: The Practical Neuroscience of Happiness, Love, and Wisdom. New Harbinger Publications, Inc, Oakland, CA, PDF e-Book.

Hernon, P., Rossiter, N., 2006. Emotional intelligence: which traits are most prized? Coll. Res. Libr. 67 (3), 260–275. Available from: <http://dx.doi.org/10.5860/crl.67.3.260> (accessed 18.11.14.)

Hopper, L., 2010. Mindful leadership. Georgia Libr. Q. 47 (2), 15–17. Available from: <http://digitalcommons.kennesaw.edu/glq/vol47/iss2/6> (accessed 18.11.14.)

Holzel, B.K., Ott, U., Gard, T., Hempel, H., Weygandt, M., Morgen, K., et al., 2007. Investigation of Mindfulness Meditation Practitioners with Voxel-Based Morphometry, vol. 3. Oxford University Press, Oxford, No. 1: pp. 55–61. Available from: <http://dx.doi.org/10.1093/scan/nsm038> (accessed 09.12.14.).

Institute for Mindful Leadership, Definitions. Last updated 2014. Available from: <http://instituteformindfulleadership.org/definitions/>.

IVAA Office, Cam 2020 the contribution of complementary and alternative medicine to sustainable healthcare in Europe. Eurocam. Last updated 2014. Available from: <http://ehtpa.eu/pdf/CAM2020-FINAL.pdf>.

Jack, A.I., Dawson, A., Begany, K., Leckie, R.L., Barry, K., Ciccia, A., et al., 2012. fMRI reveals reciprocal inhibition between social and physical cognitive domains. Neuroimage, 1–31. Available from: <http://dx.doi.org/10.1016/j.neuroimage.2012.10.061> (accessed 09.12.14.)

Jha, A.P., Kiyonaga, A., Wong, L., Gelfand, L., 2010. Examining the protective effects of mindfulness training on working memory capacity and affective experience.. Am. Psychol. Assoc. 10 (1), 54–64. Available from: <http://dx.doi.org/10.1037/a0018438> (accessed 01.10.14.)

Jha, G., British army to send 4,000 Buddhist troups to India for meditation to combat post-traumatic stress. Mail Online India. Last updated October 24, 2014. Available from: <http://www.dailymail.co.uk/indiahome/indianews/article-2246069/British-Army-send-4-000-Buddhist-troops-India-meditation-combat-post-traumatic-stress.html>.

Johns, H.E., Mosner, H.R., 1989. From trait to transformation: the evolution of leadership theories. Education 110 (1), 115–122. Available from: <http://connection.ebscohost.com/c/articles/4717838/from-trait-transformation-evolution-leadership-theories> (accessed 05.11.14.)

Kinsler, L., 2014. Born to be me… who am I again? The development of authentic leadership using evidence-based leadership coaching and mindfulness. Int. Coaching Psychol. Rev. 9 (1), 92–105.

Komives, S.P., Dugan, J.P., 2010. Contemporary leadership theories. In: Couto, R.A. (Ed.), Political and Civic Leadership, SAGE Publications, Washington, DC, pp. 111–120.

Kreitz, P.A., 2009. Leadership and emotional intelligence: a study of university library directors and their senior management teams. Coll. Res. Libr. 70 (6), 531–554. Available from: <http://dx.doi.org/10.5860/crl.70.6.531> (accessed 15.11.14.)

Langer, E., 2014. Mindfulness 25th Anniversary Edition. Da Capo Press, Boston, MA.

Langer, E.J., Moldoveanu, M., 2000. The construct of mindfulness. J. Soc. Issues 56 (1), 1–9. Available from: <http://dx.doi.org/10.1111/0022-4537.00148> (accessed 20.11.15.)

Lazar, S.W., Kerr, C.E., Wasserman, R.H., Gray, J.R., Greve, D.N., Treadway, M.T., et al., 2005. Meditation experience is associated with increased cortical thickness. Neuroreport 16 (17), 1893–1897. Available from: <http://www.ncbi.nlm.nih.gov/pmc/articles/PMC1361002/> (accessed 15.12.14.)

Lee, R.A., 2012. Accelerating the development and mitigating derailment of high potentials through mindfulness training. Ind. Organ. Psychol. 49 (3), 23–34. Available from: <http://www.siop.org/tip/jan12/04lee.aspx> (accessed 25.10.14.)

Lutz, A., Brefczynski-Lewis, J., Johnstone, T., Davidson, R.J., 2008. Regulation of the neural circuitry of emotion by compassion meditation: effects of meditative expertise. PLoS ONE 3 (3), 1–10. Available from: <http://dx.doi.org/10.1371/journal.pone.0001897> (accessed 09.12.14.)

Mason, F.M., Wetherbee, L.V., 2004. Learning to lead: an analysis of current training. Library Trends 53 (1), 187–217. Available from: <http://hdl.handle.net/2142/1723> (accessed 05.11.14.)

McKee, A., Boyatzis, R.E., 2008. Becoming a Resonant Leader: Develop Your Emotional Intelligence, Renew Your Relationships, Sustain Your Effectiveness. Harvard Business School Publishing, Boston, MA.

Moniz Jr, R.J., 2010. Practical and Effective Management of Libraries: Integrating Case Studies, General Management Theory, and Self-Understanding. Chandos Publishing, Oxford.

Naranjo, J.R., Schmidt, S., 2012. Is it me or not me? Modulation of perceptual motor awareness and visuomotor performance by mindfulness meditation. BMC Neurosci.

13 (1), 16. Available from: <http://dx.doi.org/10.1186/1471-2202-13-88> (accessed 25.10.14.)

Ray, J.L., Baker, L.T., Plowman, D.A., 2011. Organizational mindfulness in business schools. Acad. Manage. Learn. Educ. 10 (2), 188–203. Available from: <http://connection. ebscohost.com/c/articles/62798929/organizational-mindfulness-business-schools> (accessed 18.11.14.)

Robert K., Greenleaf center for servant leadership. About the Robert K. Greenleaf Center. Last updated 2014. Available from: <https://greenleaf.org/about-us/>.

Rossiter, N., Hernon, P., 2007. Making a Difference: Leadership and Academic Libraries. Libraries Unlimited, Westport, CT, PDF e-Book.

Singh, A.N.A., Kristeller, J.L., Antonino, R., Giommi, F., 2013. Advances in mindfulness research. Neuropsychiatry 3 (5), 467–470. Available from: <http://www.futuremedicine.com/doi/pdf/10.2217/npy.13.64> (accessed 05.12.14.)

Smith, E., Tapscott, L., 2010. Historic ideas into contemporary leadership theories: have formalized theories improved the field of leadership? Mid-Atl. Leadersh. Rev. 3 (1), 37. Available from: <http://cnu.edu/leadershipreview/archives/vol3iss1_smithtapscott. pdf> (accessed 15.11.14.)

Spearman, C., 1904. General intelligence, objectively determined and measured. Am. J. Psychol. 15, 201–293.

Stanely, E.A., Schaldach, J.M., 2011. Mindfulness-based mind fitness training (MMFT). Mind Fit. Train. Inst., 1–17. Available from: <http://www.mind-fitness-training.org/ MMFTOverviewNarrative.pdf> (accessed 05.12.14.)

Tang, Y.Y., Ma, Y., Wang, J., Fan, Y., Feng, S., Lu, Q., et al., 2007. Short-term meditation improves attention and self-regulation. Proc. Natl Acad. Sci. 104 (43), 17152–17156. Available from: <http://www.pnas.org/content/104/43/17152.full.pdf+html> (accessed 04.10.14.)

Vogus, T.J., Sutcliffe, K.M., 2012. Organizational mindfulness and mindful organizing: a reconciliation and path forward. Acad. Manage. Learn. Educ. 11 (4), 722–735. Available from: <http://dx.doi.org/10.5465/amle.2011.0002> (accessed 18.11.14.)

Weick, K.E., Sutcliffe, K.M., Obstfeld, D., 1999. Organizing for high reliability: processes of collective mindfulness. In: Sutton, R.S., Staw, B.M. (Eds.) Research in Organizational Behavior, Jai Press, Stanford, CT, pp. 514–524.

CHAPTER 8

The Solo Librarian

Lisa Moniz and Howard Slutzky

MINDFULNESS AND THE SOLO LIBRARIAN: AN ANTIDOTE TO BURNOUT

A solo librarian can be defined as "an isolated librarian or information collector/provider who has no professional peers within the immediate organization."[1] A couple of decades ago, the majority of solo librarians worked in smaller, specialized libraries. At the turn of the century, the Special Libraries Association estimated that between 5000 and 7000 solos were working in special libraries.[1] Today, there are more and more solo librarians working in all kinds of libraries—public, academic, school, and corporate institutions. In the United Kingdom, such a person is sometimes referred to as a "one-man band" or "one-person librarian (OPL)."[2] In Australia and New Zealand, they are called "sole-charge librarians."[1]

Some librarians choose to work alone. These are individuals who enjoy the variety of the workload, want to be independent, and prefer being the sole decision maker in their library. But at the same time, they are required to do it all, so solo librarians who take this role voluntarily would be the exception rather than the rule. Most librarians would not choose to accept the extra challenges that solo librarians face. They usually answer to supervisors who are not librarians,[1] so the nature of their work is not always understood, making it even harder to justify their worth and the value of their library programs in uncertain economic times. Solo librarians feel isolated from their peers and have less opportunity than other librarians to participate in professional development experiences because there is no one to run the program in their absence. They often have small budgets

[1] Siess, J.A., 1999. Flying solo: librarian, manage thyself. Am. Libr. 30 (2), 32.
[2] Hornung, E., 2013. On your own but not alone: one-person librarians in Ireland and their perceptions of continuing professional development. Libr. Trends 61 (3), 675. Available from: <http://muse.jhu.edu/journals/lib/summary/v061/61.3.hornung.html> (accessed 01.12.14.).

The Mindful Librarian.
© 2016 by R. Moniz, J. Eshleman, J. Henry, H. Slutzky and L. Moniz. Published by Elsevier Ltd. All rights reserved.

and limited access to networking opportunities.[3] In the past few decades, an ever increasing number of librarians have found themselves in situations where they are working alone due to budget cuts. Sadly, the uncertain economic times have forced most institutions to cut library staff along with other resources, and almost all librarians are learning to do more with less.

This scenario is never truer than in public school libraries. School libraries are perhaps the most stressful library situation to work in. In their article, "Talk Me off the Ledge: Surviving Solo Librarianship," Cynthia Karabush and Pam Pleviak refer to school librarians working alone as "the air traffic controllers of the library world, serving hundreds if not thousands of students."[4] School librarians are, first and foremost, teachers, and they are evaluated as such. Not only are they curriculum specialists, creating lesson plans and collaborating with faculty to teach information literacy and technology skills to students, school librarians are expected to implement a dynamic media program. They do the ordering, cataloging, reference work, reader advisory services, weeding of outdated materials, and budgeting; serve on school committees; plan author visits; organize book fairs; and oversee every aspect of the library. They are often asked to do other school duties as well, such as bus duty after school or monitoring students in the halls or cafeteria. School library media coordinators nearly always work alone, and they are extremely fortunate if they have a library assistant or volunteers. Those working in high-poverty schools are even less likely to have the support of volunteers from a parent organization.

In some school districts, library programs are being scrapped altogether, or library media coordinators must split their time between two schools. In her article, "The Solo Act," solo librarian Laura Bishop cites dismal results from a 2012 report on Pennsylvania's public school libraries. In Philadelphia, 103 public schools do not have libraries, and over half of Pennsylvania's students statewide do not have access to a full-time librarian.[5] In school districts such as these, stressed-out solo school librarians live with the additional worry of job security and whether their

[3] Ibid., 676.
[4] Karabush, C., Pleviak, P., 2011. Talk me off the ledge: surviving solo librarianship. Know. Quest 40 (2), 49.
[5] Bishop, L., 2013. The solo act. Know. Quest 41 (5), 32.

positions will be eliminated. "Downsizing is always around the corner, and for a solo, downsizing means you."[6]

Anne Busch, a high school librarian in Missouri, was told that her full-time library clerk was being reassigned elsewhere, and there were no plans to hire another. Once she found herself working solo, Busch had to find a way to adapt—and quickly. This required her to reflect deeply on all aspects of her media program. "It was time to prioritize, delegate, streamline, and be very realistic about the personal and educational costs of downsizing."[7] Busch's survival strategies included some tough decisions about managing her own self-care to protect herself from burnout. "An exhausted librarian is an ineffective librarian," she observed.[7] She opted to curtail library hours, including closing so that she could take a short lunch every day, because she recognized the need for a break in the day, not for idleness but as an opportunity to connect with her colleagues. She asked for help by enlisting well-trained volunteers and student aides and prioritized her lists of chores with realistic timelines. For instance, weeding was not going to happen during the school day. Busch even set a goal to get more sleep to improve her health and increase stamina.[7] In other words, while she was a solo librarian, she also intended to be a mindful one.

Librarianship is demanding work, and the profession is facing a plethora of challenges, including budget cuts at nearly every institution in spite of a growing demand for information and services. Ironically, to outsiders, the library profession can appear to be quiet, orderly, and relatively low stress. Many people are drawn to this profession because the image of libraries is that they are quiet, serene places to work. But the reality is, in an ever-increasing number of libraries, nothing could be further from the truth. Margaux DelGuidice, a high school librarian in Garden City, New York, enrolled in library school to escape, as she describes, "the cut-throat world of corporate America."[8] As a student sitting in her introductory reference course, she had to stop herself from laughing as her instructor cautioned the class about librarian burnout. "The thought that a librarian would be overwhelmed and frazzled by his or her job did not strike me as a reality."[8] It was not long after she accepted a full-time job in a school

---

[6] Siess, J.A., 1999. Flying solo: librarian, manage thyself. Am. Libr. 30 (2), 33.

[7] Busch, A., 2011. The maxed out librarian: how i learned to keep smiling and remain effective as a solo librarian. Know. Quest 40 (2), 16.

[8] DelGuidice, M., 2011. Avoiding school librarian burnout: simple steps to ensure your personal best. Libr. Media Connect., 22.

library that DelGuidice began to experience some of the stress that her professor had been talking about. Like so many other librarians in these tough economic times, she began working harder than ever to justify the value of her library program, all while serving hundreds of students.

Librarianship and teaching are professions dedicated to serving others and putting their needs first. Solo librarians who do not find ways to take care of themselves and become more mindful and self-compassionate are at the greatest risk for burnout. It is important for solo librarians to recognize the physical, behavioral, and emotional signs in order to develop proactive and mindful strategies.[9] There are physical symptoms to watch for, such as body aches, severe exhaustion, and decreased immunity to illness.[9] For example, a librarian who teaches classes all day without taking time to go to the restroom or eat properly may begin having recurring urinary tract infections, headaches, or cold symptoms that will not go away. Feelings of anxiety on the way to work about facing the day may lead to sleeplessness or nausea when pulling into the parking lot. As these symptoms intensify with stress, the librarian may need to take sick days, compounding the problem by becoming further behind in day-to-day tasks.

Emotionally, those experiencing burnout no longer derive happiness or satisfaction from their work. These are the librarians who find themselves annoyed when they are asked for help and may snap at students or coworkers. Such questions from students or colleagues are viewed as interruptions rather than opportunities to empower others. Victims of burnout may exhibit signs of depression, withdraw from others, and turn down social invitations because they are too tired to enjoy life outside work. Time outside work is spent finishing lesson plans, answering emails, worrying about the next day, or simply "recovering." Eventually, coworkers begin to avoid burned-out librarians because their attitude is so pessimistic or apathetic, according to DelGuidice.[9]

Solo librarians must mindfully take care of their physical, mental, and emotional health, or else they will be less than effective professionally, to say the least. Of all the resources that support them in their work, such as new technologies, support from colleagues, and rich library collections, "we must consider ourselves our most precious resource," according to Karabush and Pleviak.[10] Much has been written by librarians about

---

[9] Ibid., 23.
[10] Karabush, C., Pleviak, P., 2011. Talk me off the ledge: surviving solo librarianship. Know. Quest 40 (2), 52.

strategies to combat or avoid burnout, such as learning to say no, setting realistic goals, reaching out to others in professional organizations, and participating in recharging professional development experiences. An area yet to be fully explored is how practicing mindfulness could help solo librarians alleviate stress and burnout. In the field of psychology, the term *mindfulness* describes a state of awareness, and it also can refer to the practices that promote that awareness, such as meditation, yoga, and t'ai chi.[11] The concept evolved from Buddhism more than 2600 years ago, but it has recently grown in popularity due largely to the work of scientist Jon Kabat-Zinn, who studied at the Massachusetts Institute of Technology (MIT). Kabat-Zinn defines mindfulness as "awareness, cultivated by paying attention in a sustained and particular way: on purpose, in the present moment, and non-judgmentally."[12] As mentioned in earlier chapters, Kabat-Zinn is the founder of mindfulness-based stress reduction (MBSR), "a form of guided meditation where one makes time each day to practice, and over time, the practice spills over into all aspects of one's life in a natural way."[13] Kabat-Zinn originally developed MBSR to help individuals suffering from chronic pain and stress-related disorders. According to him, "Mindfulness training has been shown to be effective in reducing stress, anxiety, panic and depression."[14]

Mindfulness practice is growing in popularity—and for good reason. Researchers' interest in studying mindfulness has increased as studies reveal its beneficial effects time after time. The results of studies about mindfulness practice and its benefits speak for themselves. "Current literature points toward the potential for mindfulness to affect the structure and neural patterns present in the brain."[15] In their paper summarizing mindfulness research findings, Flaxman and Flook describe findings suggesting that doing meditation can offset cortical thinning brought about by aging and heightened empathetic awareness.[15] There are studies empirically supporting the idea that mindfulness practice boosts working memory,

[11] Davis, D.M., Hayes, J.A., What are the benefits of mindfulness? Monitor 43 (7), 64. Available from: <http://www.apa.org/monitor/2012/07-08/ce-corner.aspx>.

[12] Kabat-Zinn, J., 2012. Mindfulness for Beginners: Reclaiming the Present Moment and Your Life. Sounds True, Boulder, CO, p. 1.

[13] Ibid., p. 2.

[14] Ibid., p. 16.

[15] Flaxman, G., Flook, L., Brief summary of mindfulness research. 1. Available from: <http://marc.ucla.edu/workfiles/pdfs/MARC-mindfulness-research-summary.pdf>.

reduces stress, improves focus, and creates greater cognitive flexibility.[16] Socially, it has been proven to develop feelings of empathy and compassion toward others and reduce emotional reactivity.[17] Perhaps this is why people who are not "new age" or religious are buying into this concept because they experience such a difference in the quality of their lives.

Many organizations around the world have begun to recognize the benefits of mindfulness programs, from Fortune 500 companies and the military, to schools and universities, and even to governments.[18] In 2013, 50 members of Parliament in the United Kingdom were taking part in weekly mindfulness sessions, with 25 more members signed up for future sessions.[19] When governments embrace mindfulness programs, it is easier for other parts of that community to start mindfulness programs as well, including schools, which are often run by the government. In his book *A Mindful Nation*, Congressman Tim Ryan (D-OH) explores how mindfulness has the power to change all aspects of government and, essentially, the world. With regard to education, he asks, "What does an education system look like if a teacher approaches each student with awareness of, not only their own fears, worries, and concerns, but also those of the students? How much better could students do if, instead of worrying about what others thought of them, they mobilized their attention and could bring more relaxation and focus to the task at hand?"[20] Mindfulness can help.

Students and teachers need mindfulness practice, and so do solo librarians, many of whom are teachers (as already stated). The digital age is stressing society out, and digital technology is affecting the attention span of our students. There are students in schools all over the world studying and practicing mindfulness programs, with amazing results. "Learning to breathe through reactivity is a profoundly valuable life skill that serves children and teens in their immediate stressful environments, while providing them with a sustaining practice that they can carry into

---

[16] Davis, D.M., Hayes, J.A., 2011. What are the benefits of mindfulness? A practice review of psychotherapy-related research. Psychotherapy 48 (2), 200–201.

[17] Ibid., 201.

[18] Kabat-Zinn, J., 2012. Mindfulness for Beginners: Reclaiming the Present Moment and Your Life. Sounds True, Boulder, CO, p. 119.

[19] Brownbridge, L., 2014. Mindfulness in schools: where governments, education and mindfulness meet. Nat. Life, 18.

[20] Ryan, T., 2012. A Mindful Nation: How a Simple Practice Can Help Us Reduce Stress, Improve Performance and Recapture the American Spirit. Hay House, Carlsbad, CA, p. 21.

adulthood."[21] Indeed, mindfulness programs in schools have been proven to help both students and teachers develop coping skills to deal with stress and anxiety; encourage empathy, compassion, and a sense of community; develop clarity of thought and concentration; improve interpersonal relationships; raise awareness of habitual reactivity; create emotional regulation and balance; and leave participants feeling calmer and happier.[22] In his book *Mindfulness for Beginners*, Kabat-Zinn states that mindfulness would be helpful in any profession, but he addresses the teaching profession specifically: "If you are a teacher at any level, from preschool through graduate school, mindfulness may be a valuable ally in so many different aspects of your work and calling. It may also satisfy something deep within yourself that hungers for authenticity, connectivity, and creativity that emerges as more than the sum of its individual components."[18]

One formal practice of mindfulness is meditation, and in meditation, there is an awareness of one's breath. Our lives depend on breathing. Meditators use breathing as a tool for bringing them back into the present moment "because we are only breathing now—the last breath is gone, the next one hasn't come yet—it is always a matter of this one."[23] Yet, it is not the breathing that is the focus of meditation, but the awareness of each moment. As Kabat-Zinn says, "If you can be mindful in this moment, it is possible for the next moment to be hugely and creatively different—because you are aware and not imposing anything on it in advance."[24]

Dr Howard Slutzky on Conquering Irrational Beliefs

Albert Ellis, the father of cognitive-behavioral therapy and founder of rational emotive behavior therapy (REBT), discovered that people's beliefs strongly affected their emotional functioning. He proposed that it is our beliefs, rather than events or situations, that cause our emotional and behavioral difficulties. In this approach, which he called "The A, B, C's and D's of Emotions," the *A* stands for the *activating event* (e.g., a break-up). The *B* stands for our irrational or maladaptive *beliefs* (e.g., "There must be something wrong with me." "No one else will ever love me."). The *C* stands for the emotional and behavioral *consequences* (e.g., depression, social withdrawal, and alcohol abuse). The *D* stands for *disputing* the irrational

---

[21] Brownbridge, L., 2014. Mindfulness in schools: where governments, education and mindfulness meet. Nat. Life, 19.

[22] Ibid., 20.

[23] Ibid., p. 11.

[24] Ibid., p. 16.

and maladaptive beliefs (e.g., "There are plenty of other fish in the sea." "You deserve better than that."). One aspect of mindfulness involves identifying and disputing the maladaptive beliefs that are negatively influencing our emotions and our behaviors. This is often quite difficult because our beliefs have become so automatic. They usually reside just beneath the surface of our conscious awareness, but deep enough to avoid any evaluation or modification.

Cognitive therapy has been most widely used for the treatment of depressive disorders, but it also can be applied to a host of other issues, including adult anxiety disorders. In my clinical experience, and in my work with students, I also find it useful for issues such as jealousy in relationships, anger management issues, grief and loss, and even academic challenges. One of the most common forms of anxiety is that which is associated with (not caused by) presenting in front of an audience. Most of my students are surprised when I tell them that I used to suffer severe panic attacks when speaking in front of an audience. Some students have told me that if they learn that there is a presentation requirement for a course, they will transfer out and take the class with a professor who has no such requirement as part of their course agenda. So, in this situation, the activating event is clearly the course requirement of presenting in front of a class. One might suspect that the emotional (and physiological) response is associated with a fear of failure, pressure to succeed, and concern of a bad grade. While this might be part of the picture, this fear reaction is problematic, even for those who have presentations that are weighted very low (e.g., 5% of the course grade), and for those for whom there is no grade at all (e.g., getting called on in class to respond to a question, to read aloud, or even to introduce themselves to the class as part of an icebreaker activity on the first day of the term). So mindfulness in this scenario involves identifying the beliefs that underlie the fear and panic, challenging the validity of those beliefs, and offering alternative beliefs that are more rational, adaptive, and valid.

In the scenario of presentation anxiety, for example, the beliefs that typically predominate are concerns of judgment, scrutiny, and criticism by members of the audience. Is it possible that one or more audience members will react this way? Sure. But then what? What does that mean for the individual afflicted with paralyzing anxiety? The process of belief identification can be a multilevel process of exploration. While our mind and body react to these beliefs as if the situation is life or death, the reality is not quite so dangerous (and this should be part of the process of disputing the maladaptive beliefs).

In fact, I touch on this in my Introductory Psychology class during a section on the sympathetic nervous system. Among its multiple functions is the triggering of the fight-or-flight response. Whether we perceive a real or imagined threat, our sympathetic nervous system reflexively shifts into survival mode and quickly mobilizes our body's resources in preparation for fight or flight. In the case of presentation anxiety, I inform students that while they are trying to force their body to "fight" through the presentation, their body is telling them to "Run! Run as fast as you can!" Specifically, their heart rate has increased to provide more oxygen to their muscles so they can run faster and longer. Their breathing has increased to provide more oxygen to the blood. Adrenaline has increased to allow them more stamina and strength. And endorphins have increased to reduce the experience of any pain resulting from the infliction of injury from the "predator" or the act of trying to outrun it (e.g., a twisted ankle). None of these things are designed to improve one's presentation skills! While I am not suggesting that students honor their sympathetic response by running out of the classroom, educating them about this process is a useful tool for gaining mindfulness into their struggle with presentation anxiety. It can be a useful tool in helping them to dispute their maladaptive beliefs by first normalizing their panic reaction, and then adjusting those beliefs so that they reflect a more realistic interpretation of the "danger" associated with public speaking.

So with this approach, mindfulness involves identifying the set of beliefs underlying the emotional and behavioral challenges that we have become conditioned to activate when certain triggers arise. The first step toward this aspect of mindfulness involves an introduction to the concept of cognitive therapy and the ABC's (and D's) of emotions. This initial educational component is an important step because it helps prepare the client (or recipient) for the work that follows and ideally helps to lower the defenses so the person is better able to identify any maladaptive and irrational beliefs. The next steps involve the identification of the beliefs themselves, and then disputing them. This can often be the most challenging part, as these beliefs are so automatic and out of one's immediate conscious awareness. Based on my work as a clinical psychologist, I strongly believe that psychotherapy offers the best context in which to accomplish this aspect of mindfulness practice. Self-help books offer an additional area of resources. Two suggestions are *Feeling Good: The New Mood Therapy*, by David Burns, and *Mind Over Mood: Changing How You Feel by Changing the Way You Think*, by Dennis Greenberger and Christine Padesky.

As solo librarians, practicing mindfulness to stay in the present moment is a powerful strategy that combats anxiety. Because they are often multitasking, solo librarians experience a barrage of thoughts and anxious feelings that everything cannot be accomplished. "What if I don't have the budget proposal ready by the deadline?" "What if I lose my job?" Practicing mindfulness meditation allows one to step out of the anxiety for a time and turn off worries about the future, allowing a person to switch from "doing mode" to "being mode." Kabat-Zinn states, "Most of our lives, we are absorbed in doing; in getting things done, in going rapidly from one thing to the next, or in multitasking—attempting to juggle a bunch of different things at the very same time."[25] But what kind of quality of life is this? Is it really living, to rush around in a state of half-attention, not really listening to others, eating and drinking without tasting, or living with a constant feeling of frustration that one cannot accomplish enough?

One major feeling of frustration for solo librarians is that there is not enough time in the day. Ironically, the antidote to this feeling is to take time to practice meditation, and those who feel they don't have the time are the ones who would benefit the most. Ihnen and Flynn (2008) states: "Time spent in inner stillness shifts your perception of time."[26] Mindfulness takes dedication and practice to start with, so in the beginning, the solo librarian must acknowledge that time must be set aside each day to reap the benefits. For example, participants in an MBSR program go through an 8-week training session where they practice meditation for at least 45 min a day. One does not just say, "Okay, I'm going to be more aware of each moment." It has to be learned, implemented, and sustained through ongoing, regular practice. The solo librarian may be reluctant to add one more event to an already busy day, but the results are well worth the time and effort.

It takes patience, but the good news is that mindfulness in the workplace can be practiced in small doses. The first step is making the decision to give full attention, as often as possible, to what is happening around you. One does not have to be an MBSR participant or an expert at meditation to begin making and experiencing changes. In his blog, "Staying Present in the Classroom," Chase Mielke gives some simple but powerful strategies for teachers to use to bring themselves back to the present in the middle of a hectic day. The first, and most important, step is conscious breathing. Simply notice your breathing.[27] Step 2 is to find daily mindfulness triggers to help you remember to breathe, such as a designated location in the classroom (or library) marked with a sign that says "Breathe"; the mindful consumption of a cup of coffee or tea, where one truly savors the flavor; or

[25] Ibid., p. 18.

[26] Ihnen, A., Flynn, C., 2008. The Complete Idiot's Guide to Mindfulness. Penguin, New York, NY, p. 238.

[27] Mielke, C., 2015. Staying present in the classroom: practicing mindful teaching. We Are Teachers (blog). Available from: <http://www.weareteachers.com/blogs/post/2015/03/03/staying-present-in-the-classroom-practicing-mindful-teaching>.

even the school bells ringing between classes. All of these can be powerful reminders to stop—and breathe in and breathe out.[27] Sharon Salzberg, a meditation teacher, blogged, "Within ourselves, we have many resources to become more productive and feel happier at work and beyond. Foremost among them is meditation—a portable practice that commonly relies on the breath. Meditation can open up space in our minds and hearts to help us reframe problems at work as sources of clarity and strength."[28]

According to Kabat-Zinn, there are seven fundamental attitudes of mindfulness practice: nonjudging, patience, beginner's mind, trust, non-striving, acceptance, and letting go.[29] As individuals practice mindfulness, these attitudes permeate their lives and transform their work. Examining these attitudes in the context of solo librarianship in a school library setting creates a convincing argument for overworked librarians to consider the practice of mindfulness as a remedy for burnout.

Attitude 1: Nonjudging

Nonjudging is when an individual discovers that every thought is a judgment of one kind or another. It is enough to just be aware and recognize these thoughts and judgments. In her book *Self-Compassion*, Kristin Neff includes a quote by the famous psychologist, Carl Rogers, who said, "The curious paradox is that when I accept myself just as I am, then I can change."[30] Solo librarians who are struggling with feelings of inadequacy often have a dialogue inside their heads, with thoughts such as, "I can't do all of this. It's impossible." There is defeating self-talk playing in one's head that the individual may not even be aware of. The stillness that comes with meditation allows one to become aware of one's thoughts. Once that happens, one can release them, or even change them. At the heart of mindfulness is an attitude of gentleness and compassion toward oneself.[31]

[28] Salzberg, S., 2014. How to find happiness at work, even if you don't like your job. Sharon Salzberg, Meditation Teacher & Author (blog). Available from: <http://www.sharonsalzberg.com/find-happiness-work-even-dont-like-job/>.

[29] Kabat-Zinn, J., 2012. Mindfulness for Beginners: Reclaiming the Present Moment and Your Life. Sounds True, Boulder, CO, pp. 122–123.

[30] Neff, K., 2011. Self-Compassion: The Proven Power of Being Kind to Yourself. HarperCollins, New York, NY, p. 159.

[31] Kabat-Zinn, J., 2012. Mindfulness for Beginners: Reclaiming the Present Moment and Your Life. Sounds True, Boulder, CO, p. 79.

In her blog "Kindness and the Solo Librarian," Nancy Murrey-Settle describes a philosophy grounded in the acronym K.I.N.D.[32] The *K* stands for *kindness*. "Be kind to yourself if you get off track from your goals," she advises.[32] The *I* stands for *importance*. "Pick goals that are important to you personally that you are sure to accomplish."[32] The *N* stands for *noticeable*. Post goals visibly and stay visible so that others will notice the work being done. Finally, the *D* is for *developing*. One should embrace goals as developing. Some will fail or need to be adjusted. But the overall philosophy is one of nonjudgment with regard to what a solo librarian can and cannot accomplish. "The only way to create a kind school library where young people feel accepted and appreciated is 'to start with the way we treat ourselves.' If we are realistic about the competing demands for our time as a solo librarian, we can begin to set realistic goals that we can and will achieve."[32] Settle makes an important point: If the solo librarian is kind to himself or herself, the library itself will be a friendly, compassionate place. With practice, the nonjudging attitude encourages a feeling of loving kindness that spills over into other areas of life, allowing mindfulness participants to view others differently. If we are less judgmental of ourselves, we are also less likely to be judgmental of others. In libraries and in teaching, relationships are key. If patrons do not want to be in the library or are intimidated to ask for help, then the library and librarian have no purpose and will cease to exist. As covered in detail in Chapter 3, studies have shown that some library patrons get library anxiety and are reluctant to ask for help because they do not want to admit that they need the help or they fear being judged as incompetent. It is much more likely that patrons will approach and receive help from a librarian who is not likely to pass judgment or make them feel inferior. "Feelings of compassion and loving-kindness toward others can be developed and refined," along with those feelings directed toward oneself.[33]

Attitude 2: Patience

To be productive members of society, we are socialized to be impatient and driven. Solo librarians are often required to multitask, yet at the same time, it is the nature of the work to be constantly interrupted. This can be frustrating and make it easy to lose focus. A key part of mindfulness

[32] Murrey-Settle, N., 2014. Kindness and the solo librarian. YALSA (blog). Available from: <http://yalsa.ala.org/blog/2014/08/18/kindness-for-the-solo-librarian/>.
[33] Kabat-Zinn, J., 2012. Mindfulness for Beginners: Reclaiming the Present Moment and Your Life. Sounds True, Boulder, CO, p. 90.

practice is learning how to step out of "clock time"[34] and learn to focus on one moment at a time. *Patience* is very important quality in professions such as librarianship, where you serve or teach others. People are struggling with whatever it is that they need, such as finding resources for a research paper, and they are relying on librarians to help them. Librarians must have patience when being interrupted. If the librarian is impatient or comes across as feeling bothered, a student or patron will become discouraged and is not going to approach the librarian for help.

An even greater amount of patience is required of school librarians who work with small children; and the younger the child, the more patience is required. Mindfulness teaches us that things unfold in their own time. Those who choose to work with children cannot be impatient. Children are not products like those created in the business world. They are little people who are growing and developing over many years. Children are innocent and often do not have the necessary background knowledge or skills to figure things out without a great deal of help. They do not understand it when a teacher (or librarian) loses patience with them, and it is not their fault. Young children also tend to worry if they see that a teacher is unhappy or in a bad mood, and they may feel they have done something wrong to cause it.

Solo librarians who are terribly stressed out must find a way to overcome negative feelings and exude a positive attitude, lest a student perceive them as unapproachable or possibly even scary. The goal is for students to want to come to the library and to empower them to become lifelong library users. School librarians must be mindful that the students they serve are coming from diverse backgrounds and have varied skill levels. If they are impatient, they are going to miss valuable teachable moments with students and miss signs of their progress. For example, rather than hurrying to the shelf and grabbing the book that Jimmy wants, the patient librarian is going to walk Jimmy through the steps of searching the online catalog and watching Jimmy's beaming face as he pulls the book off the shelf, proud because he found it partly on his own. The good news is that most students and teachers (including children) recognize when an overworked librarian is doing the best that he or she can, and having a patient attitude is contagious. Solo librarian Anne Busch reflected, "I found that if I am patient and doing my best to cover all the bases, most of the teachers and students will be patient, too."[35]

[34] Ibid., p. 124.
[35] Busch, A., The maxed out librarian: How I learned to keep smiling and remain effective as a solo librarian. Know. Quest 40 (2), 17.

Attitude 3: Beginner's Mind

Beginner's mind is about resting in the awareness of not knowing.[36] Our ideas, opinions, and knowledge can actually get in the way of recognizing what we do not know. According to Kabat-Zinn, "Beginners come to new experiences not knowing so much and therefore open. This openness is very creative… The trick is never to lose it. You can remember from time to time that each moment is fresh and new."[37] In practicing mindfulness, one calls on the beginner's mind repeatedly. Librarians who are burned out need a fresh way of looking at their work. They have, in essence, lost sight of their contribution to the world. They are so overwhelmed with stress that they have forgotten why they chose the profession in the first place and need to be reminded of how much they have learned, how far they have come, and also how much opportunity for growth and potential lies ahead. "One of the most direct ways in which we change the world is through our livelihood. Through mindfulness practice, we can come to see more clearly our skills, our purpose, our unique contribution and how they fit into the world."[38]

Beginner's mind is an important concept for those solo librarians working with children. Children naturally have a beginner's mind. Sometimes teachers and school librarians forget that children do not have the background knowledge or experience to fully understand new ideas. They are the ultimate open books, and it is helpful to look at the world as children experience it, learning new things for the first time. When children are very young, they are going to need more assistance from the library staff in finding materials in the library or learning to use a database. Librarians who teach children while keeping the attitude of beginner's mind will be able to teach information skills more thoroughly, approaching the lesson as if it were brand new. They will also notice when the children respond to the lesson with understanding, exhibiting a joyful excitement about learning. This observation can create an awareness of the value of libraries and library work. It is a reminder to librarians who may be at risk of burning out that the work that they are doing is shaping lives.

---

[36] Kabat-Zinn, J., 2012. Mindfulness for Beginners: Reclaiming the Present Moment and Your Life. Sounds True, Boulder, CO, p. 124.

[37] Ibid., p. 9.

[38] Ihnen, A., Flynn, C., 2008. The Complete Idiot's Guide to Mindfulness. Penguin, New York, NY, p. 257.

Attitude 4: Trust

Deep listening is the essence of mindfulness.[39] When people are over-worked, they do not take the time to listen to their thoughts or their bod-ies, and they lose touch with themselves. Mindfulness is about *trusting* our bodies and being in touch with our senses. For instance, much has been much written about mindful eating. How many times do solo librarians inhale lunch at their desks without tasting the food? It happens too often. Or perhaps this scenario is familiar: Susie is exhausted, driving home after an especially stressful day working in an elementary school library, and she is feeling like she needs a reward. She pulls up at a fast food drive-through window for a milkshake, which she drinks while driving the rest of the way home. As Susie pulls into her driveway, she realizes that she did not even taste the sweet drink, and she feels full and bloated rather than rewarded. What Susie's body really needed was a nap, but she was not paying atten-tion to the signals until she arrived at home. By then, she had made some wrong choices for herself. This example illustrates that only when one is mindful and listening to his or her body, can an individual determine what he or she really needs and make effective decisions about self-care.

When people are overworked and multitasking, they also cannot lis-ten deeply to others, which is a crucial skill for librarians. As stated earlier, relationships are key and patrons are relying on librarians to help them. Deep listening is imperative for a successful reference interview or readers' advisory services. How can one determine what is really needed if listen-ing is not taking place? When people are not being mindful, they may nod as someone is speaking and then walk away, realizing that they did not really hear what was being said.

Attitude 5: Nonstriving

Professionals are taught that to make progress, get *somewhere*. Just for a few minutes, what would it be like to have permission to just be, and not feel the crazy pressure to get it all accomplished? Sometimes one needs to just let oneself be in, in Kabat-Zinn's words, "the timeless quality of the pres-ent moment we call now" with no place to go, nothing to do, nothing to attain.[40] The *nonstriving* attitude sounds like a paradox to the busy life of a solo librarian. One might think it means not taking care of responsibilities,

[39] Kabat-Zinn, J., 2012. Mindfulness for Beginners: Reclaiming the Present Moment and Your Life. Sounds True, Boulder, CO, p. 5.
[40] Ibid., p. 129.

but that is not the case at all. It is about taking time to be in stillness and being fully in the moment through the experience of meditation, and as a result, intimately knowing one's own mind through systematic cultivation, "and that cultivation itself comes out of the discipline of attending. ... It is the how of coming to our senses moment by moment."[41] Rather than trying to get someplace else or waiting for life to begin, it is living life now, in each moment.

The attitude of nonstriving and living each moment can spill over into untold areas of life in a positive way. Perhaps solo librarians could allow themselves to take a break or spend moments in stillness, without judgment. Everyone needs breaks; in fact, breaks can actually make workers more productive. The solo librarian with no assistant may come to recognize that breaks are necessary and valuable. For example, rather than eating at the desk, a solo librarian may consider closing the library and eating lunch with other colleagues. This decision would not be a waste of time. The librarian is forging relationships with colleagues and getting a needed change of scenery. Or perhaps the librarian will choose to eat lunch alone and take a few minutes to meditate and refresh the mind, incorporating the practice of mindfulness and reaping its benefits during the remainder of the workday.

Attitude 6: Acceptance

The attitude of *acceptance* is often misunderstood. It does not mean passive resignation, but rather an awareness of a situation or circumstance that "can give you a place to stand, an orientation for taking appropriate action in the next moment."[42] Librarians are encouraged to make time for reflective practice, which is essential to growth as a professional. With an attitude of acceptance, solo librarians can find peace with their situation, or see things as they really are without denial in order to make changes. One cannot plan for the future, set goals, or solve problems unless there is a true picture of what the library program is like and what is needed now. When people slow down and looks at things as they are, they can see what is really important, what really needs doing, what can wait another day, and what cannot be done at all.[43] This is critical, because when time is limited, one must prioritize goals and make choices. In her article

---

[41] Ibid., p. 80.
[42] Ibid., p. 130.
[43] Ihnen, A., Flynn, C., 2008. The Complete Idiot's Guide to Mindfulness. Penguin, New York, NY, p. 49.

"The Solo Act," Laura Bishop describes setting S.M.A.R.T. goals, which stands for specific, measurable, attainable, relevant, and timebound.[44] Her first recommendation for what she has learned as a solo librarian is to be realistic about time and to pace oneself. Accept that there are circumstances beyond one's control, and become comfortable with the idea of limitations. It is difficult to acknowledge the reality that everything will not get done, but solo librarians must accept that they cannot be all things to all people.[45] With regard to goal setting, Bishop recommends having a clear plan and strategizing, down to the most minute detail. When one is constantly busy, there is no time to prioritize what is important and plan beyond the next day, but prioritizing and focus are of utmost importance to survival.[44] Mindfulness allows solo librarians to reflect on the situation, accept it, and then set goals to be proactive rather than reactive.

Attitude 7: Letting Go

Letting go means having an attitude of nonattachment to the outcome. This attitude can give one a liberating sense of resilience, or, as Kabat-Zinn puts it, "the freedom to choose how to respond inwardly to our circumstances—even if our outer circumstances are beyond our control."[46] With regard to stress management, this line of thought is truly liberating. Practicing mindfulness can actually help turn off the stress response. This is key because it gets to the root of stress—it is not just treating the symptoms.[47] People spend money on blood pressure medications or take sleeping pills, but those just treat the symptoms of stress, not the root of it. Stress comes from the inside out, so if one can change his response to it, then one can control it.[47] Practicing mindfulness does not mean that one will get a free pass from suffering. Unfortunately, suffering is part of the human condition. But part of letting go and living moment to moment is acknowledging that there is a law of impermanence: "the fact that everything, without exception, is always changing, that things will not, cannot stay the same forever."[46] The knowledge that things won't always be a certain way can be a comforting thought to a librarian who is unhappy with

---

[44] Bishop, L., 2013. The solo act. Know. Quest 41 (5), 32.

[45] Ibid., 31.

[46] Kabat-Zinn, J., 2012. Mindfulness for Beginners: Reclaiming the Present Moment and Your Life. Sounds True, Boulder, CO, p. 97.

[47] Olpin, M., Bracken, S., Unwind! 7 Principles for a Stress-Free Life. Franklin Covey, New York, NY, p. 4.

his or her situation. According to Sharon Salzberg, one can literally train oneself to feel happier by practicing mindfulness. She says, "Mindfulness redefines our attention so we can connect more fully to the present moment, and let go of biases, habits, fears, and so on."[48] Librarians who are happy in their work are far more likely to create thriving library programs.

CONCLUSION

In conclusion, although solo librarians may need to be reminded of their worth, their work makes a valuable difference in the lives of patrons. They are experts in all aspects of librarianship, from cataloging to teaching information literacy concepts. No one in the organization knows everything they know, and they accomplish great things despite many obstacles. The hard truth is that solo librarians may not be able to control many aspects of their situations, such as dwindling resources and endless responsibilities. But the great news is that mindfulness can help control how they respond and feel about their work in life-changing ways. The great writer Maya Angelou once said, "You may not control all the events that happen to you, but you can decide not to be reduced by them." Practicing mindfulness can help solo librarians manage stressful work environments and rediscover the joys of promoting literacy and empowering minds.

RECOMMENDED RESOURCES

Kabat-Zinn, J., 2012. Mindfulness for Beginners. Sounds True, Boulder, CO.

BIBLIOGRAPHY

Bishop, L., 2013. The solo act. Knowl. Quest 41 (5), 30–35.
Brownbridge, L., 2014. Mindfulness in schools: where governments, education and mindfulness meet. Nat. Life (May/June), 18–22.
Burns, D., 1983. Feeling Good: The New Mood Therapy. HarperCollins, New York, NY.
Busch, A., 2011. The maxed out librarian: how I learned to keep smiling and remain effective as a solo librarian. Knowl. Quest 40 (2), 14–17.
Davis, D.M., Hayes, J.A., 2011. What are the benefits of mindfulness? A practice review of psychotherapy-related research. Psychotherapy 48 (2), 198–208.
DelGuidice, M., 2011. Avoiding school librarian burnout: simple steps to ensure your personal best. Libr. Media Connect 29 (4), 22–23.

[48] Salzberg, S., 2014. How to find happiness at work, even if you don't like your job. Sharon Salzberg, Meditation Teacher & Author (blog). Available from: <http://www.sharonsalzberg.com/find-happiness-work-even-dont-like-job/>.

Flaxman, G., Flook, L. Brief summary of mindfulness research. 1. Available from: <http://marc.ucla.edu/workfiles/pdfs/MARC-mindfulness-research-summary.pdf> (accessed 22.03.15.).

Greenberger, D., Padesky, C., 1995. Mind Over Mood: Changing How You Feel by Changing the Way You Think. Guilford Press, New York, NY.

Hornung, E., 2013. On your own but not alone: one-person librarians in Ireland and their perceptions of continuing professional development. Libr. Trends 61 (3), 675–702.

Ihnen, A., Flynn, C., 2008. The Complete Idiot's Guide to Mindfulness. Penguin, New York, NY.

Kabat-Zinn, J., 2012. Mindfulness for Beginners. Sounds True, Boulder, CO.

Karabush, C., Pleviak, P., 2011. Talk me off the ledge: surviving solo librarianship. Knowl. Quest 40 (2), 48–53.

Mielke, C., March 6, 2015. Staying present in the classroom: practicing mindful teaching. We Are Teachers (blog) Available from: <http://www.weareteachers.com/blogs/post/2015/03/03/staying-present-in-the-classroom-practicing-mindful-teaching>

Murrey-Settle, N., August 18, 2014. Kindness and the solo librarian. YALSA (blog) Available from: <http://yalsa.ala.org/blog/2014/08/18/kindness-for-the-solo-librarian/>

Neff, K., 2011. Self-Compassion: The Proven Power of Being Kind to Yourself. HarperCollins, New York, NY.

Olpin, M., Bracken, S., 2014. Unwind! 7 Principles for a Stress Free Life. Franklin Covey, New York, NY.

Ryan, T., 2012. A Mindful Nation: How a Simple Practice Can Help Us Reduce Stress, Improve Performance and Recapture the American Spirit. Hay House, Carlsbad, CA.

Salzberg, S., How to find happiness at work, even if you don't like your job. Sharon Salzberg, Meditation Teacher & Author (blog), October 20, 2014. Available from: <http://www.sharonsalzberg.com/find-happiness-work-even-dont-like-job/>.

Siess, J., February 1, 1999. Flying solo: librarian, manage thyself. Am. Libr. 30 (2), 32–34.

Conclusion

If you are reading this, we hope that you have already gained some insight and useful tips that make your life and your work as a librarian more mindful, and hence more meaningful and enjoyable. In closing, we thought we would summarize some of the key points made and leave you with some thoughts for reflection.

We began this book with a basic introduction to mindfulness and the practices associated with it. While many of these practices have existed for thousands of years, it is notable that it is really only in relatively recent times that human beings have had the technology to demonstrate with any scientific rigor the benefits of these practices. Some might say that the science of mindfulness is still in its infancy and shows great promise moving forward. While much of mindful practice, such as mindfulness-based stress reduction (MBSR) programs, evolved within the context of health care, it has become apparent that its benefits can be enjoyed by all.

After laying out the case for mindfulness, we explored contemplative practices in education. This seems like an area that is ripe for change and has tremendous possibilities. There are many creative experiments going on, and there seem to be more adherents within academia every day. Our schools and colleges can be stressful places for students, faculty, staff, and librarians. Mindfulness provides all parties with practical tools for managing stress and appreciating our lives more as they happen. It seems as though K–12 educators and librarians, armed with this understanding, have a unique opportunity to shape the minds and the emotional intelligence of future generations. In higher education, we have many exciting experiments underway as well. Traditional-age college students are budding adults that will hopefully develop lifelong learning habits, as well as lifelong strategies or approaches to life that are positive and meaningful. Likewise, older, non-traditional students, as discussed earlier, have a greater ability to adapt and change than once believed. Those of us in education can have a significant impact through modeling mindfulness practices and introducing them to others.

As we continued our journey through writing this book, we learned a lot ourselves. Some of the middle chapters, especially those concerned with conducting research, the new Framework for Information Literacy for Higher Education created by the Association of College and Research

Libraries (ACRL), and the *Guidelines for Behavior for Behavioral Performance of Reference and Information Service Providers* as established by the Reference and User Services Association (RUSA), got us really excited. We felt that these areas have a natural connection to mindful practice. That is, as librarians, our specific library-related practices and services as spelled out in these chapters can benefit greatly from coupling our professional standards to the tenets of mindfulness. We are also in a unique position to positively influence others in these areas, such as when we are involved in library instruction, taking part in reference interactions, or meeting with students to assist them with research projects.

The book continues in Chapters 6 and 7 with an emphasis on *intra*personal relationships and how the improvement of these can also lead to better *inter*personal relationships. The focus on the role played by academic library liaisons and library leaders speaks to the necessity for building strong relationships in general. Relationships are often an extension of who we are. If they are to be good relationships, they require us to be genuine, authentic human beings who seek to serve others and model positive approaches to our life and work. Academic library liaisons and administrators can make all the difference when their approach to communicating and leading is grounded in mindful practices.

Speaking of making a difference, perhaps the greatest potential for "mindful warriors" within our profession lies with the school librarian or solo librarian. In the final chapter, we explored the unique impact that school librarians in particular have on their schools and students, as well as the heavy burden they often carry. As librarians, we should appreciate the way that these individuals stand up and serve as champions for their students. They need to do all of the things that are often found in separate positions in other libraries. They need to develop and catalog collections, build relationships with faculty, and deliver meaningful instruction to students, in addition to numerous other activities "as assigned." We believe that these individuals are perhaps at the greatest risk for burnout within our profession, so they may enjoy the greatest benefit from adopting a mindfulness lens. Self-care is so important a concept, especially when it comes to school librarians. An approach that incorporates self-care and mindfulness in general as a way of being is summarized by Sharon Salzberg:

> *Mindfulness is a relational quality, in that it does not depend on what is happening, but is how we are relating to what is happening. That's why we say that mindfulness can go anywhere. We can be mindful of joy, sorrow, pleasure and pain, beautiful music and a screech...it means that old, habitual ways of relating—perhaps holding on fiercely to pleasure, so that, ironically, we are actually enjoying*

it less; or resenting and pushing away pain, so that, sadly, we suffer a lot more; or not fully experiencing times that seem unexciting because we're oblivious or take for granted the ordinary and the everyday—all these self-defeating, limiting reactions don't have to dominate.[1]

One last overarching element of our book that we would like to touch upon is the contribution made by Howard Slutzky. While he came on board primarily because of his clinical experience and the work he does to help people essentially become more mindful and live happier lives, it was his expertise as a faculty member that really stood out. His unique ability to apply the kind of compassion and concern to situations related to education and then transpose that to the librarian–patron interaction were especially helpful. One excellent book that we came across in the research and writing process, which again emphasizes the kind of self-compassion that Dr. Howard Slutzky believes in fostering, is Kristin Neff's *Self-Compassion: The Proven Power of Being Kind to Yourself.* In recognizing how challenging self-kindness can be, she states:

We don't need to be perfect to feel good about ourselves, and our lives don't need to be any certain way for us to be content. Every one of us has the capacity for resilience, growth, and happiness, simply by relating to our ever-arising experience with both compassion and appreciation…Each new moment presents an opportunity for a radically different way of being.[2]

Dr. Slutzky added another layer of understanding and depth to our discussions and debates, while compiling the text, which we feel was invaluable. He also shared what we feel are useful/insightful sidebars in each chapter.

Finally, we hope to have provided readers with some new opportunities for introspection and reflection in the area of mindfulness. Mindfulness starts with understanding of self and the acceptance that meditation and mindful practice can make a difference. For librarians, it is a useful and enriching disposition for all aspects of work, from stress reduction to enhanced communication to reference work to quality leadership. If you have not meditated, we hope that you will give it a try and keep at it. As noted by Lodro Rinzler, "The purpose of meditation practice is to blur the lines between meditation and postmeditation practice, so that we live all of our waking hours being present to whatever the world presents to us."[3] He goes on to point out we should not be

[1] Salzberg, S., Real Happiness at Work, p. 12.
[2] Neff, K., Self-Compassion, pp. 282–283.
[3] Rinzler, L., Walk Like a Buddha, p. 9.

quickly discouraged, stating, "Because it is so gradual a path, you need to be patient and put in the hours to let it have an effect on you."[4] If you already meditate, we hope to have given you some insight on not only how it can help, but how it can be applied from a librarian's perspective. So take a deep breath, hold it, and exhale. May the mindfulness journey begin now!

BIBLIOGRAPHY

Neff, K., 2011. Self-Compassion: The Proven Power of Being Kind to Yourself. Harper Collins, New York, NY.

Rinzler, L., 2013. Walk Like a Buddha. Shambala, Boston, MA.

Salzberg, S., 2014. Real Happiness at Work: Meditations for Accomplishment, Achievement, and Peace. Workman Publishing, New York, NY.

[4] Ibid., 13.

INDEX

Printed in the United States
By Bookmasters